FRED BASSET YEARBOOK 2018

Summersdale Publishers Ltd
46 West Street
Chichester
West Sussex
PO19 1RP
UK

www.summersdale.com

Printed and bound in the Czech Republic

ISBN: 978-1-78685-075-1

Substantial discounts on bulk quantities of Summersdale books are available to corporations, professional associations and other organisations.
For details contact general enquiries: telephone: +44 (0) 1243 771107, fax: +44 (0) 1243 786300 or email: enquiries@summersdale.com.

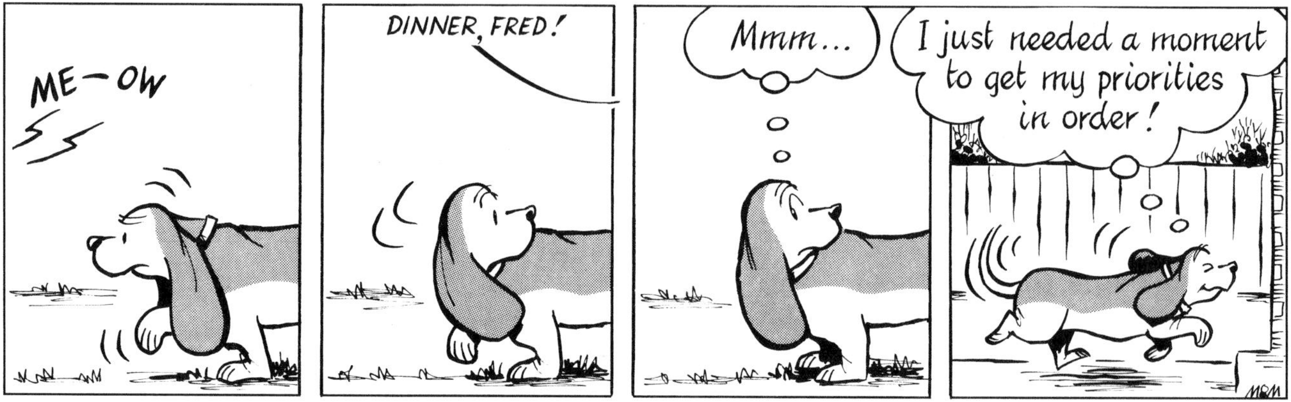
ME-OW
DINNER, FRED!
Mmm...
I just needed a moment to get my priorities in order!

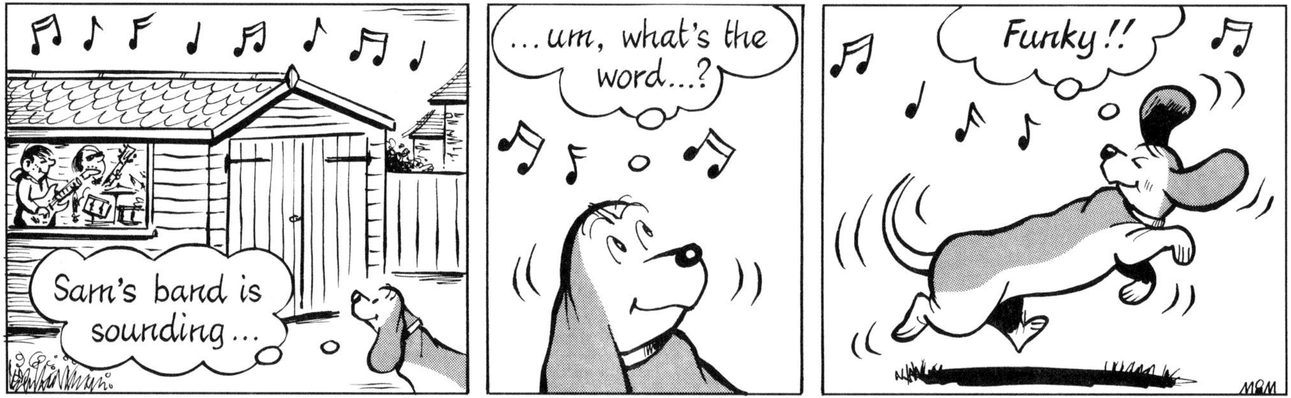
Sam's band is sounding...
...um, what's the word...?
Funky!!

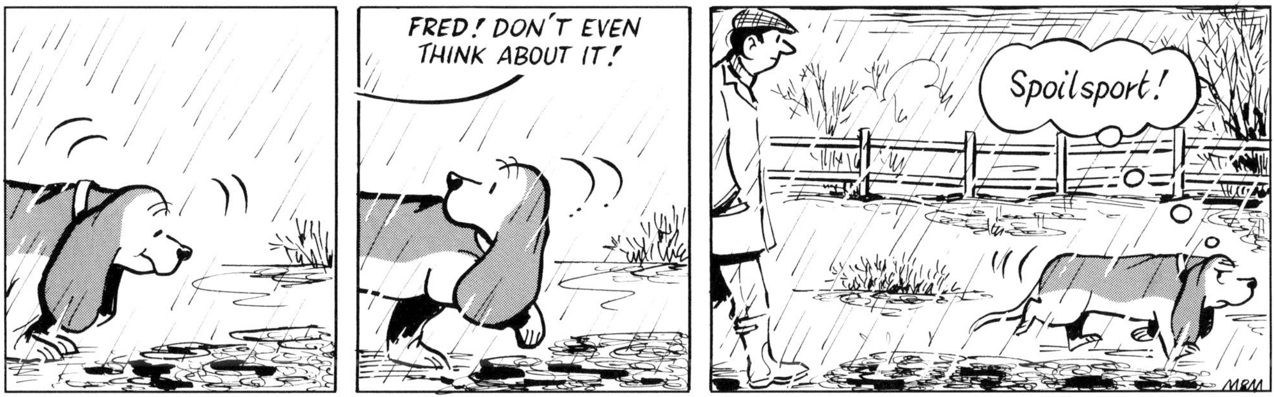
FRED! DON'T EVEN THINK ABOUT IT!
Spoilsport!

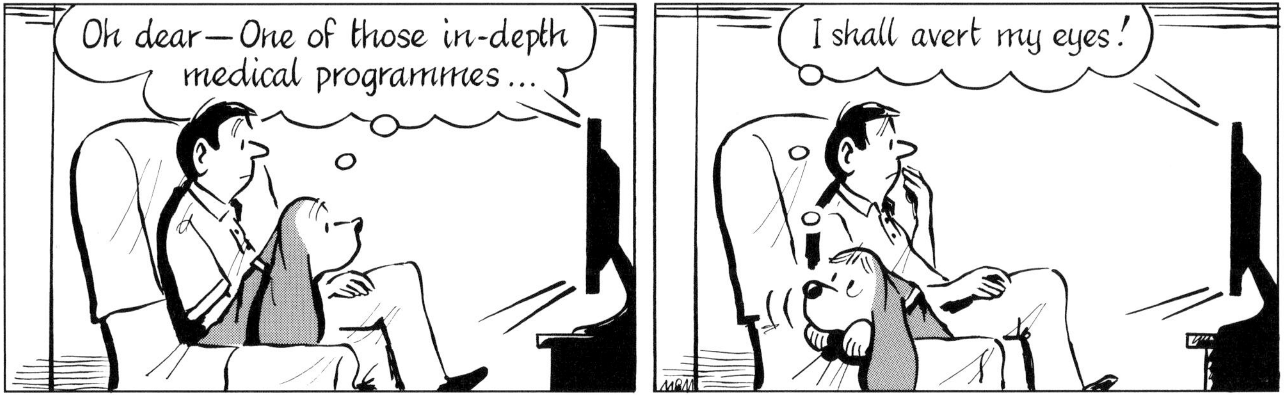
Oh dear—One of those in-depth medical programmes ...
I shall avert my eyes!

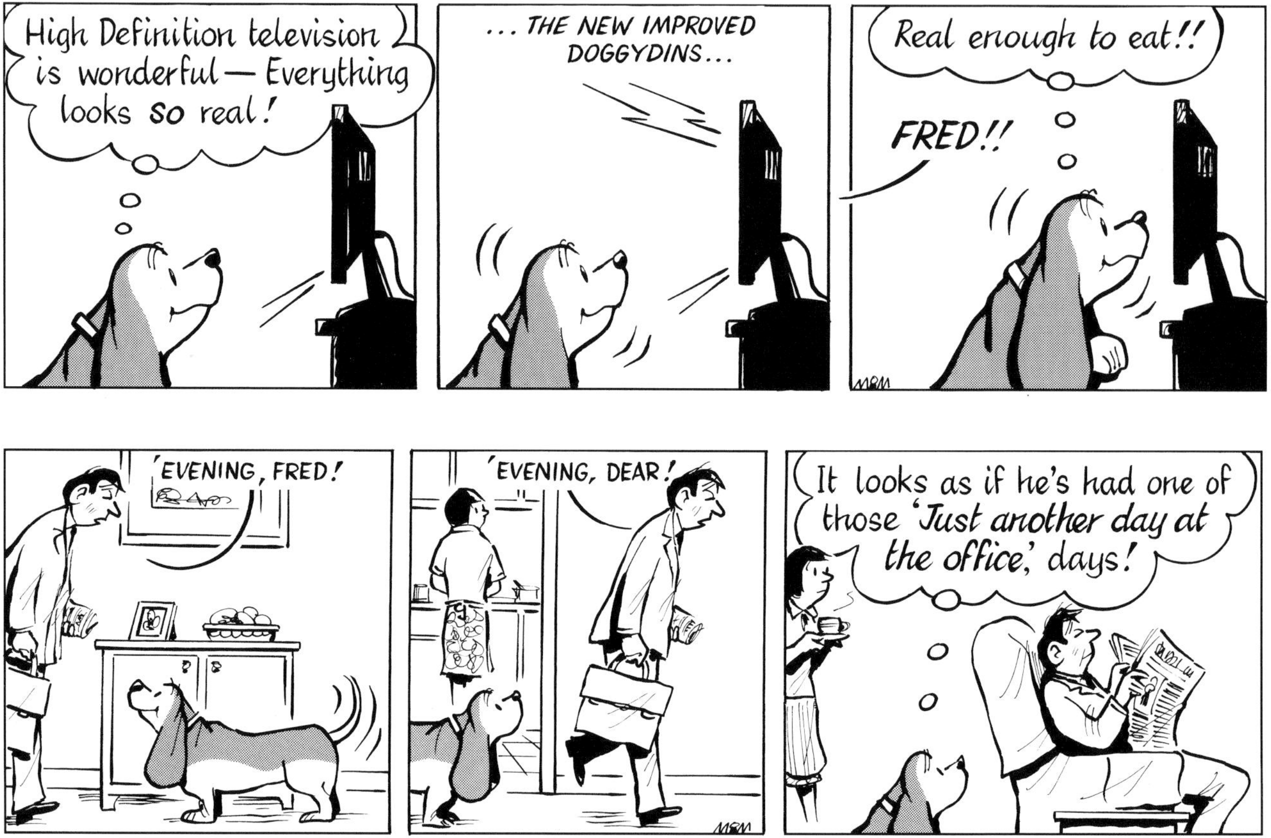
High Definition television is wonderful— Everything looks so real!
...THE NEW IMPROVED DOGGYDINS...
Real enough to eat!!
FRED!!
MBM
'EVENING, FRED!
'EVENING, DEAR!
MBM
It looks as if he's had one of those 'Just another day at the office,' days!

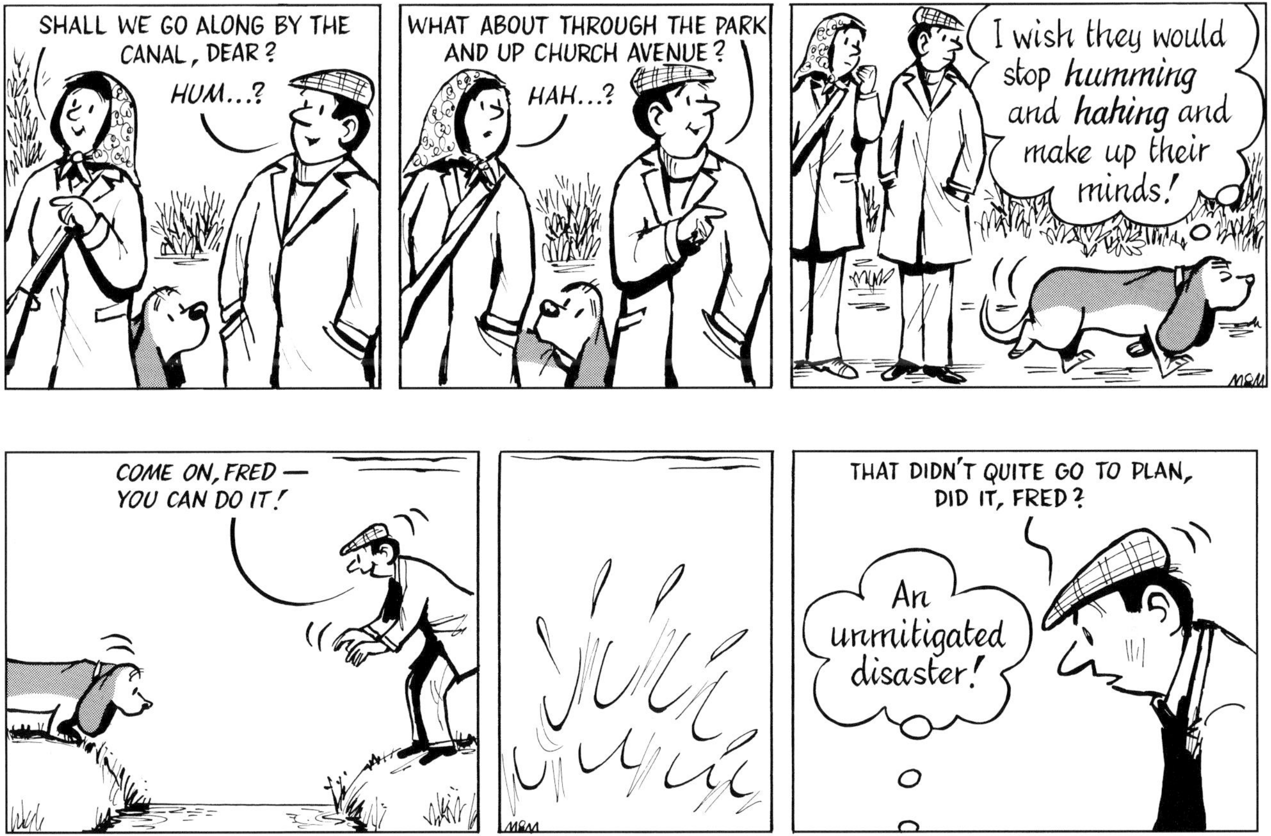
SHALL WE GO ALONG BY THE CANAL, DEAR?
HUM...?
WHAT ABOUT THROUGH THE PARK AND UP CHURCH AVENUE?
HAH...?
I wish they would stop humming and hahing and make up their minds!
COME ON, FRED — YOU CAN DO IT!
THAT DIDN'T QUITE GO TO PLAN, DID IT, FRED?
An unmitigated disaster!

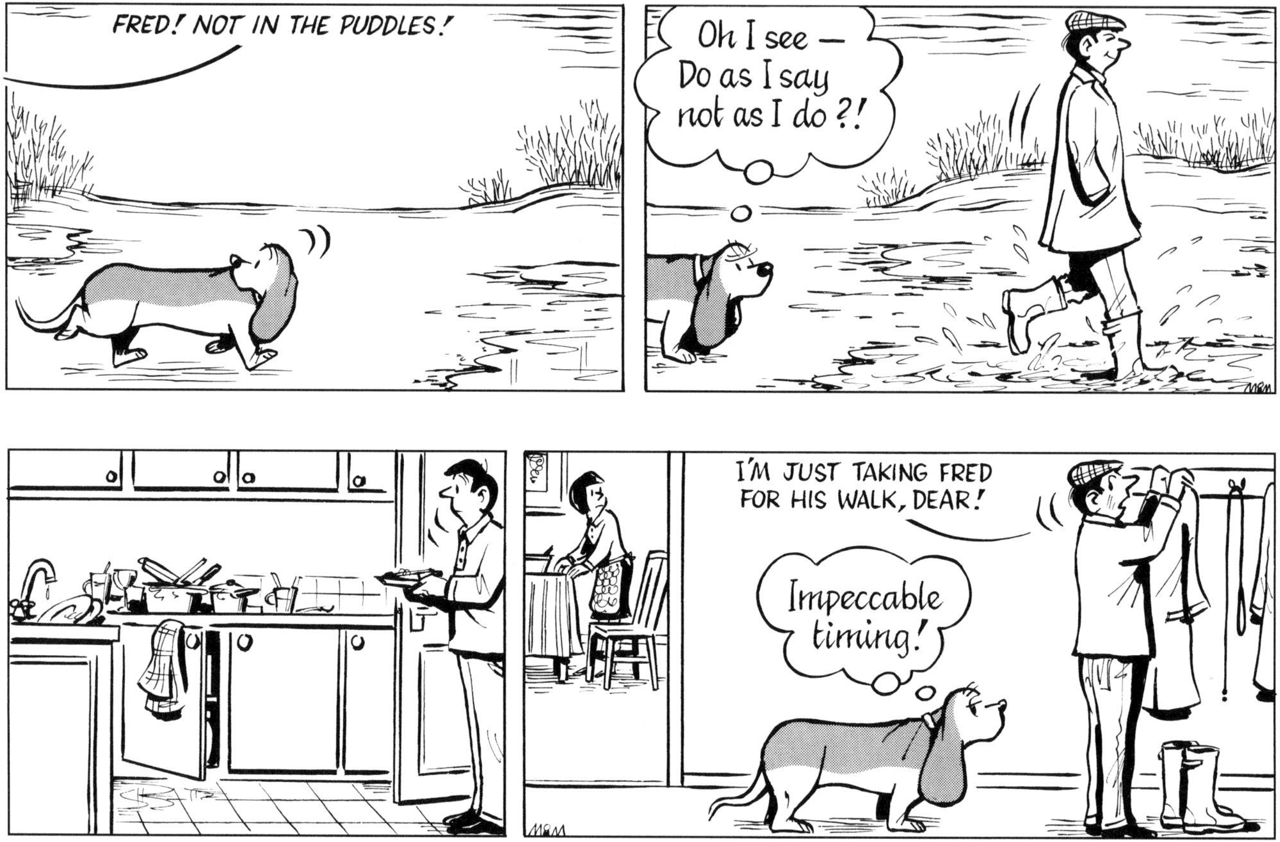
FRED! NOT IN THE PUDDLES!
Oh I see – Do as I say not as I do?!
I'M JUST TAKING FRED FOR HIS WALK, DEAR!
Impeccable timing!

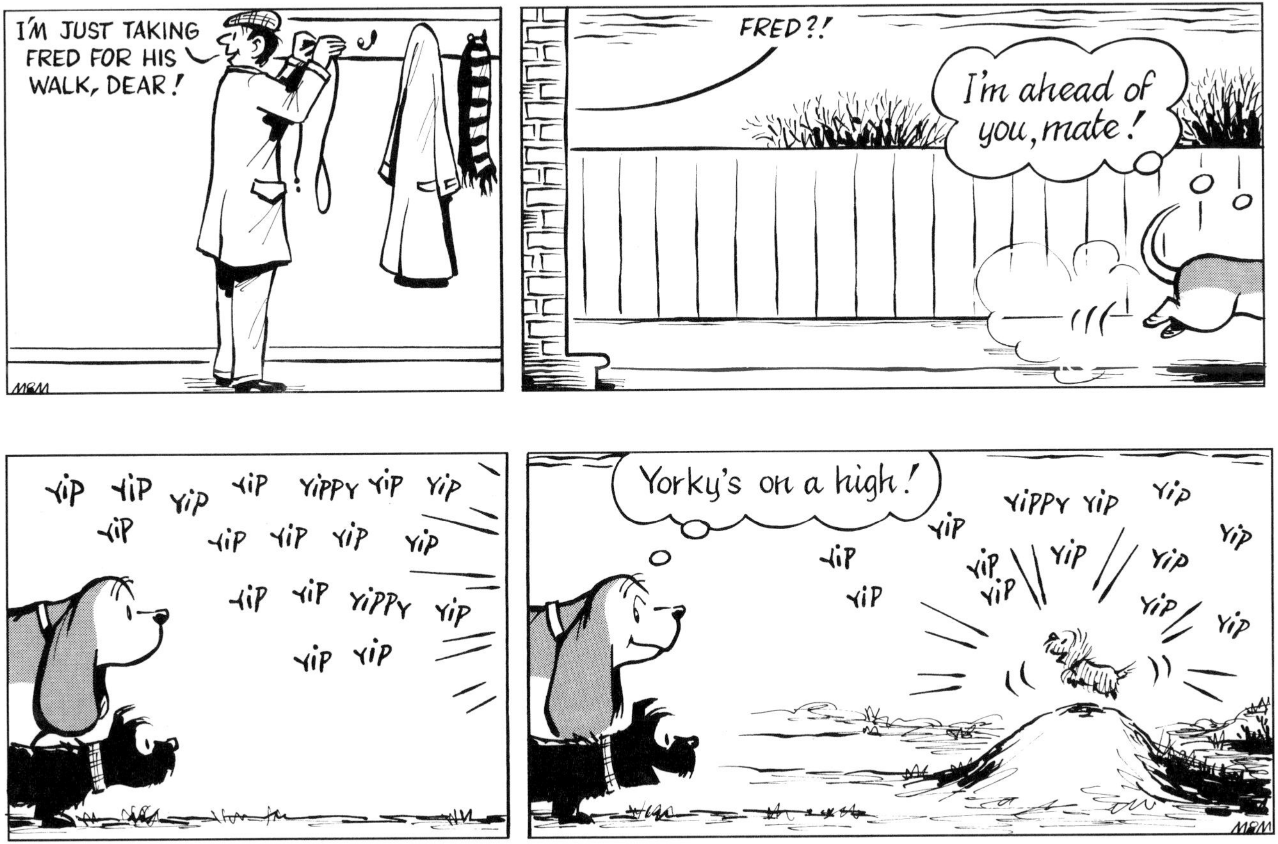
I'M JUST TAKING FRED FOR HIS WALK, DEAR!
FRED?!
I'm ahead of you, mate!
YIP YIP YIP YIP YIPPY YIP YIP
YIP
YIP YIP YIP YIP
YIP YIP YIPPY YIP
YIP YIP
Yorky's on a high!
YIPPY YIP YIP
YIP
YIP YIP YIP YIP
YIP YIP YIP YIP
YIP YIP YIP

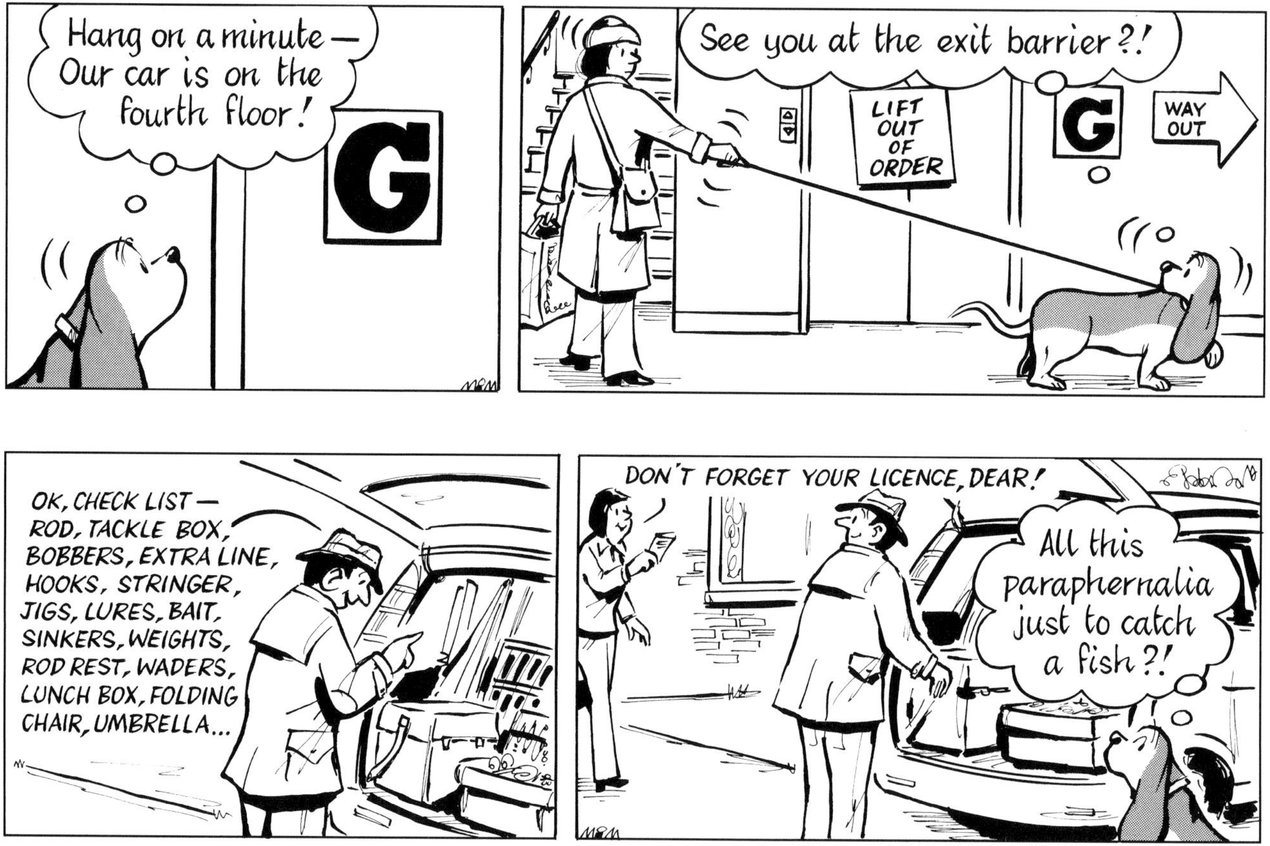
Hang on a minute — Our car is on the fourth floor!
G
See you at the exit barrier?!
LIFT OUT OF ORDER
G
WAY OUT
OK, CHECK LIST — ROD, TACKLE BOX, BOBBERS, EXTRA LINE, HOOKS, STRINGER, JIGS, LURES, BAIT, SINKERS, WEIGHTS, ROD REST, WADERS, LUNCH BOX, FOLDING CHAIR, UMBRELLA...
DON'T FORGET YOUR LICENCE, DEAR!
All this paraphernalia just to catch a fish?!

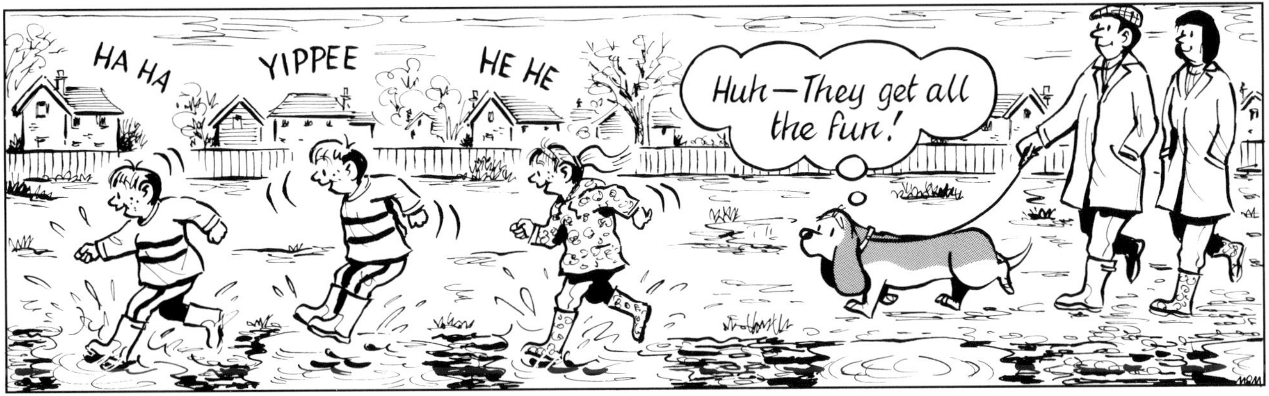
HA HA
YIPPEE
HE HE
Huh—They get all the fun!

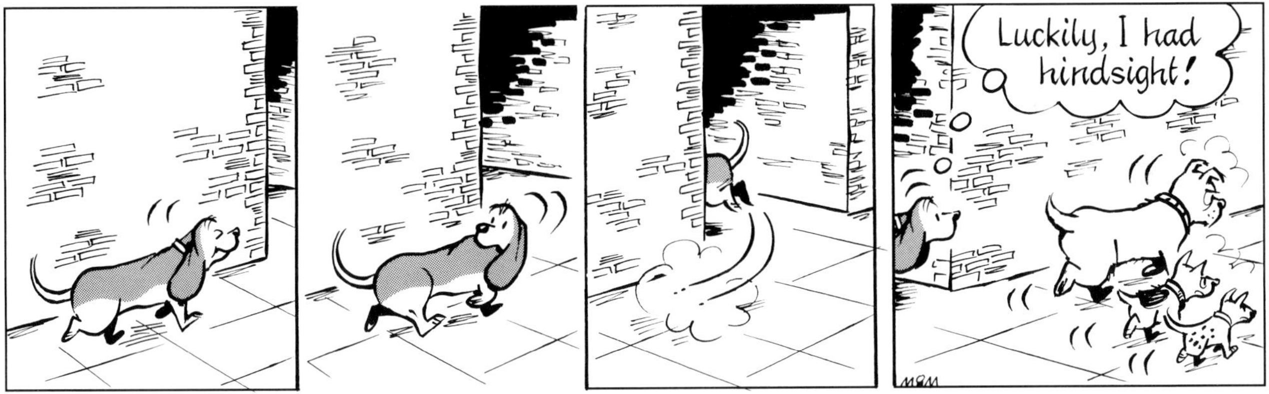
Luckily, I had hindsight!

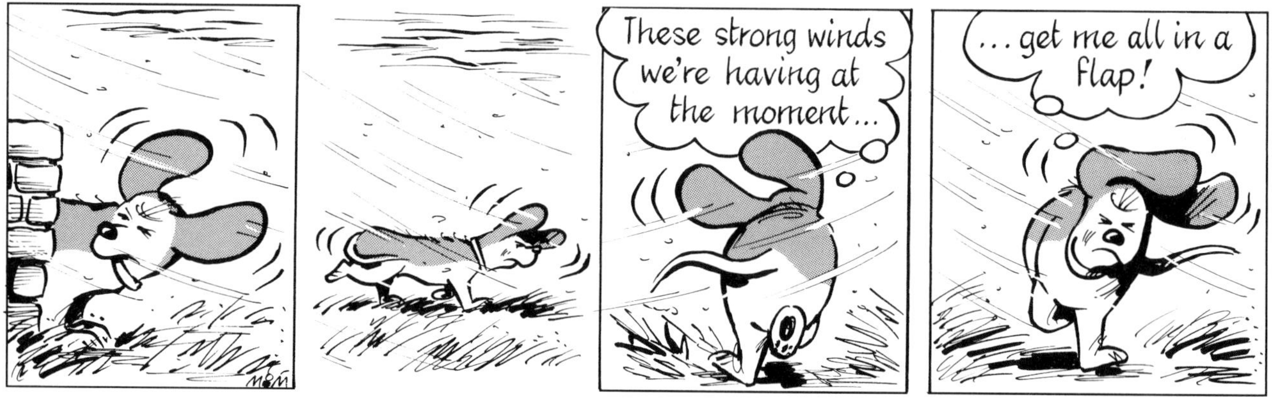
These strong winds we're having at the moment...
... get me all in a flap!

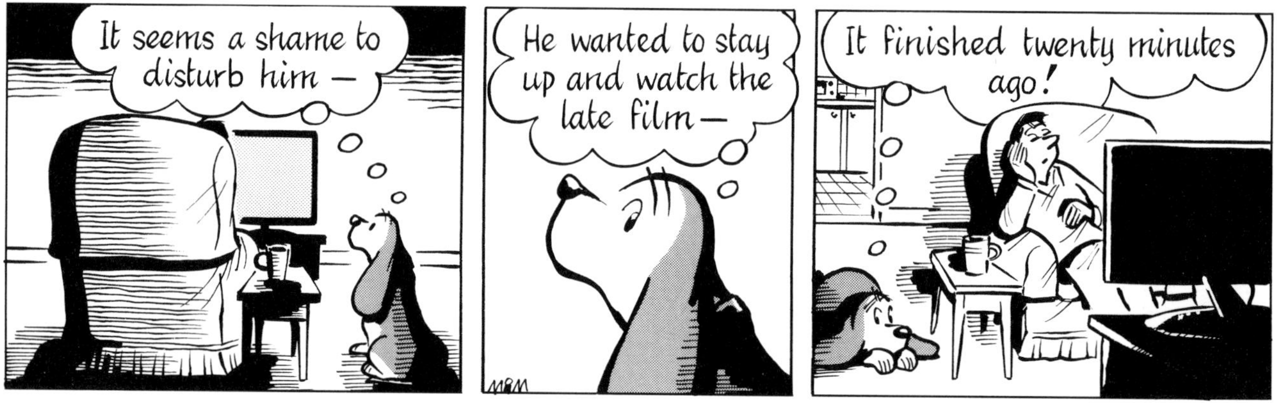
It seems a shame to disturb him –
He wanted to stay up and watch the late film –
It finished twenty minutes ago!

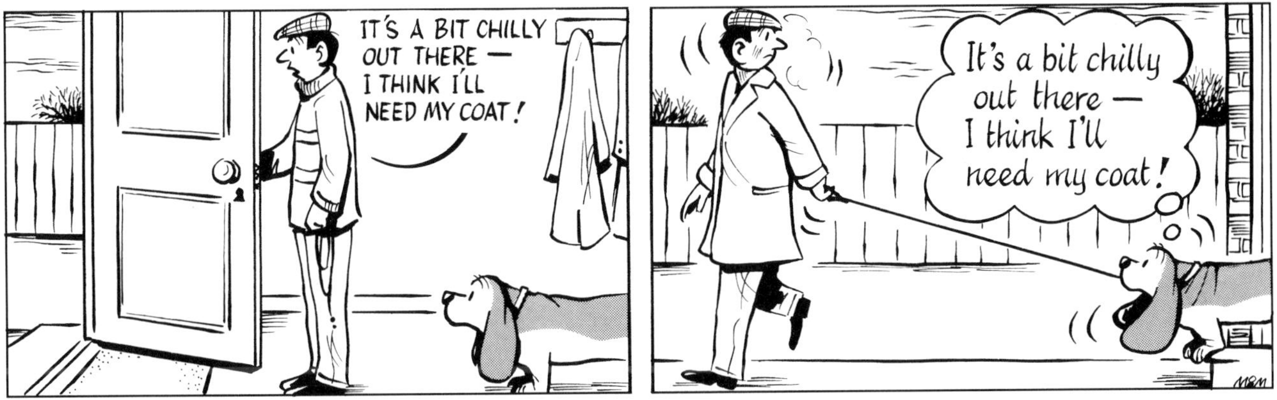
IT'S A BIT CHILLY OUT THERE — I THINK I'LL NEED MY COAT!
It's a bit chilly out there — I think I'll need my coat!

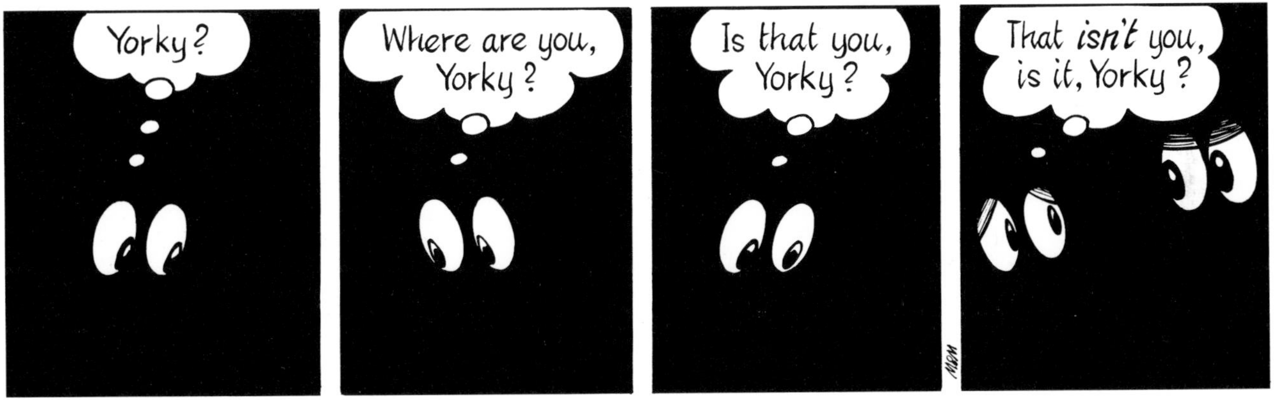
Yorky?
Where are you, Yorky?
Is that you, Yorky?
That *isn't* you, is it, Yorky?

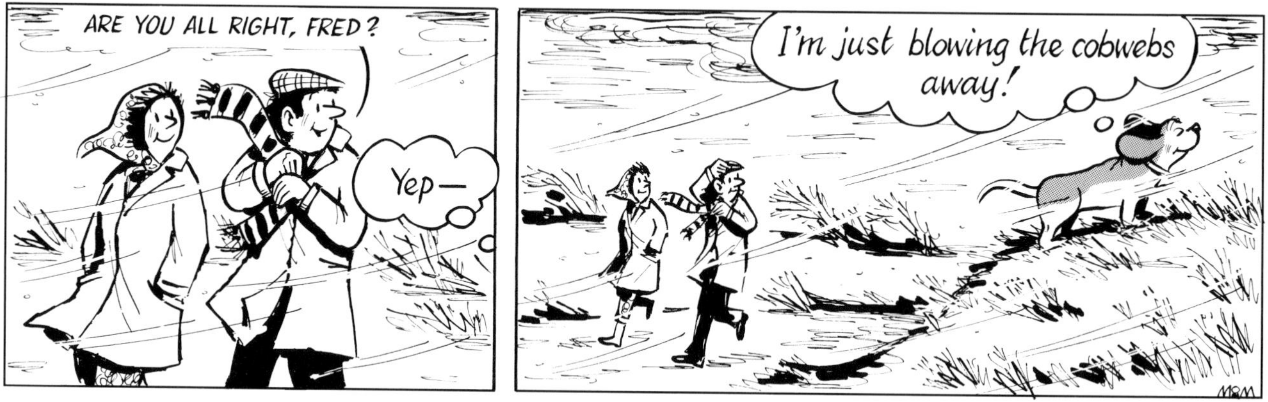
ARE YOU ALL RIGHT, FRED?
Yep—
I'm just blowing the cobwebs away!

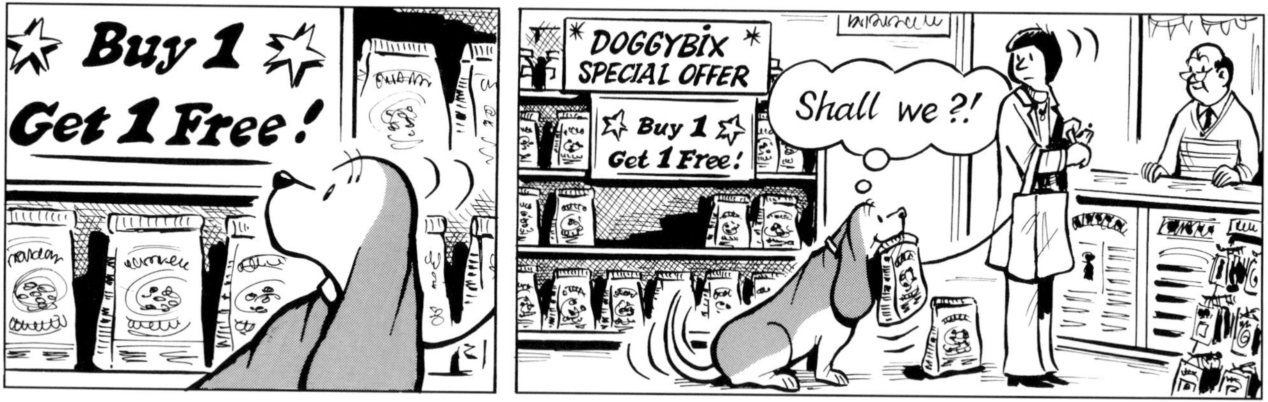
Buy 1 Get 1 Free!
DOGGYBIX SPECIAL OFFER
Buy 1 Get 1 Free!
Shall we?!

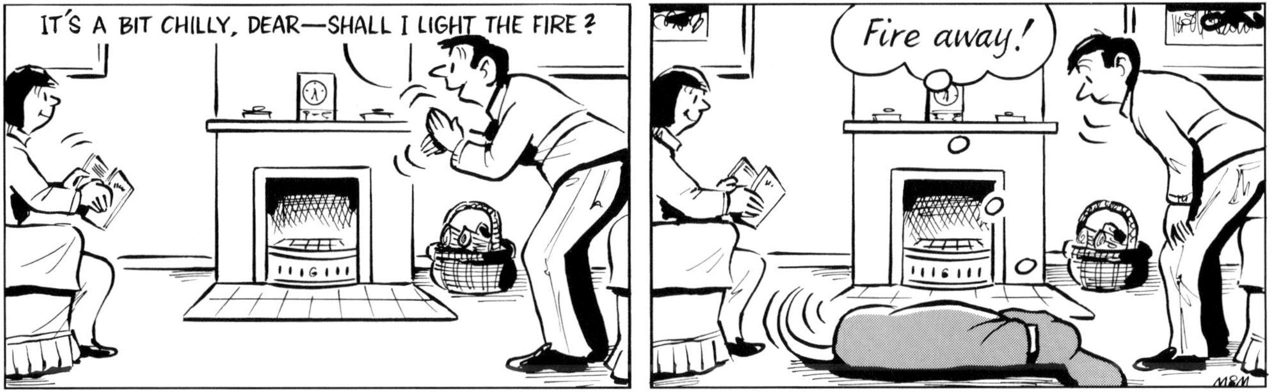
IT'S A BIT CHILLY, DEAR—SHALL I LIGHT THE FIRE?
Fire away!

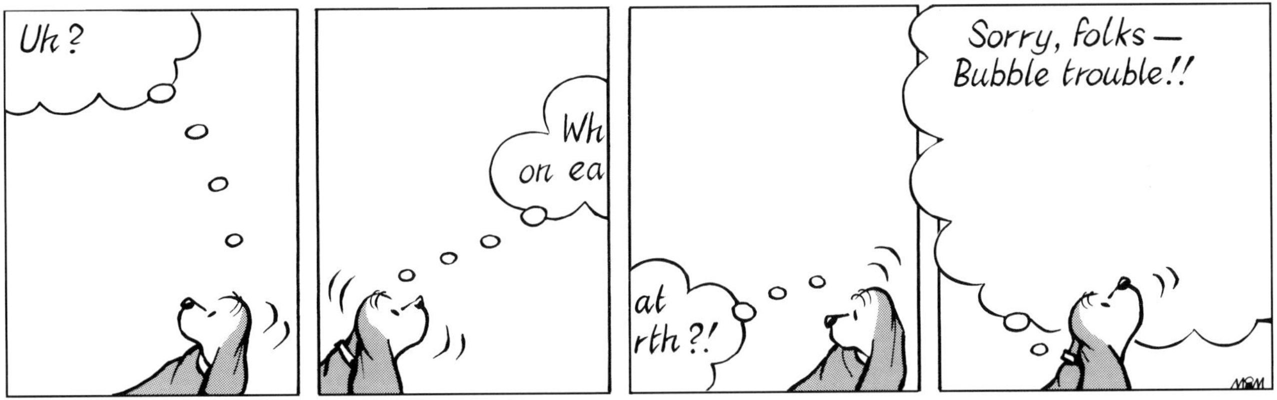
Uh?
Wh
on ea
at
rth?!
Sorry, folks—
Bubble trouble!!

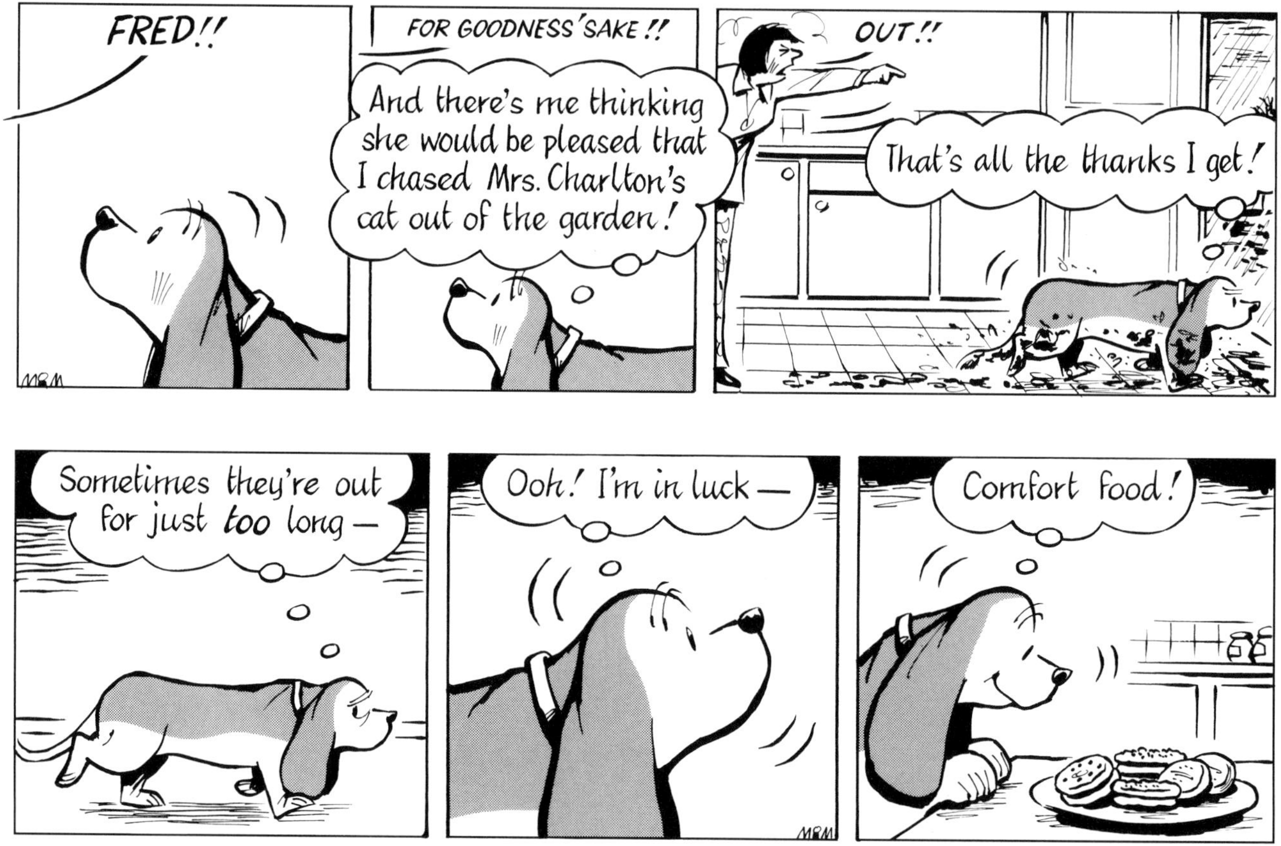
FRED!!
FOR GOODNESS'SAKE!!
And there's me thinking she would be pleased that I chased Mrs. Charlton's cat out of the garden!
OUT!!
That's all the thanks I get!
Sometimes they're out for just *too* long —
Ooh! I'm in luck —
Comfort food!

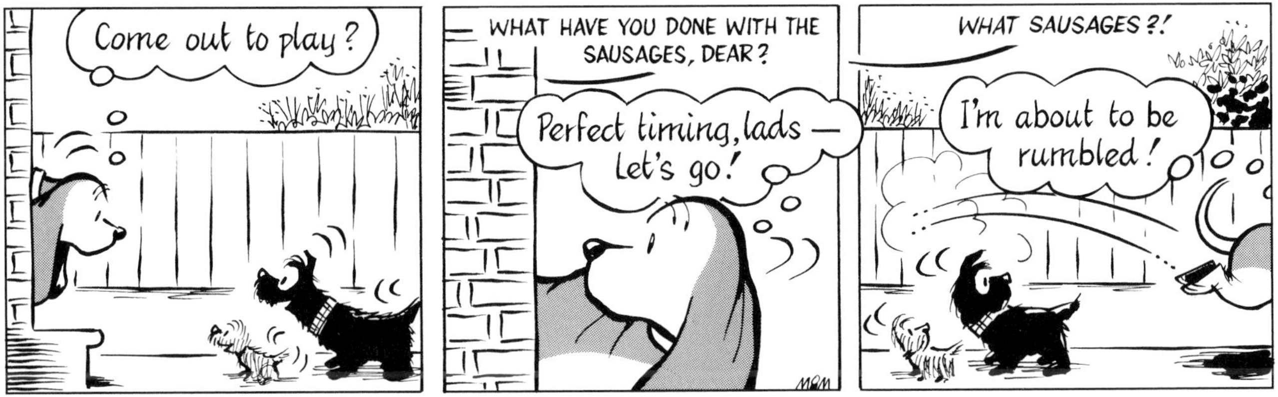
Come out to play?
WHAT HAVE YOU DONE WITH THE SAUSAGES, DEAR?
Perfect timing, lads — let's go!
WHAT SAUSAGES?!
I'm about to be rumbled!

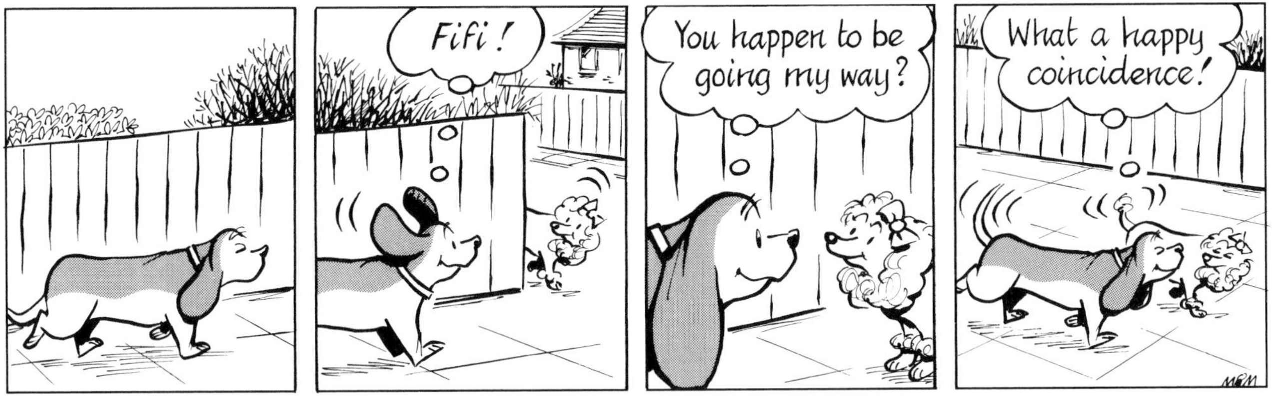
Fifi!
You happen to be going my way?
What a happy coincidence!

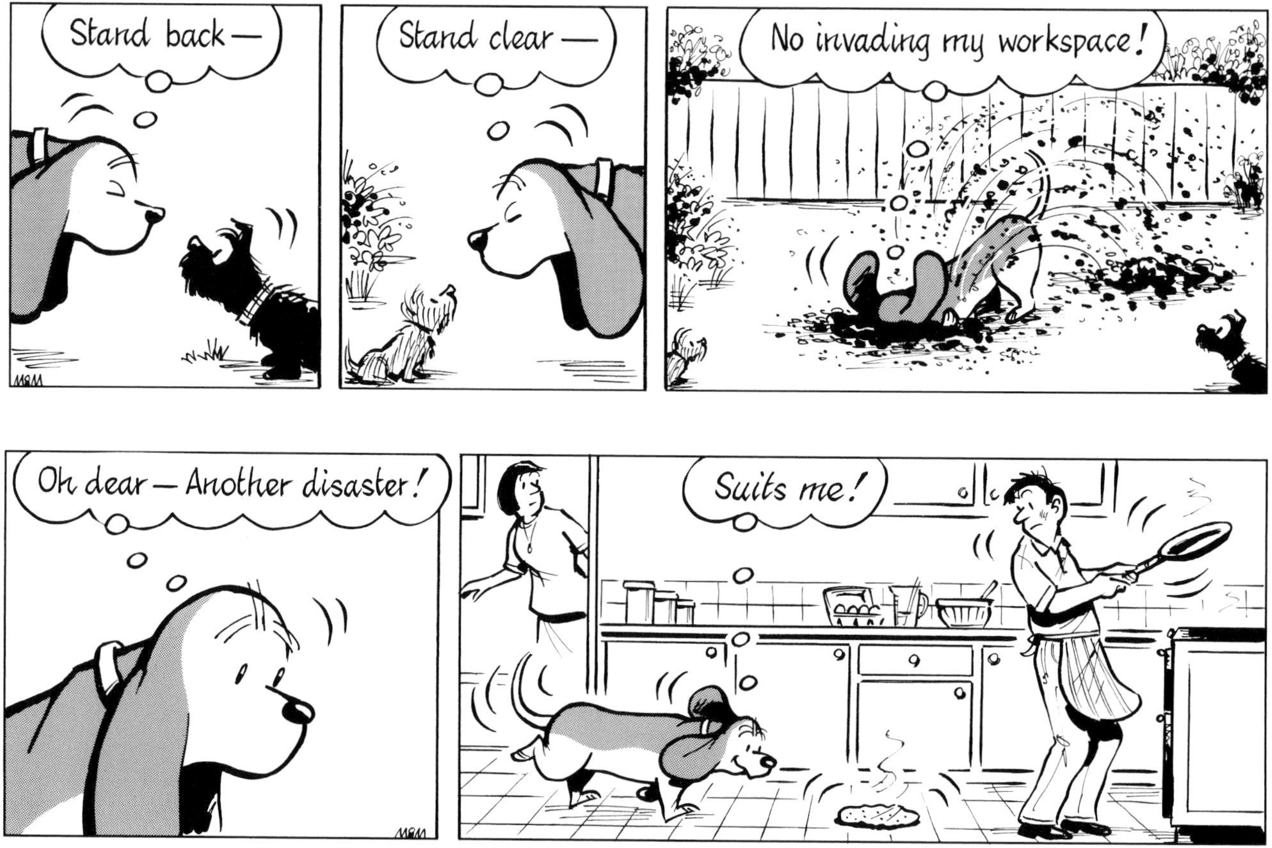
Stand back —
Stand clear —
No invading my workspace!
Oh dear — Another disaster!
Suits me!

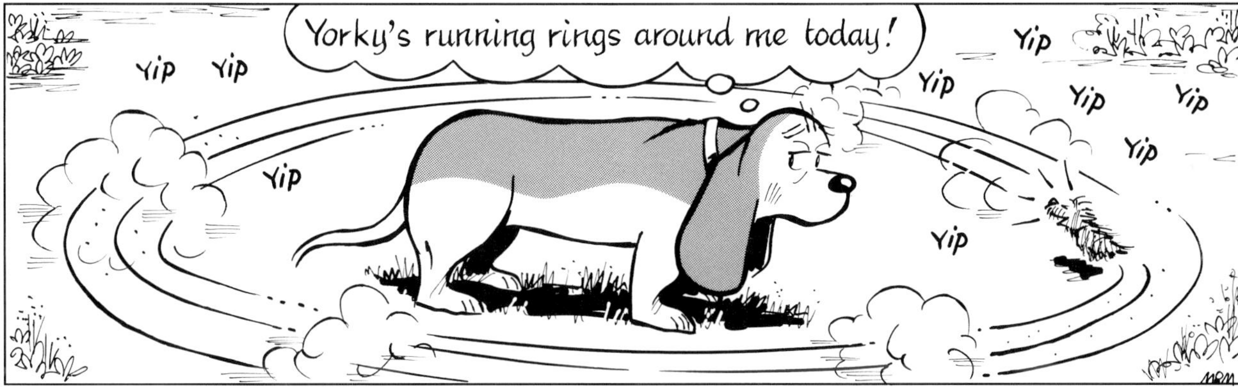
Yorky's running rings around me today!
Yip Yip
Yip
Yip
Yip
Yip
Yip
Yip
Yip

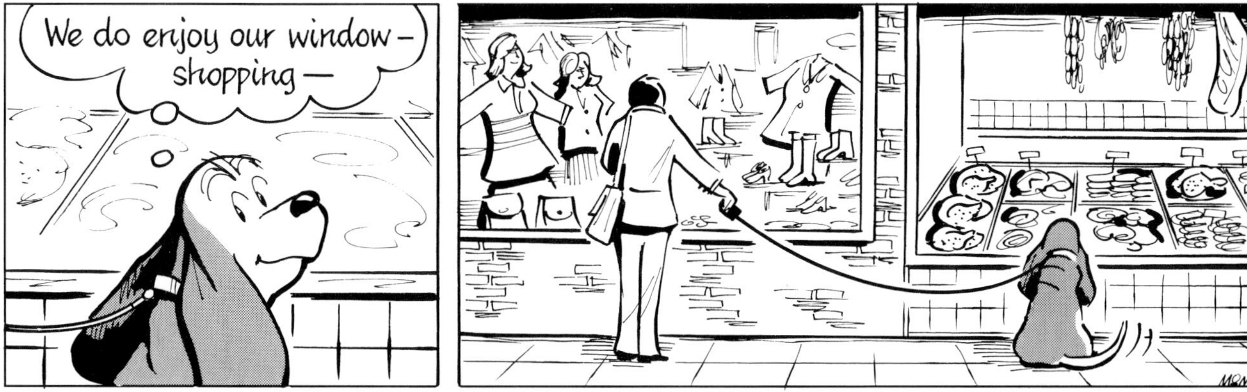
We do enjoy our window-shopping—

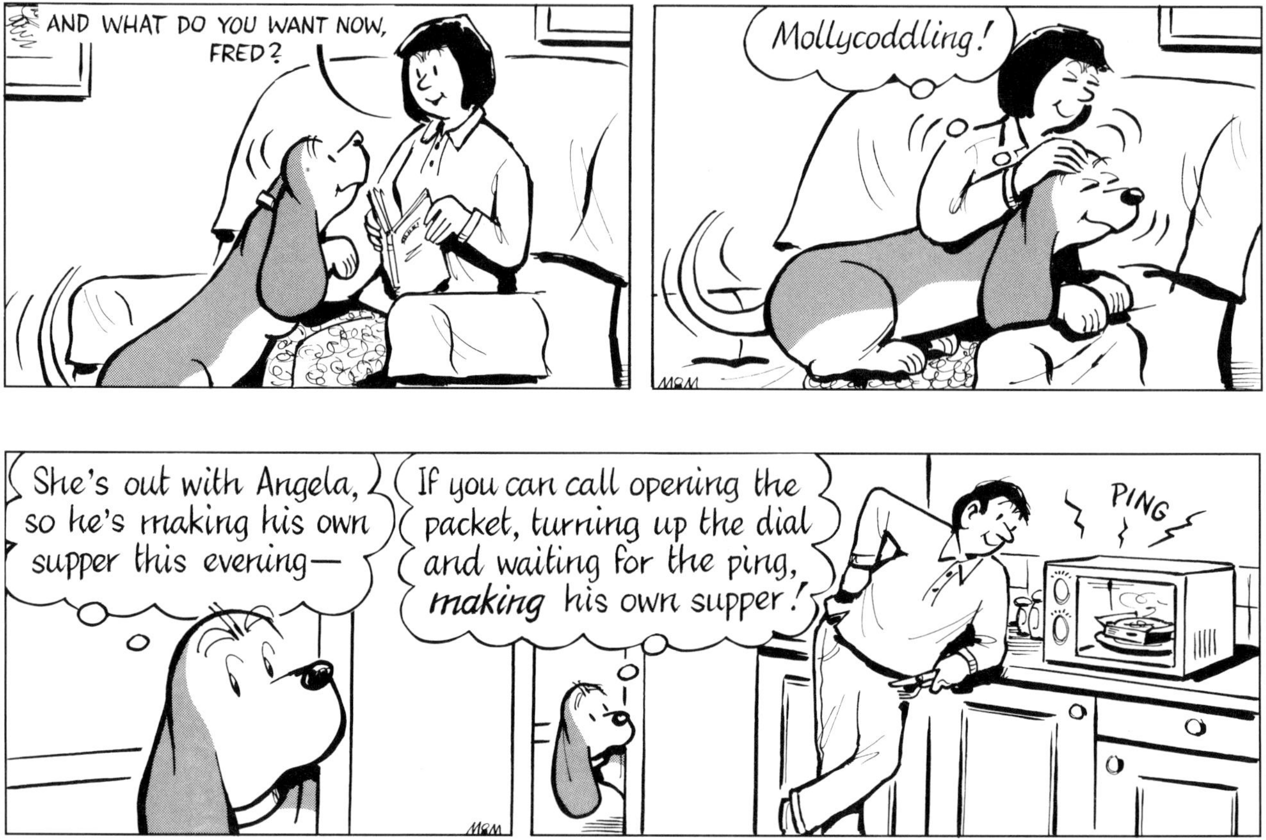
AND WHAT DO YOU WANT NOW, FRED?
Mollycoddling!
She's out with Angela, so he's making his own supper this evening—
If you can call opening the packet, turning up the dial and waiting for the ping, *making* his own supper!
PING

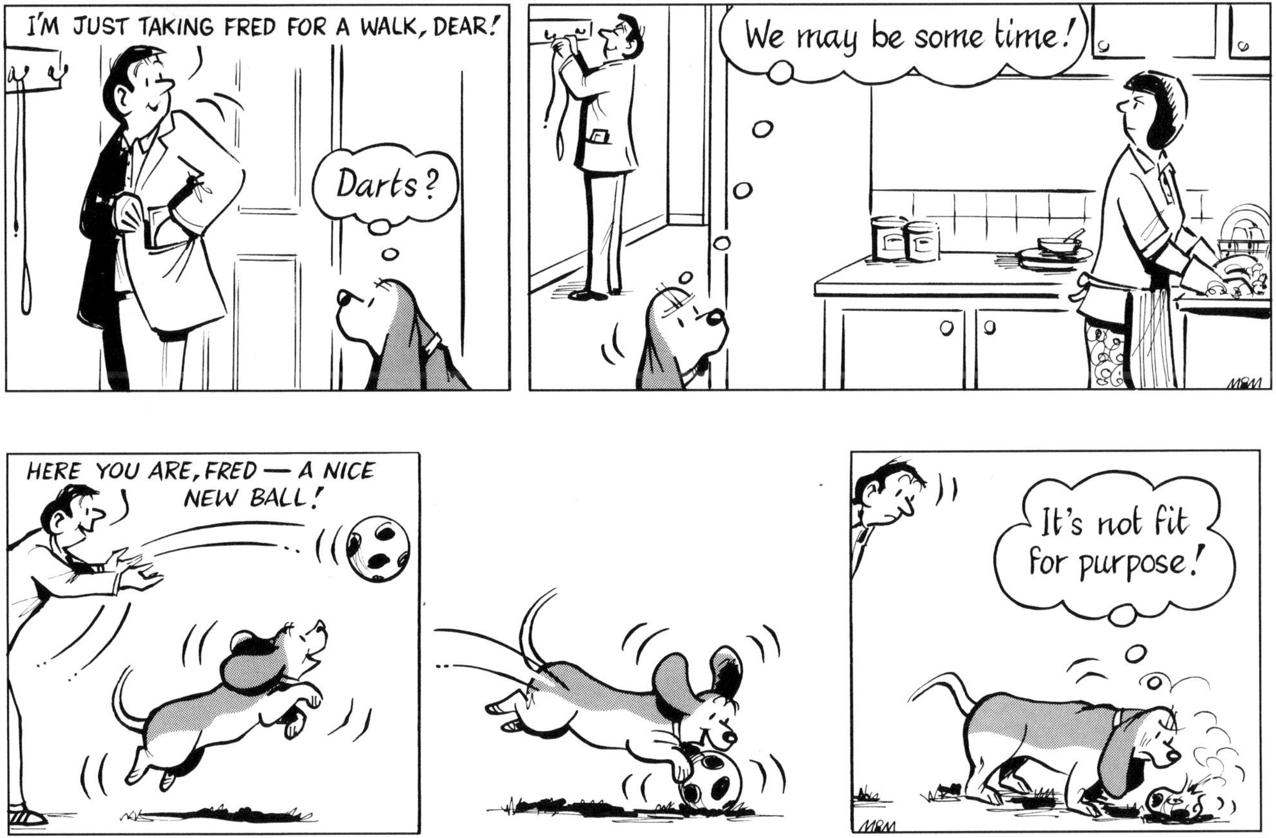
I'M JUST TAKING FRED FOR A WALK, DEAR!
Darts?
We may be some time!
M&M
HERE YOU ARE, FRED — A NICE NEW BALL!
It's not fit for purpose!
M&M

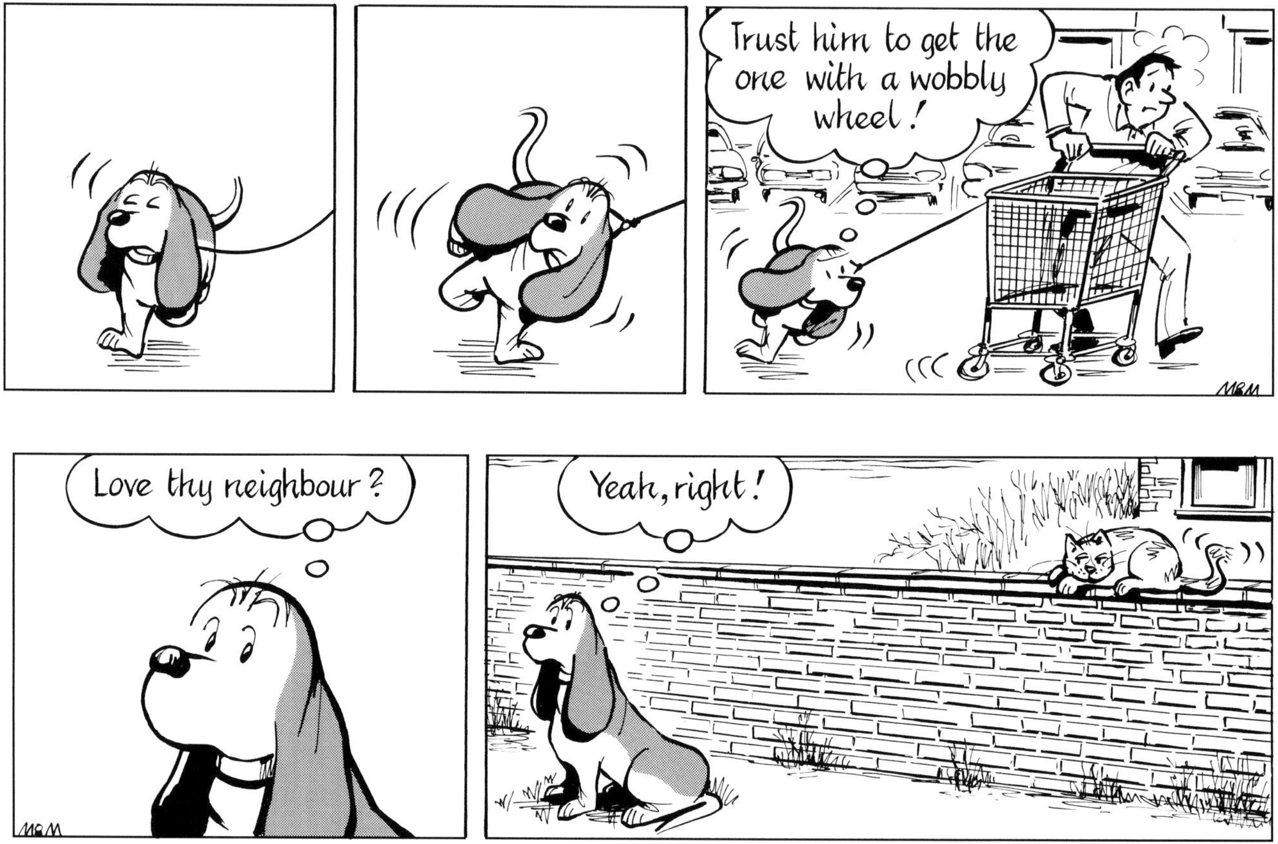
Trust him to get the one with a wobbly wheel!
Love thy neighbour?
Yeah, right!

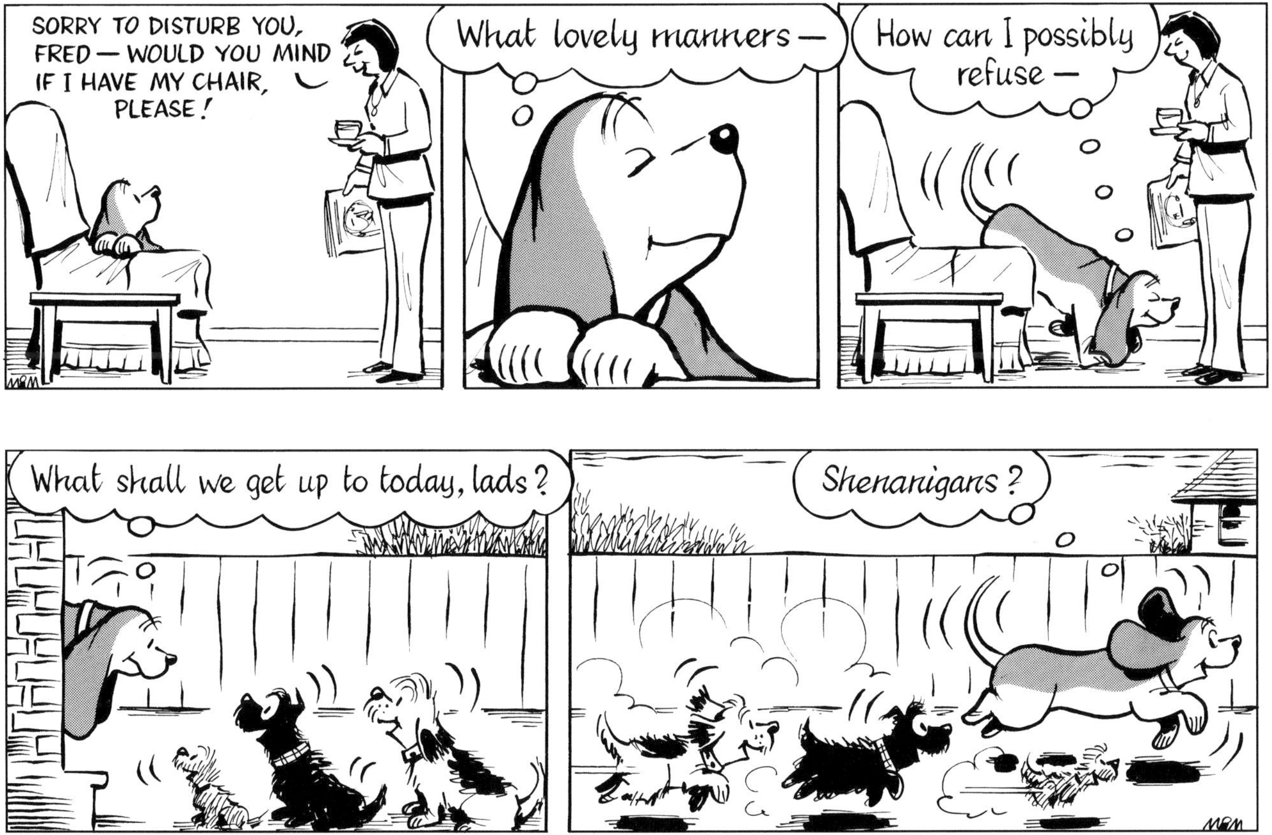
SORRY TO DISTURB YOU, FRED — WOULD YOU MIND IF I HAVE MY CHAIR, PLEASE!
What lovely manners —
How can I possibly refuse —
What shall we get up to today, lads?
Shenanigans?

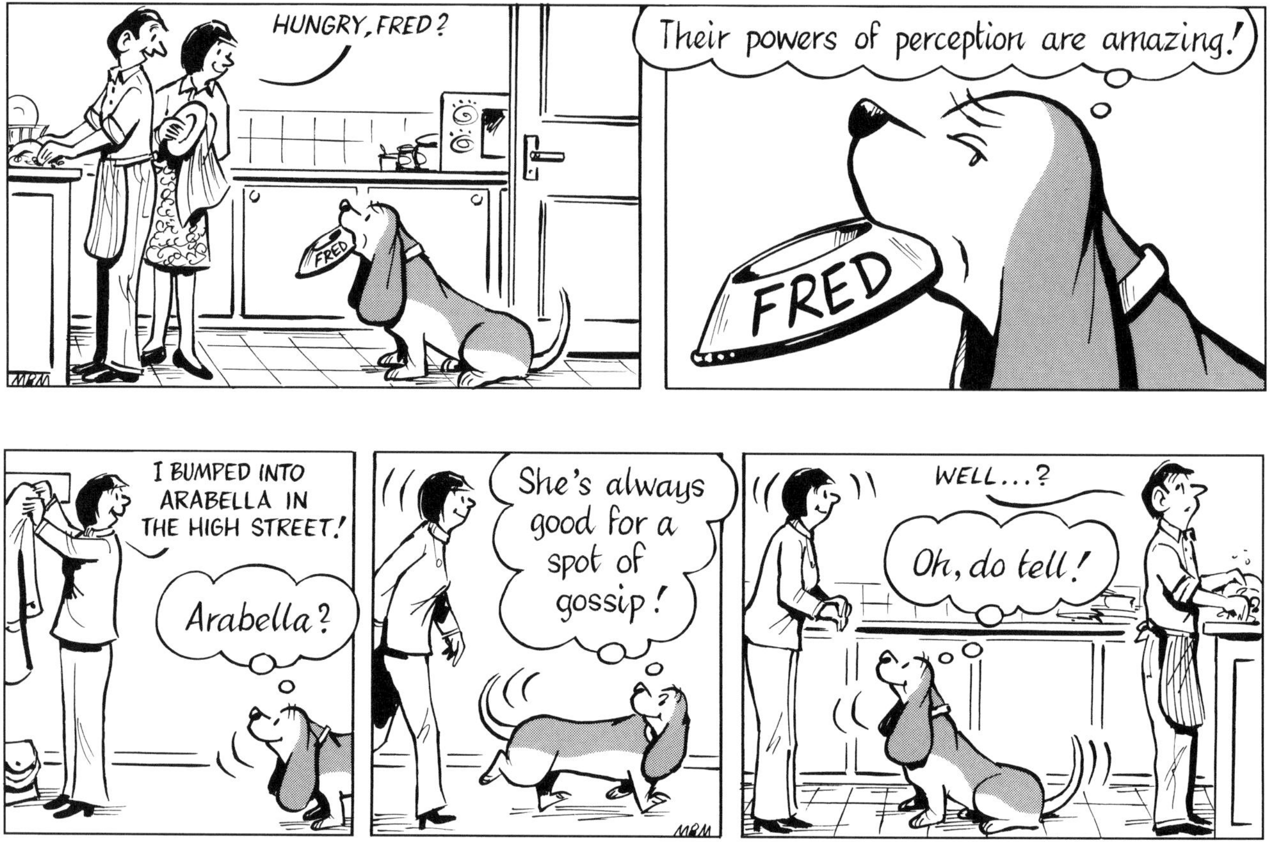
HUNGRY, FRED?
FRED
Their powers of perception are amazing!
FRED
I BUMPED INTO ARABELLA IN THE HIGH STREET!
Arabella?
She's always good for a spot of gossip!
WELL...?
Oh, do tell!

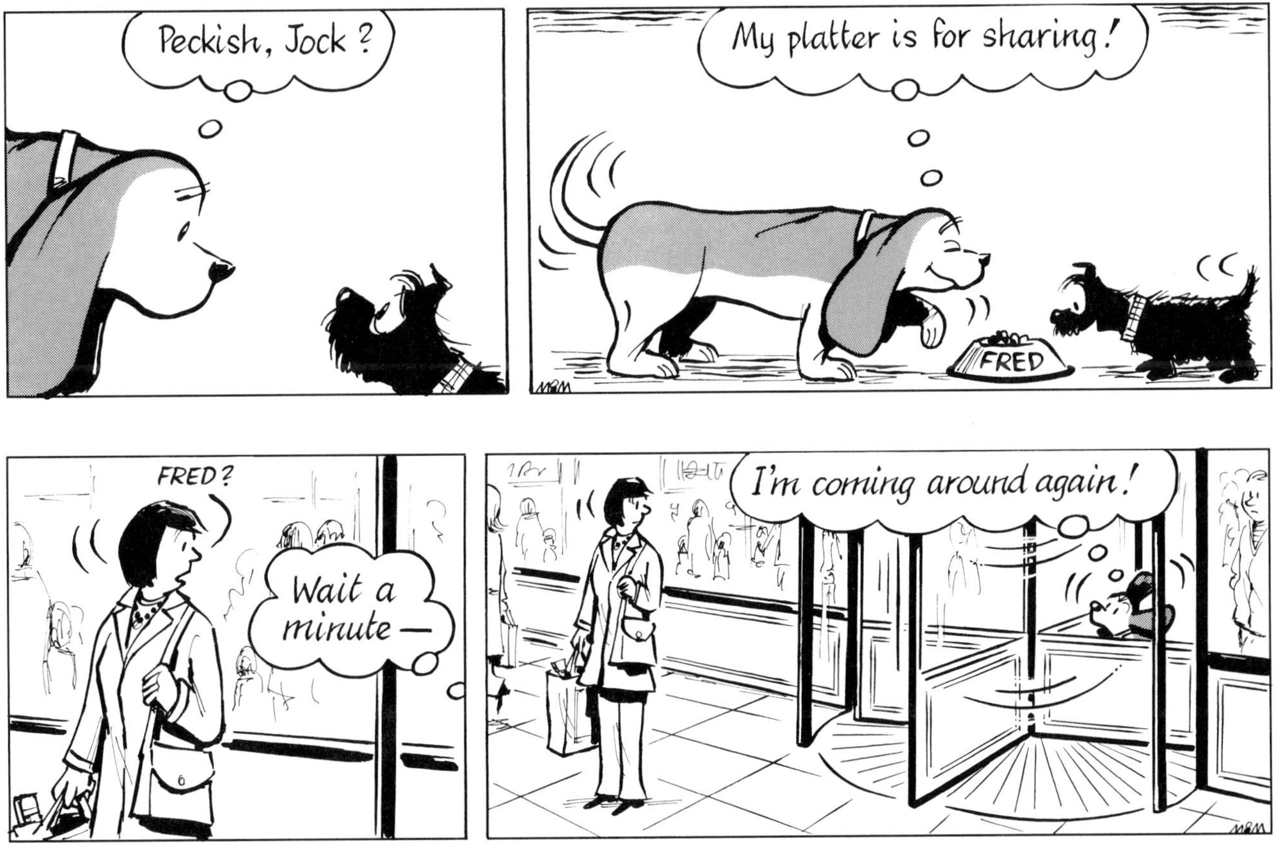
Peckish, Jock ?
My platter is for sharing!
FRED
MBM
FRED?
Wait a minute—
I'm coming around again!
MBM

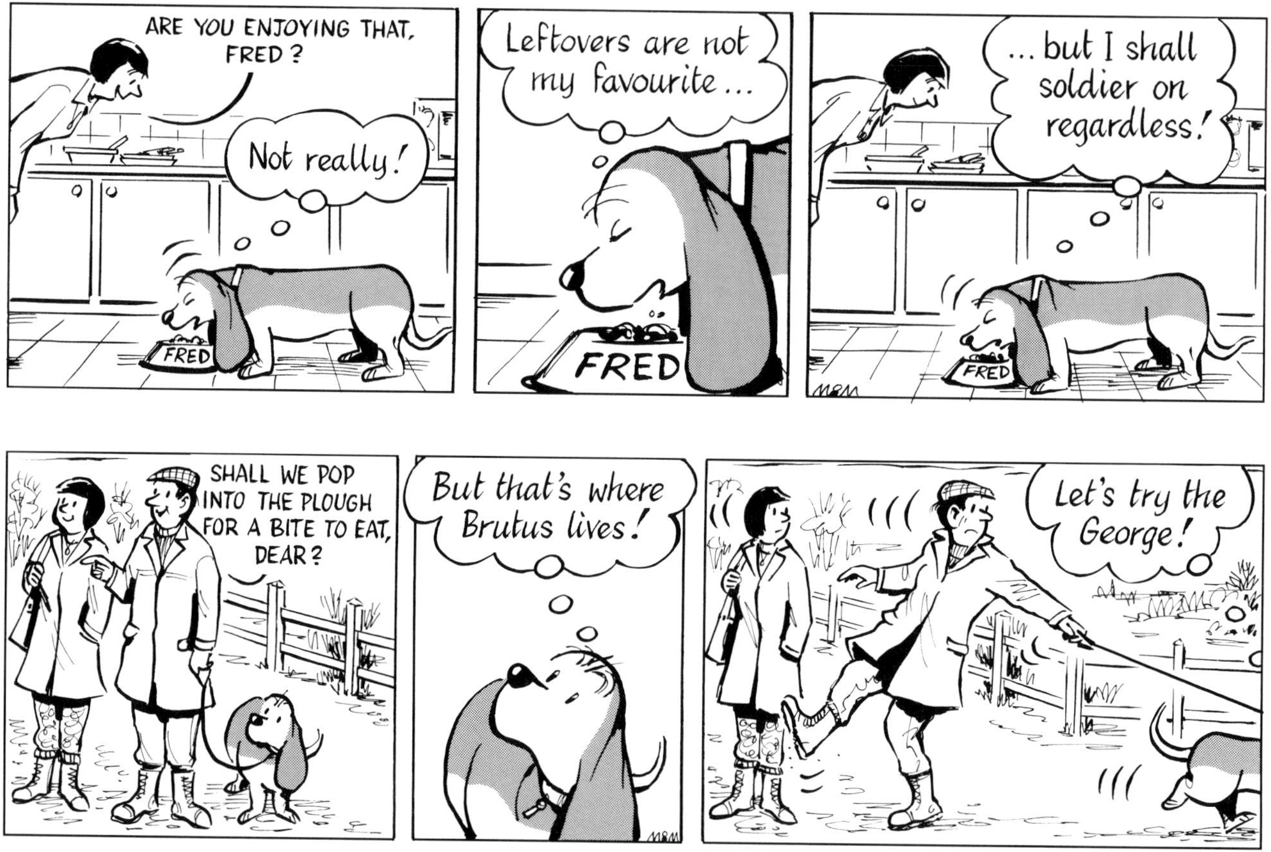
ARE YOU ENJOYING THAT, FRED?
Not really!
FRED
Leftovers are not my favourite ...
FRED
... but I shall soldier on regardless!
FRED
M&M
SHALL WE POP INTO THE PLOUGH FOR A BITE TO EAT, DEAR?
But that's where Brutus lives!
M&M
Let's try the George!

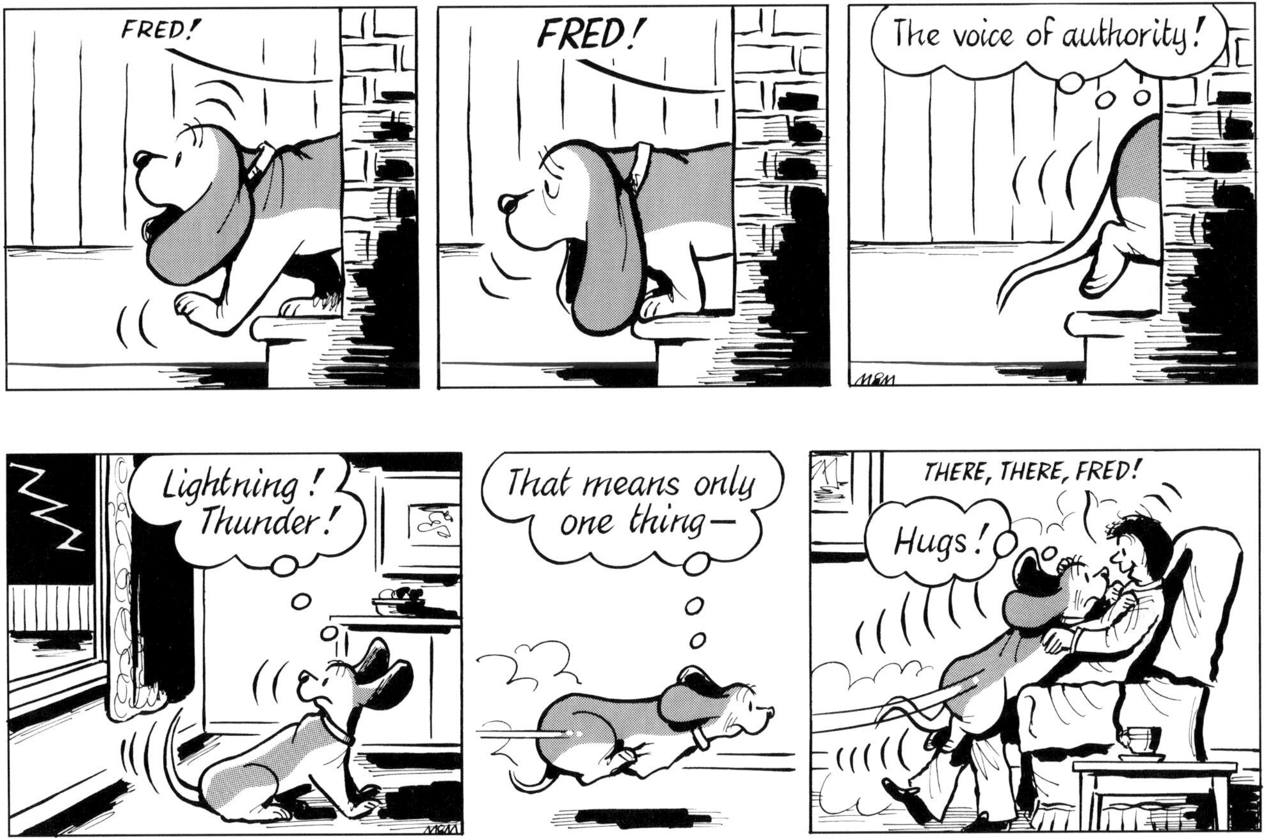
FRED!
FRED!
The voice of authority!
MGM
Lightning! Thunder!
That means only one thing—
THERE, THERE, FRED!
Hugs!
MGM

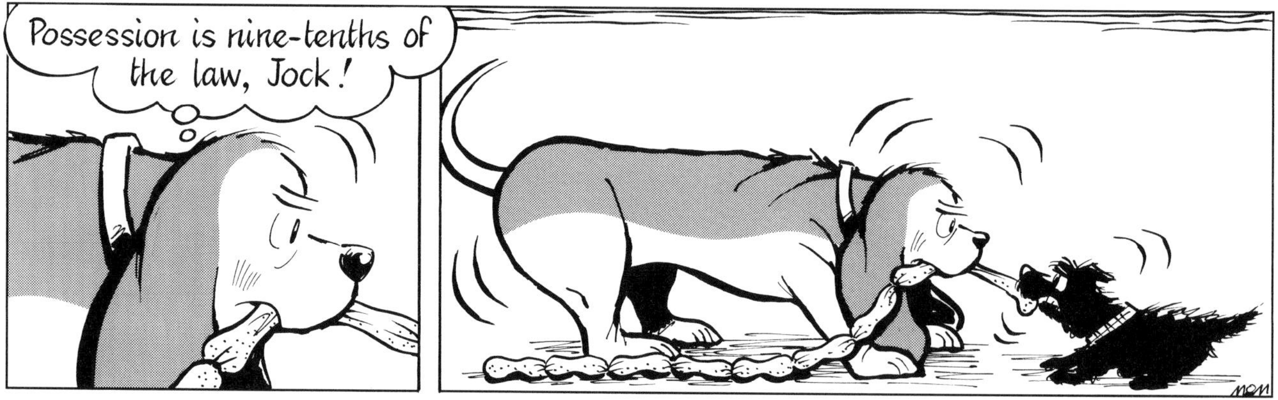
Possession is nine-tenths of the law, Jock!

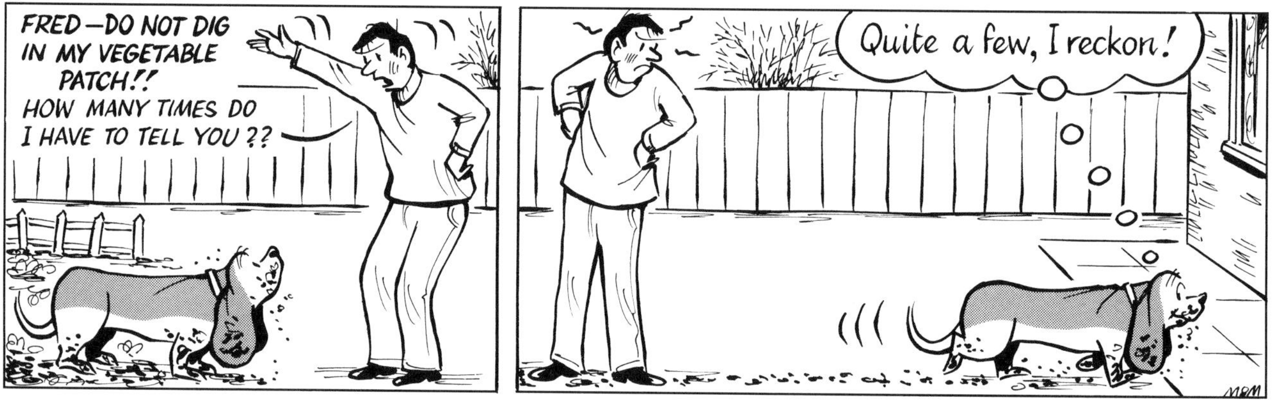
FRED—DO NOT DIG IN MY VEGETABLE PATCH!!
HOW MANY TIMES DO I HAVE TO TELL YOU??
Quite a few, I reckon!

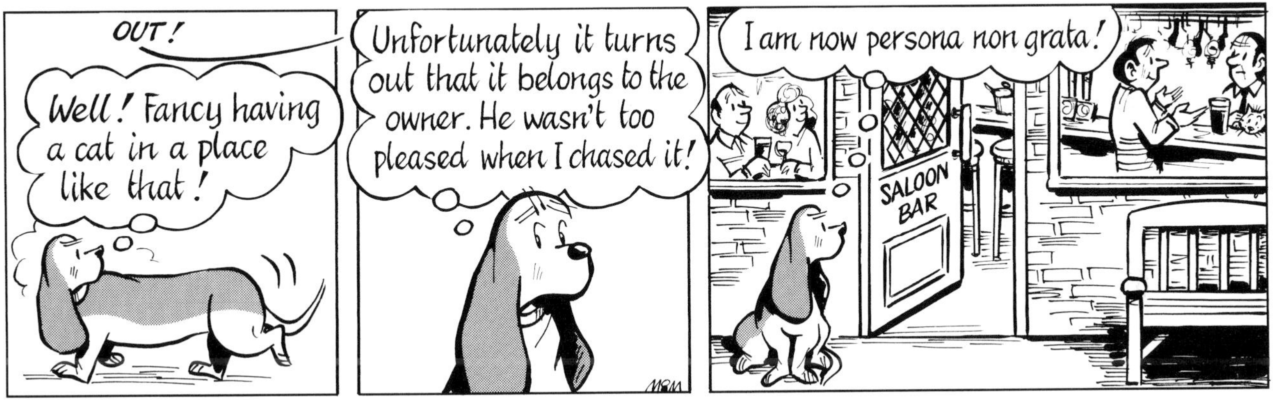
OUT!
Well! Fancy having a cat in a place like that!
Unfortunately it turns out that it belongs to the owner. He wasn't too pleased when I chased it!
I am now persona non grata!
SALOON BAR
M&M

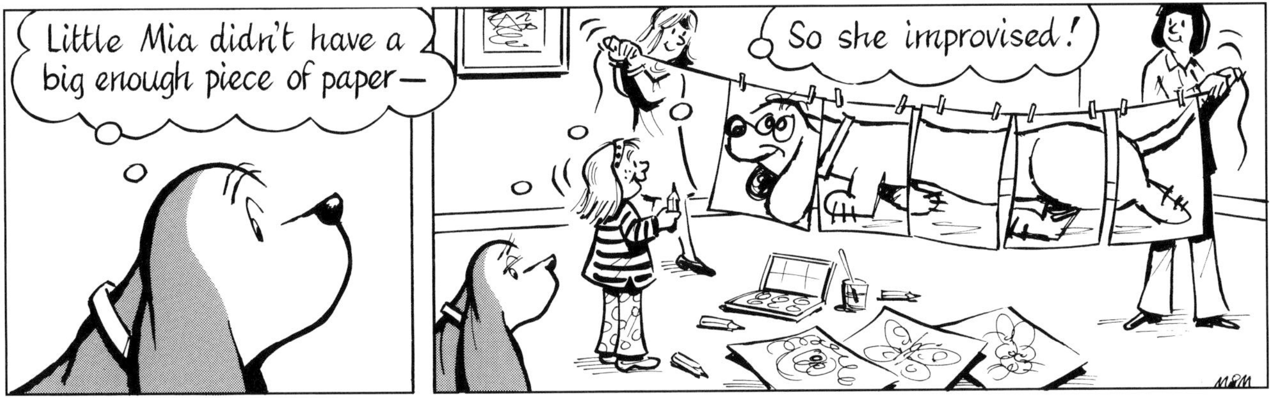
Little Mia didn't have a big enough piece of paper—
So she improvised!
M&M

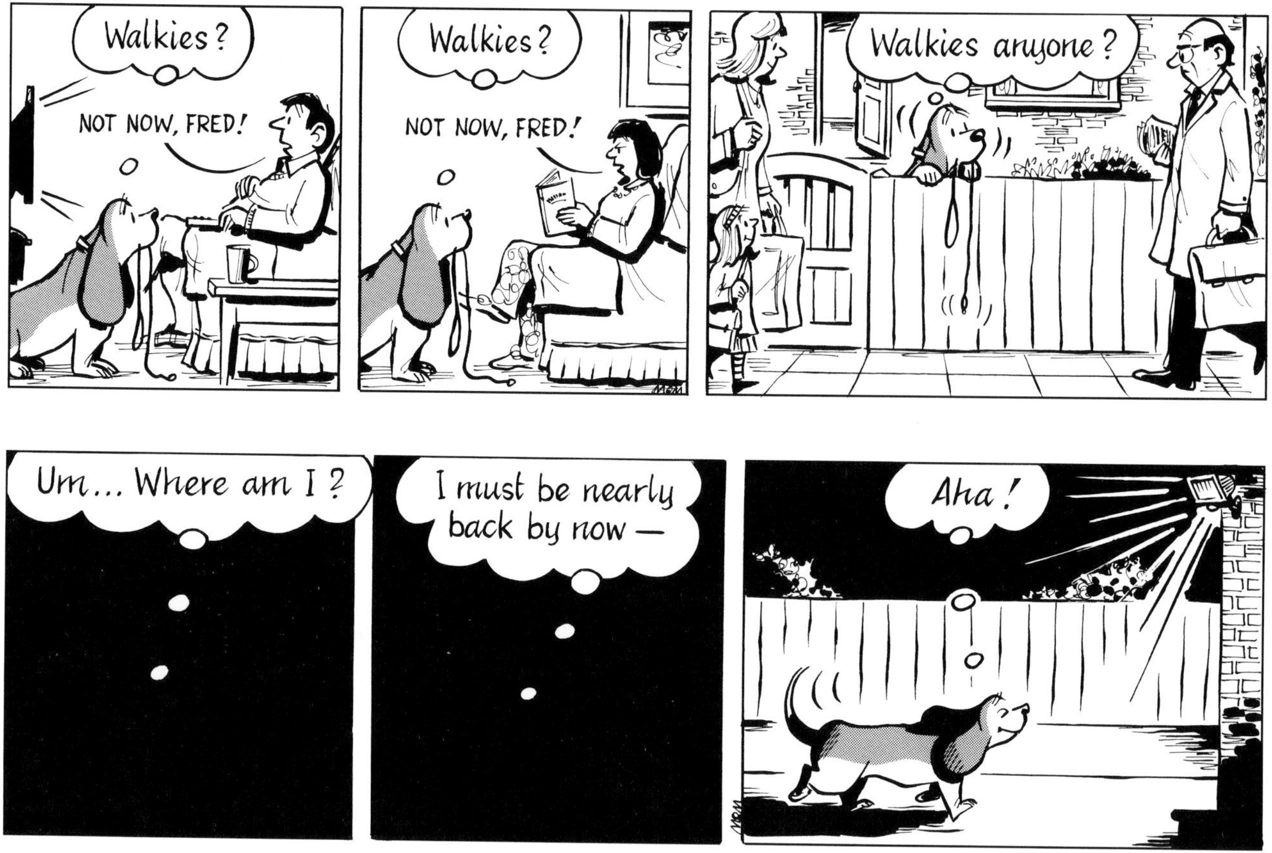
Walkies?
NOT NOW, FRED!
Walkies?
NOT NOW, FRED!
Walkies anyone?
Um... Where am I?
I must be nearly back by now —
Aha!

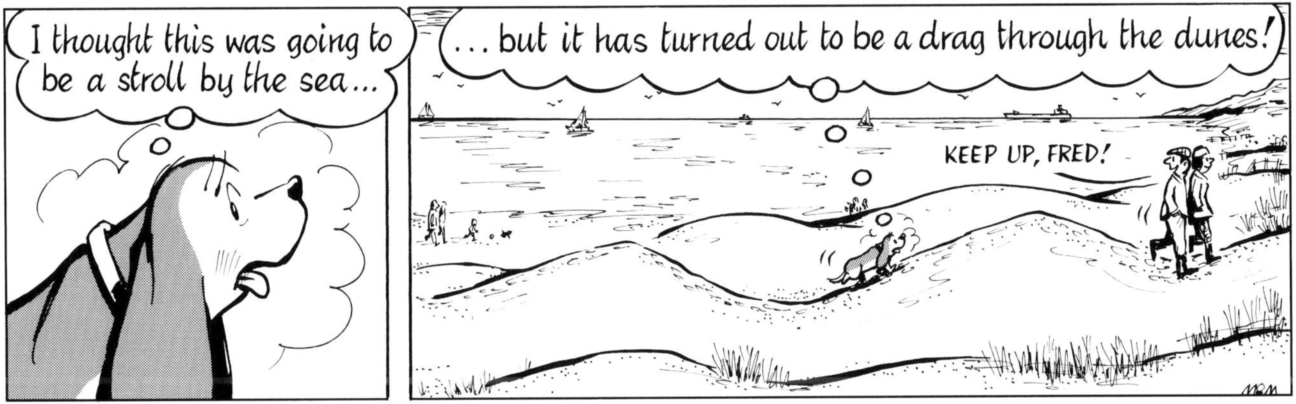
I thought this was going to be a stroll by the sea...
... but it has turned out to be a drag through the dunes!
KEEP UP, FRED!
MGM

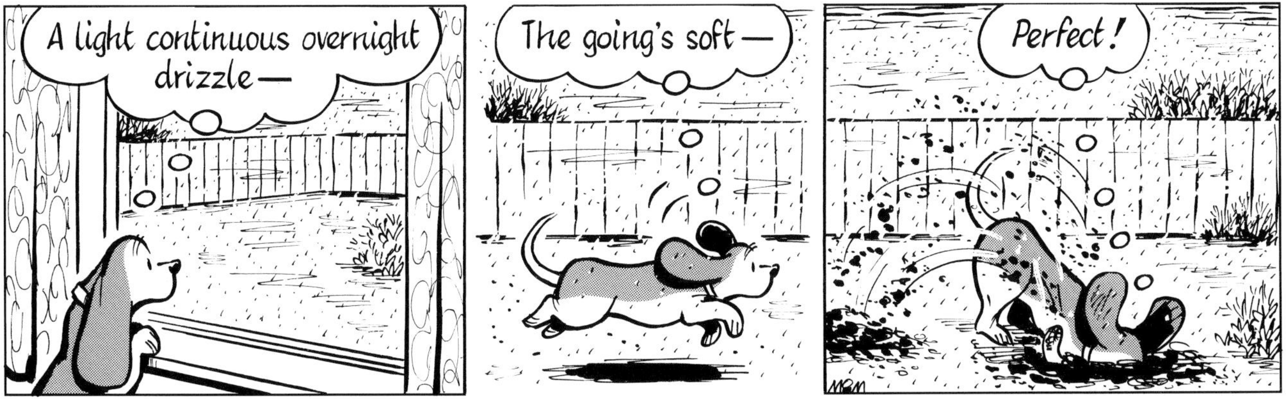
A light continuous overnight drizzle—
The going's soft—
Perfect!
MGM

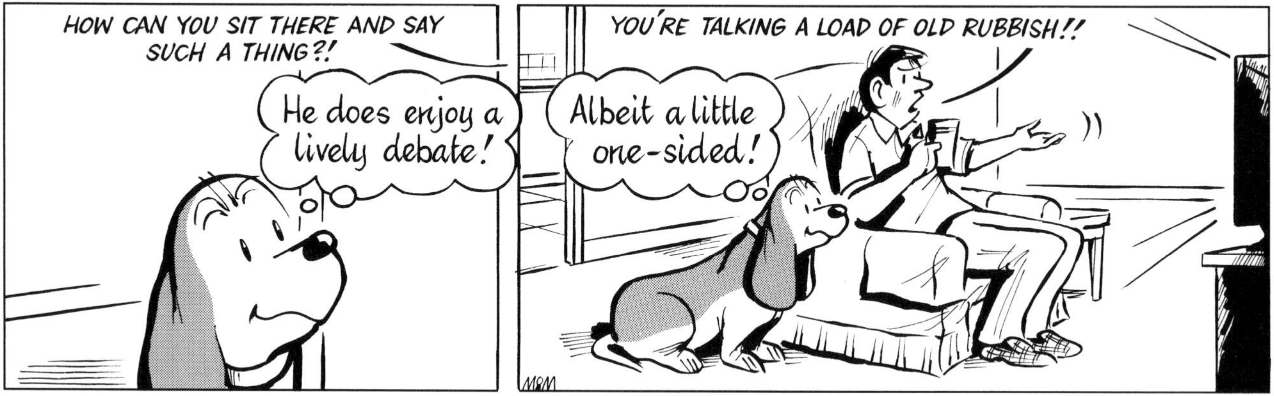
HOW CAN YOU SIT THERE AND SAY SUCH A THING?!
He does enjoy a lively debate!
YOU'RE TALKING A LOAD OF OLD RUBBISH!!
Albeit a little one-sided!

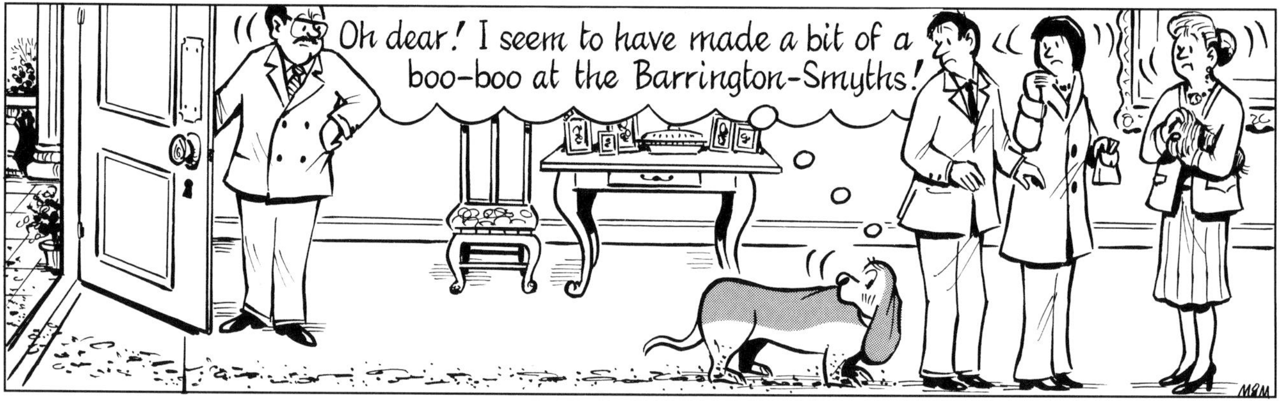
Oh dear! I seem to have made a bit of a boo-boo at the Barrington-Smyths!

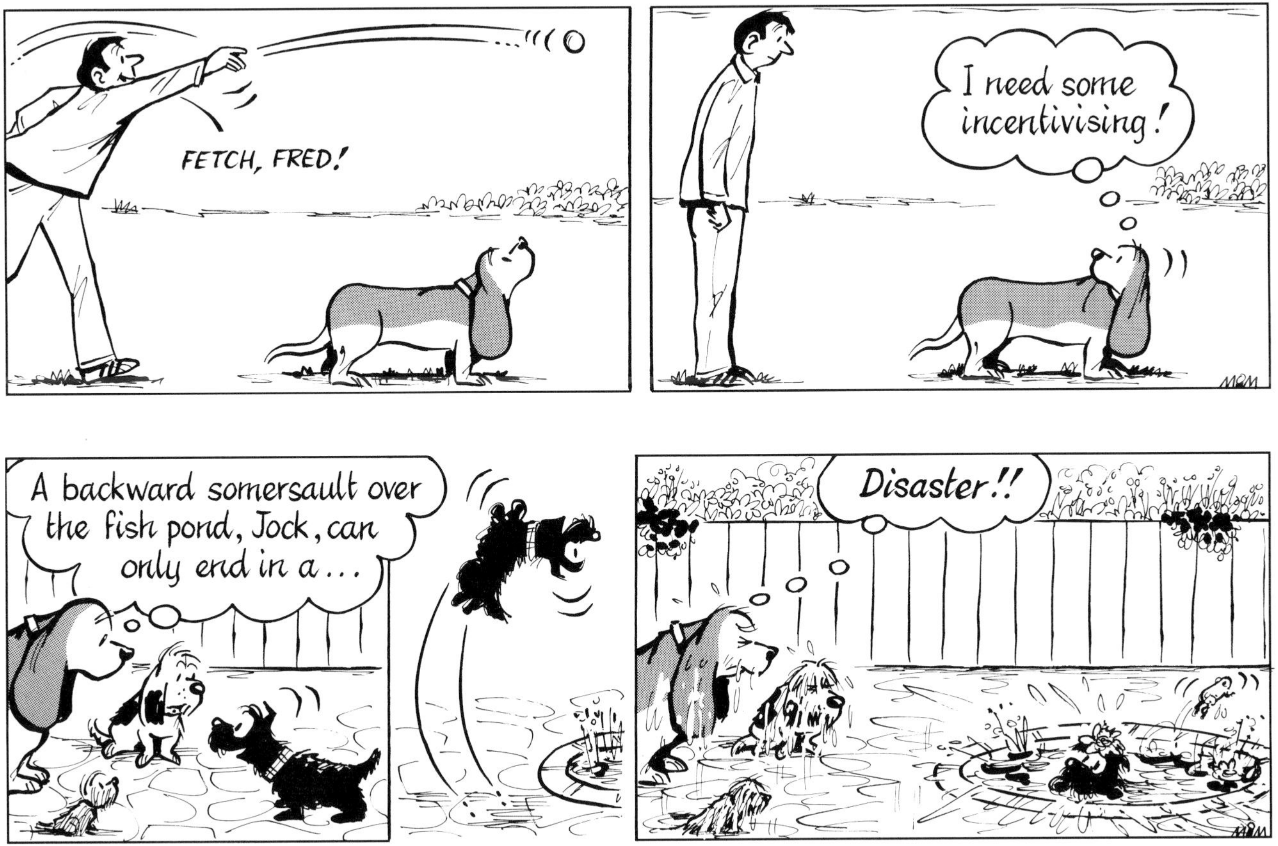
FETCH, FRED!
I need some incentivising!
A backward somersault over the fish pond, Jock, can only end in a . . .
Disaster!!

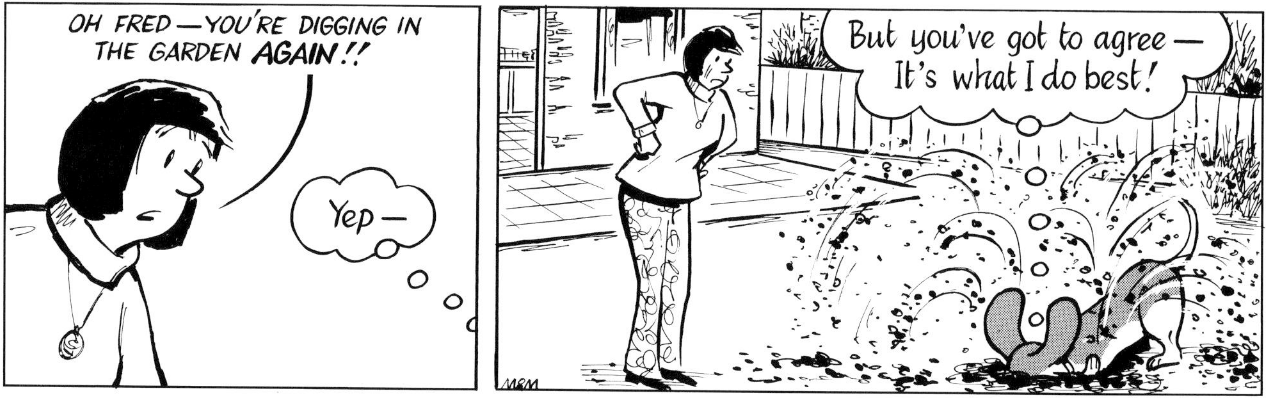
OH FRED—YOU'RE DIGGING IN THE GARDEN AGAIN!!
Yep—
But you've got to agree—It's what I do best!

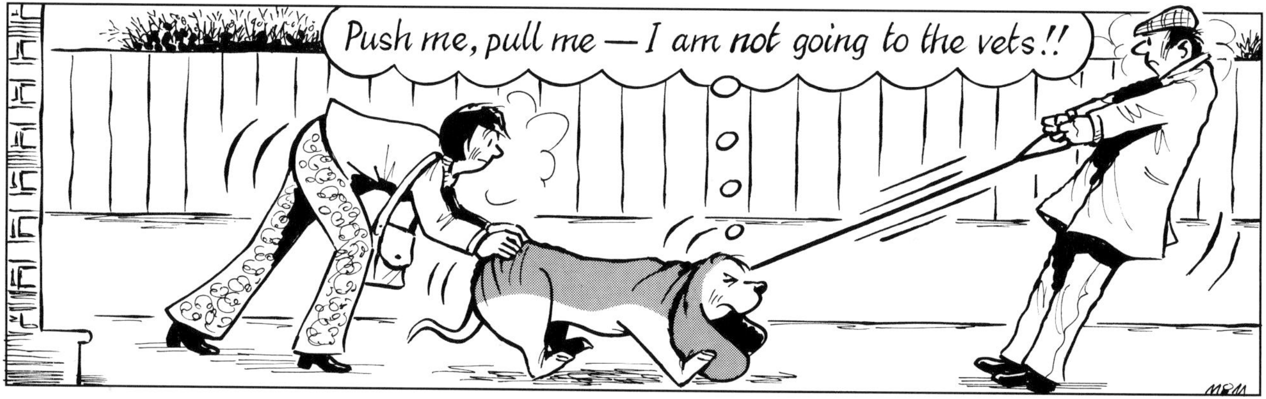
Push me, pull me—I am not going to the vets!!

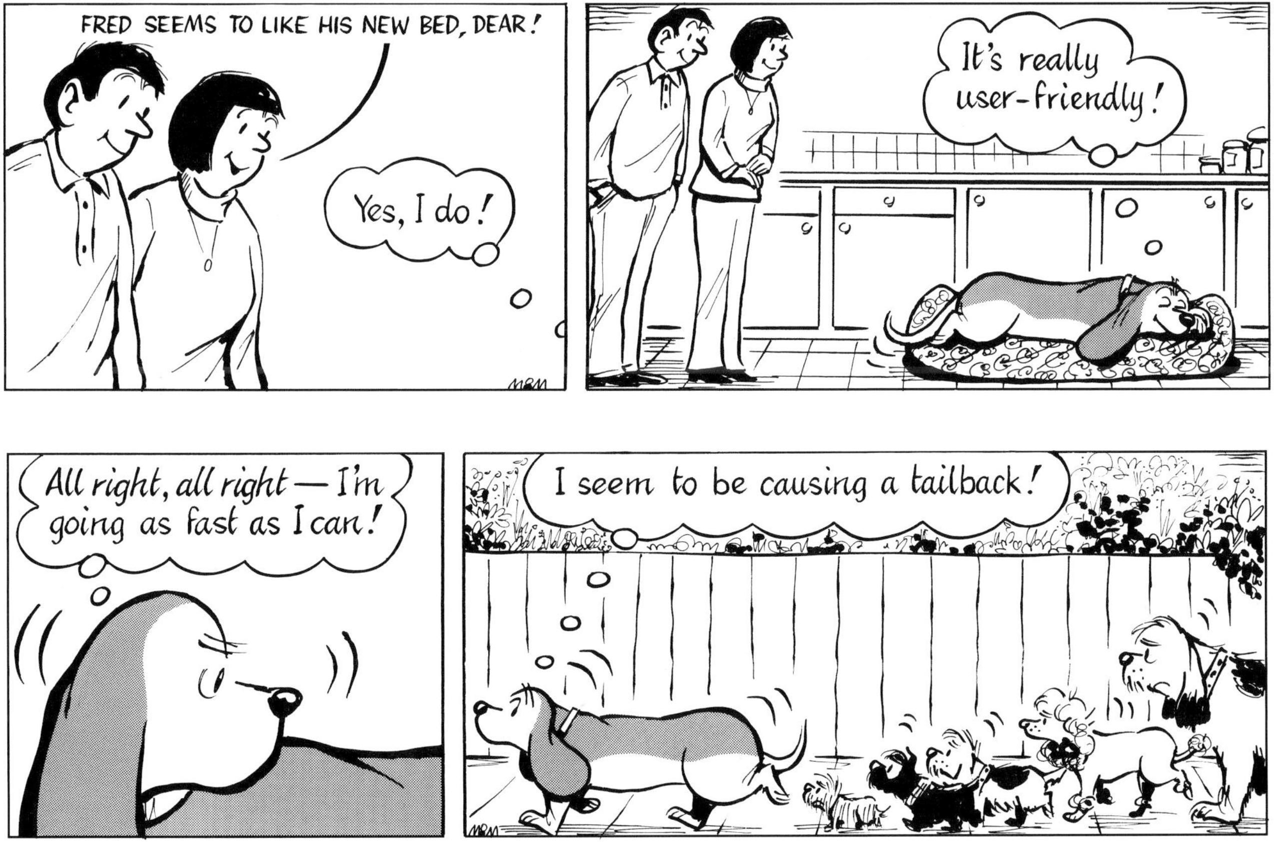
FRED SEEMS TO LIKE HIS NEW BED, DEAR!
Yes, I do!
It's really user-friendly!
All right, all right — I'm going as fast as I can!
I seem to be causing a tailback!

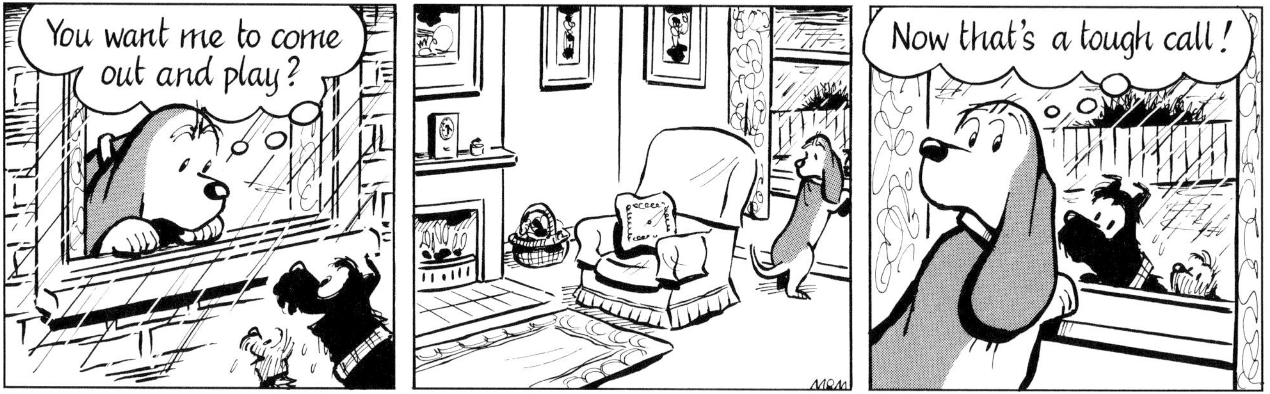
You want me to come out and play?
Now that's a tough call!

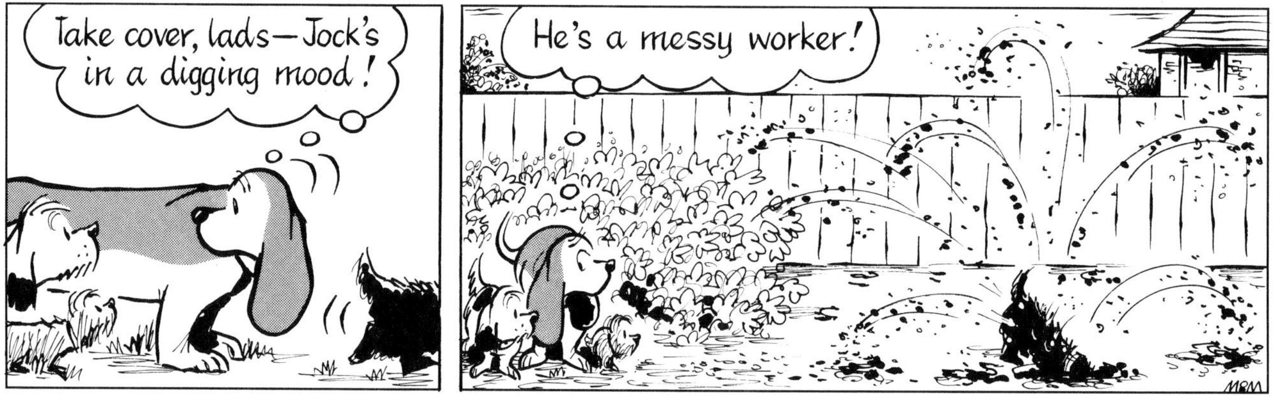
Take cover, lads—Jock's in a digging mood!
He's a messy worker!

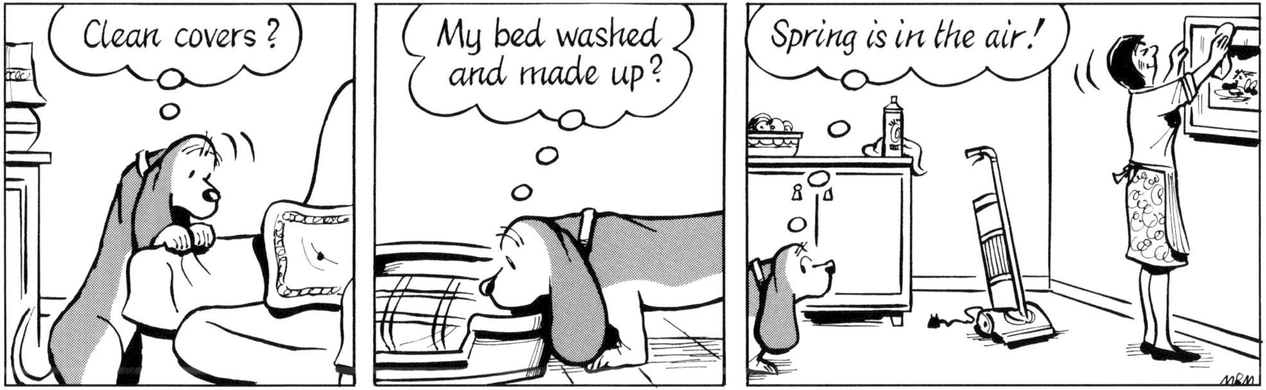
Clean covers?
My bed washed and made up?
Spring is in the air!

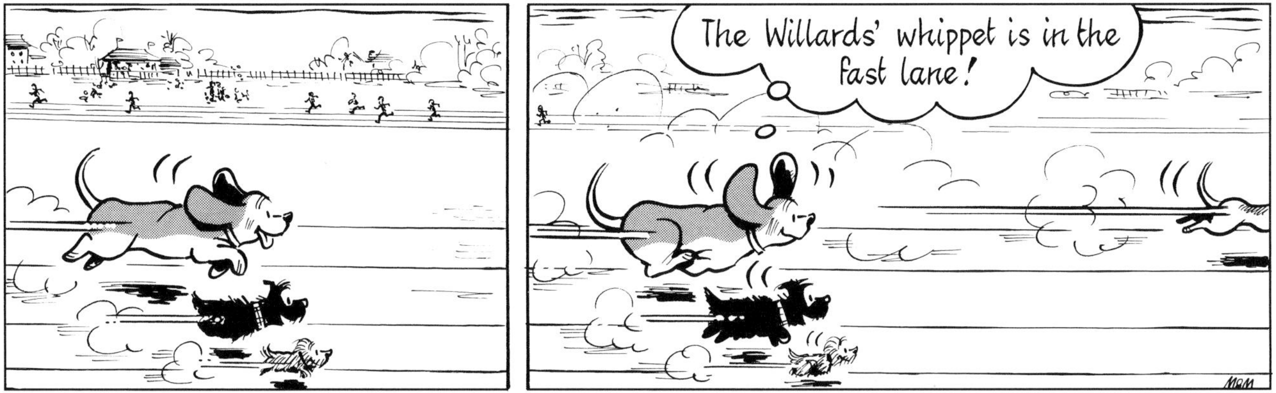
The Willards' whippet is in the fast lane!

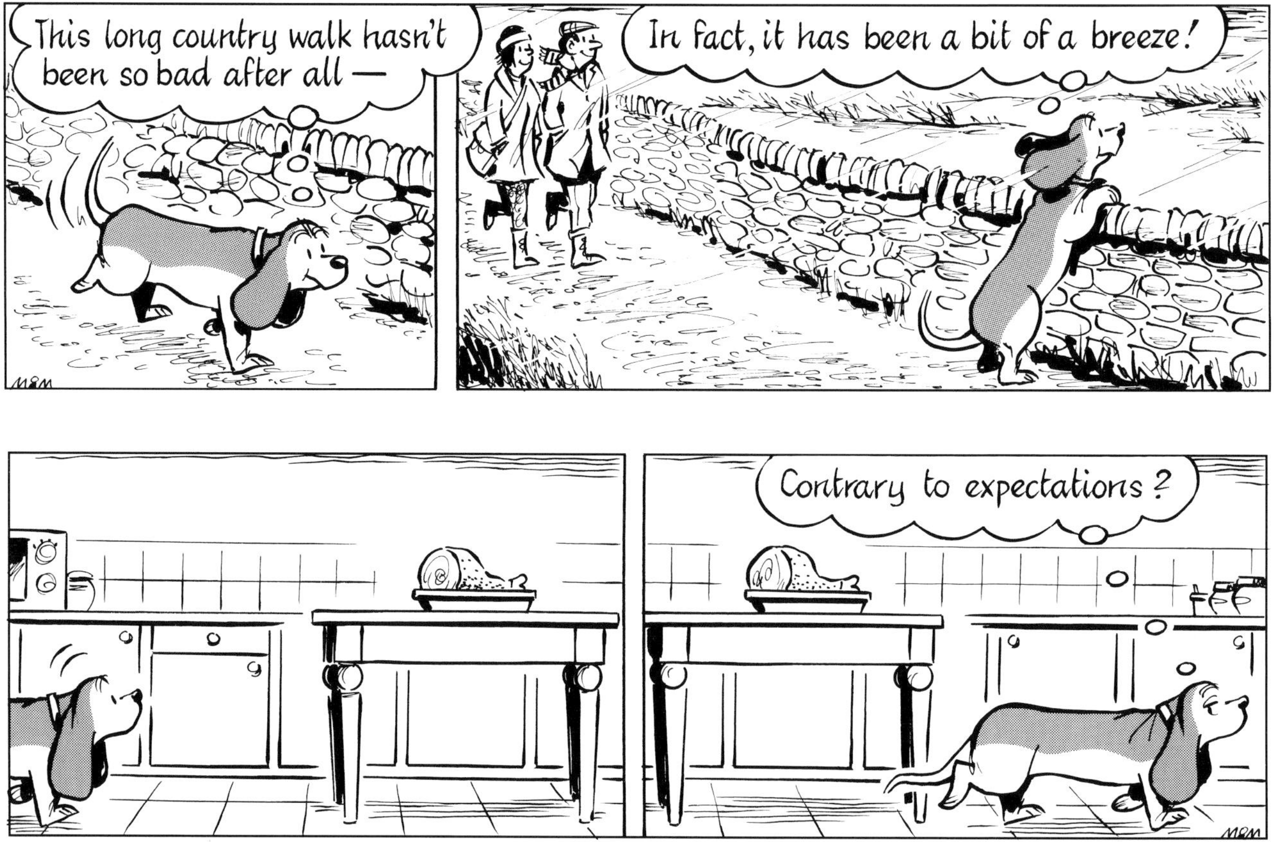
This long country walk hasn't been so bad after all —
In fact, it has been a bit of a breeze!
Contrary to expectations?

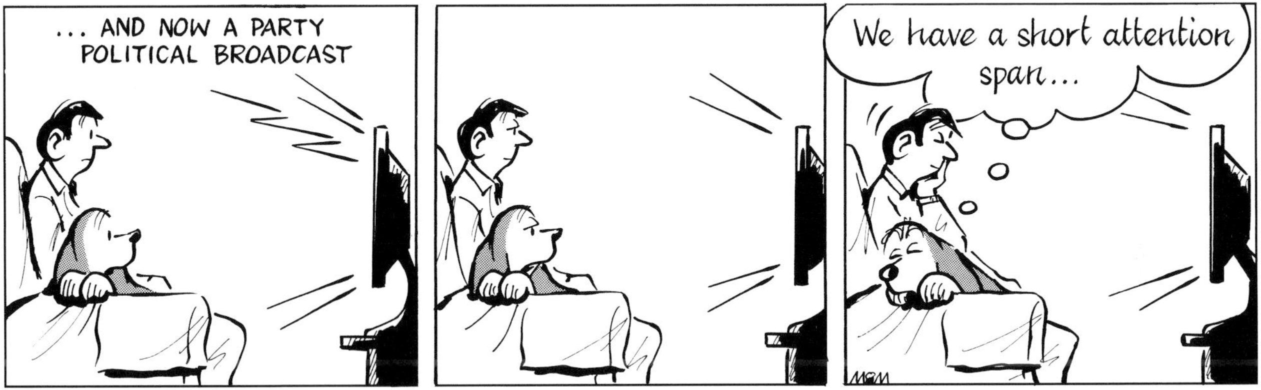

... AND NOW A PARTY POLITICAL BROADCAST
We have a short attention span...
MGM

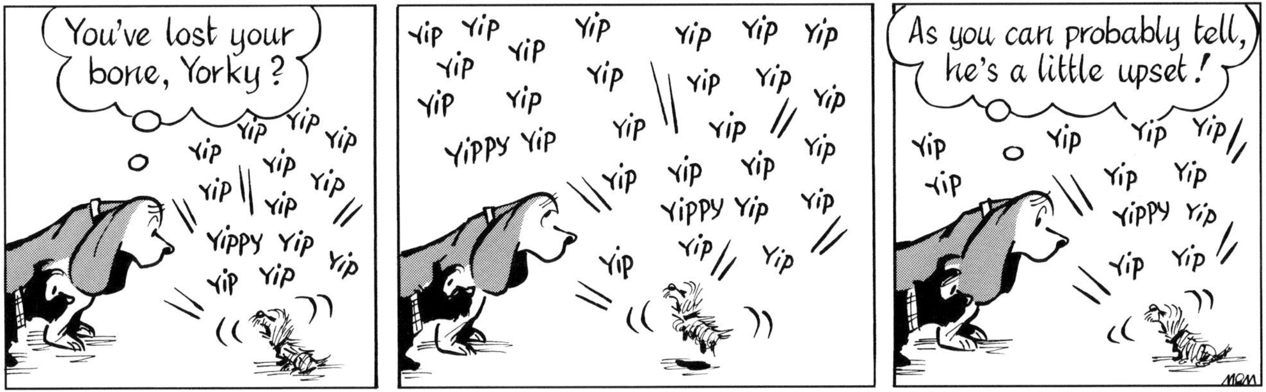

You've lost your bone, Yorky?
Yip Yip Yip Yip Yip Yip Yip Yip Yip Yippy Yip Yip Yip Yip Yip
Yip Yip Yip Yip Yip Yip Yip Yip Yip Yip Yip Yip Yippy Yip Yip Yip Yip Yip Yip Yip Yip Yip Yip Yippy Yip Yip Yip Yip Yip
As you can probably tell, he's a little upset!
Yip Yip Yip Yip Yip Yip Yip Yippy Yip Yip Yip
MGM

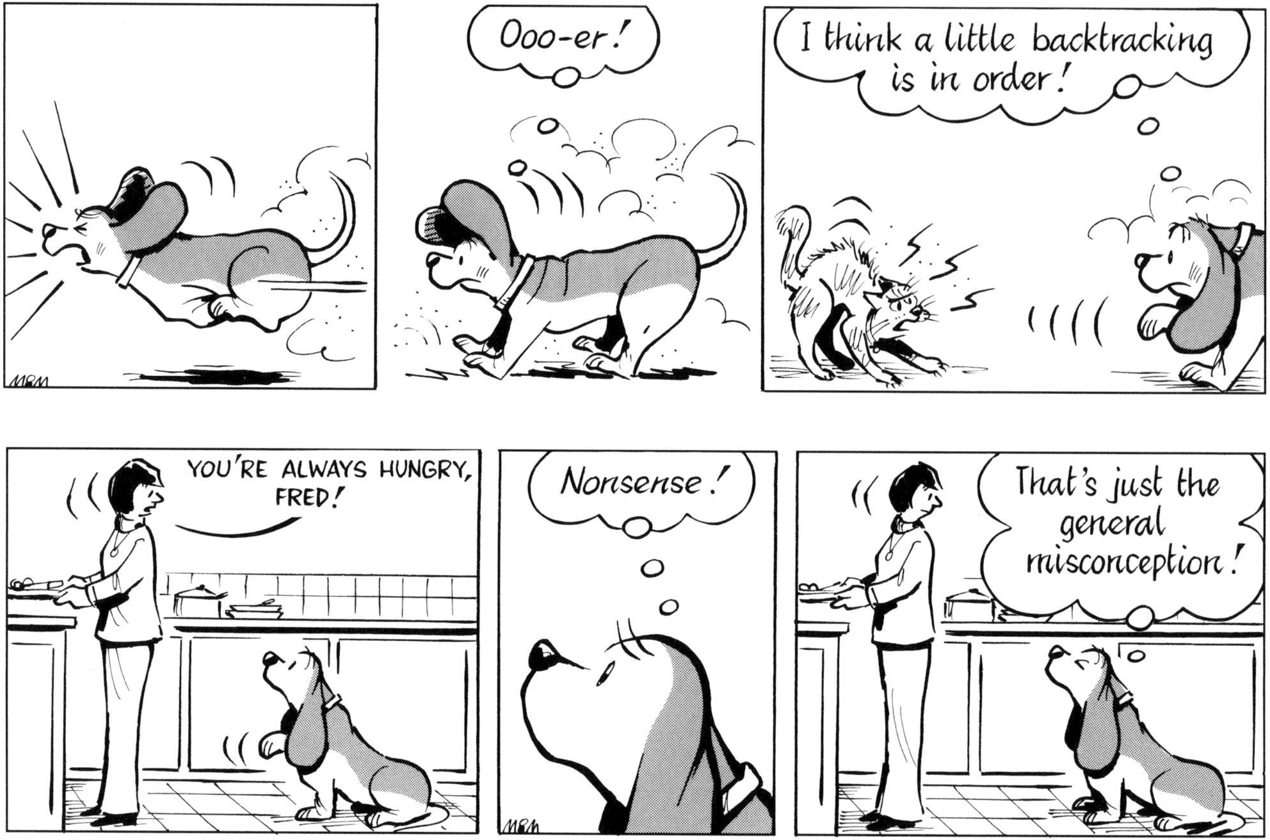
Ooo-er!
I think a little backtracking is in order!
YOU'RE ALWAYS HUNGRY, FRED!
Nonsense!
That's just the general misconception!

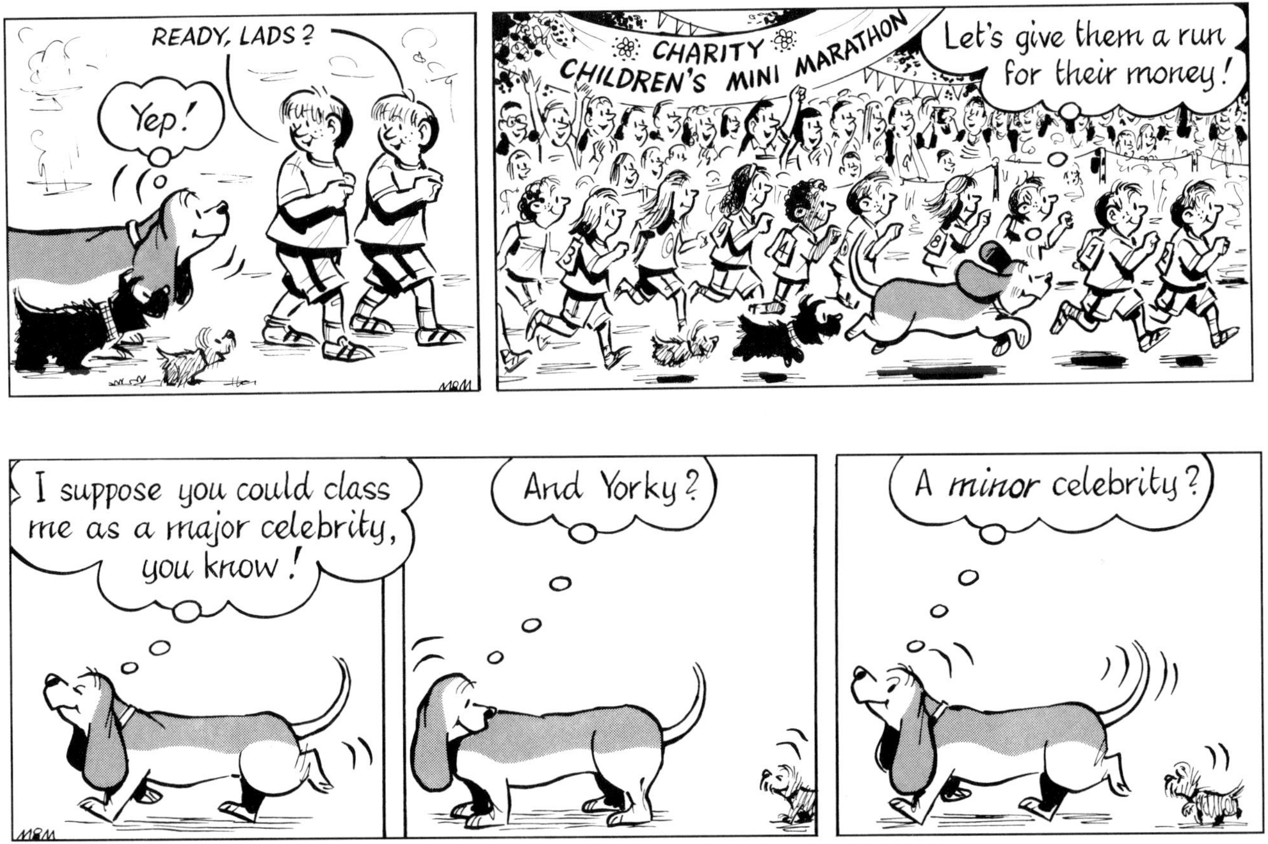
READY, LADS?
Yep!
CHARITY CHILDREN'S MINI MARATHON
Let's give them a run for their money!
I suppose you could class me as a major celebrity, you know!
And Yorky?
A *minor* celebrity?

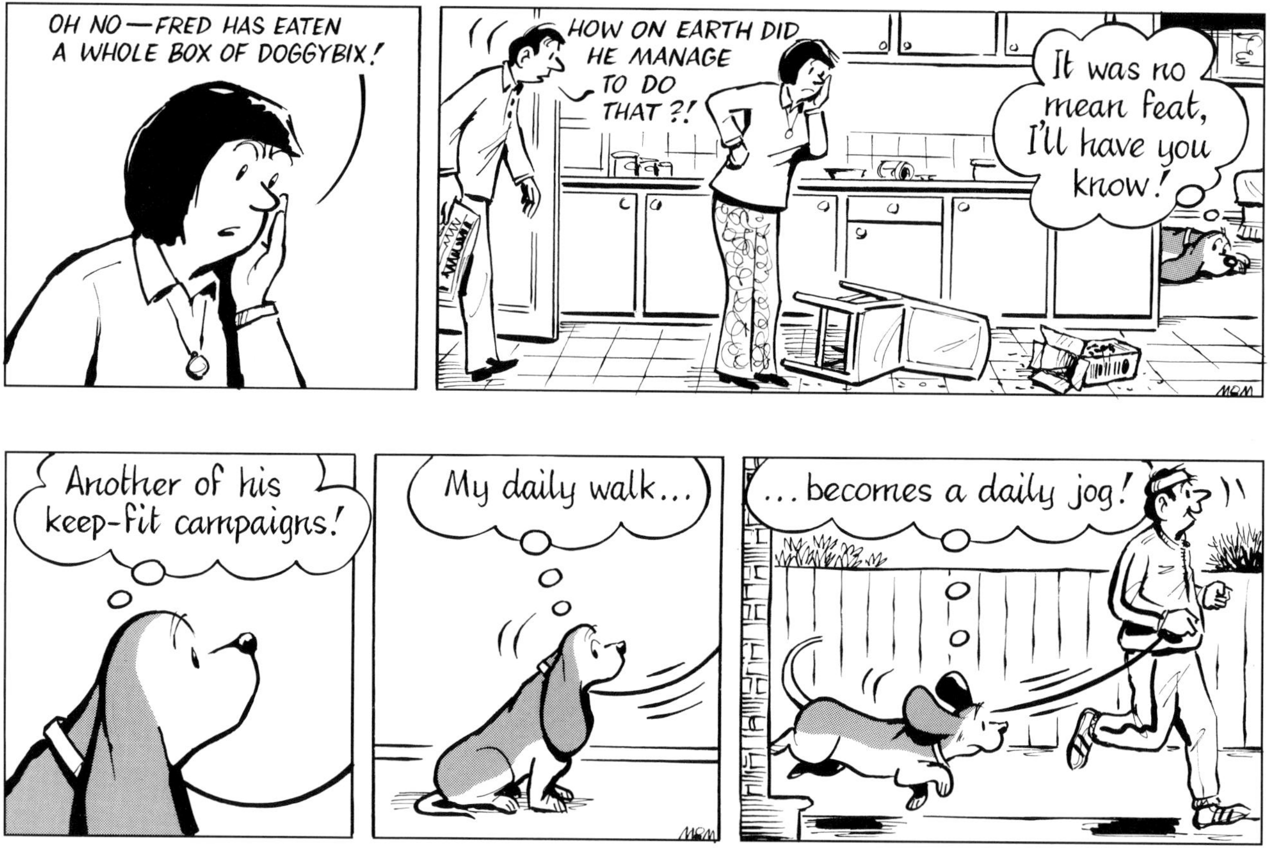
OH NO — FRED HAS EATEN A WHOLE BOX OF DOGGYBIX!
HOW ON EARTH DID HE MANAGE TO DO THAT ?!
It was no mean feat, I'll have you know!
Another of his keep-fit campaigns!
My daily walk...
... becomes a daily jog!

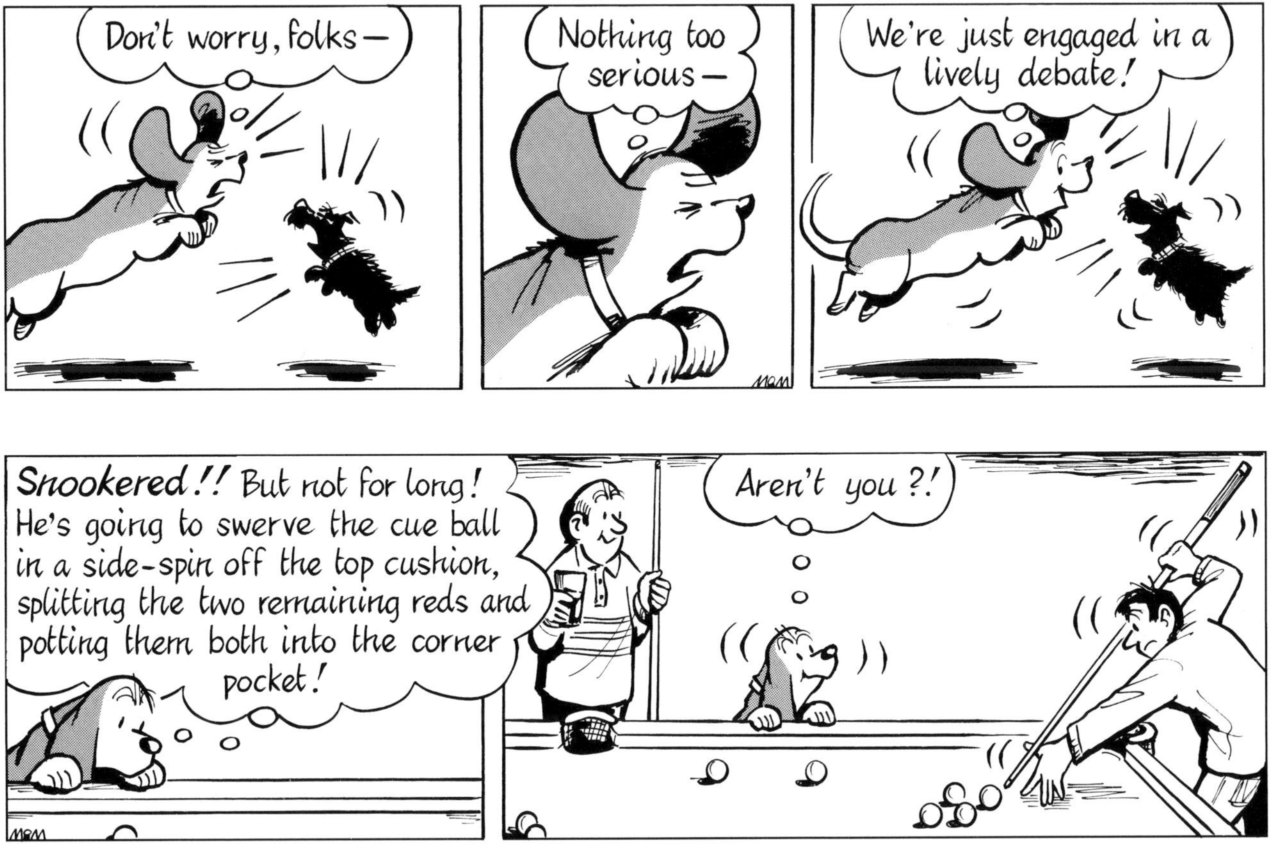
Don't worry, folks—
Nothing too serious—
We're just engaged in a lively debate!
MGM
Snookered!! But not for long! He's going to swerve the cue ball in a side-spin off the top cushion, splitting the two remaining reds and potting them both into the corner pocket!
Aren't you?!
MGM

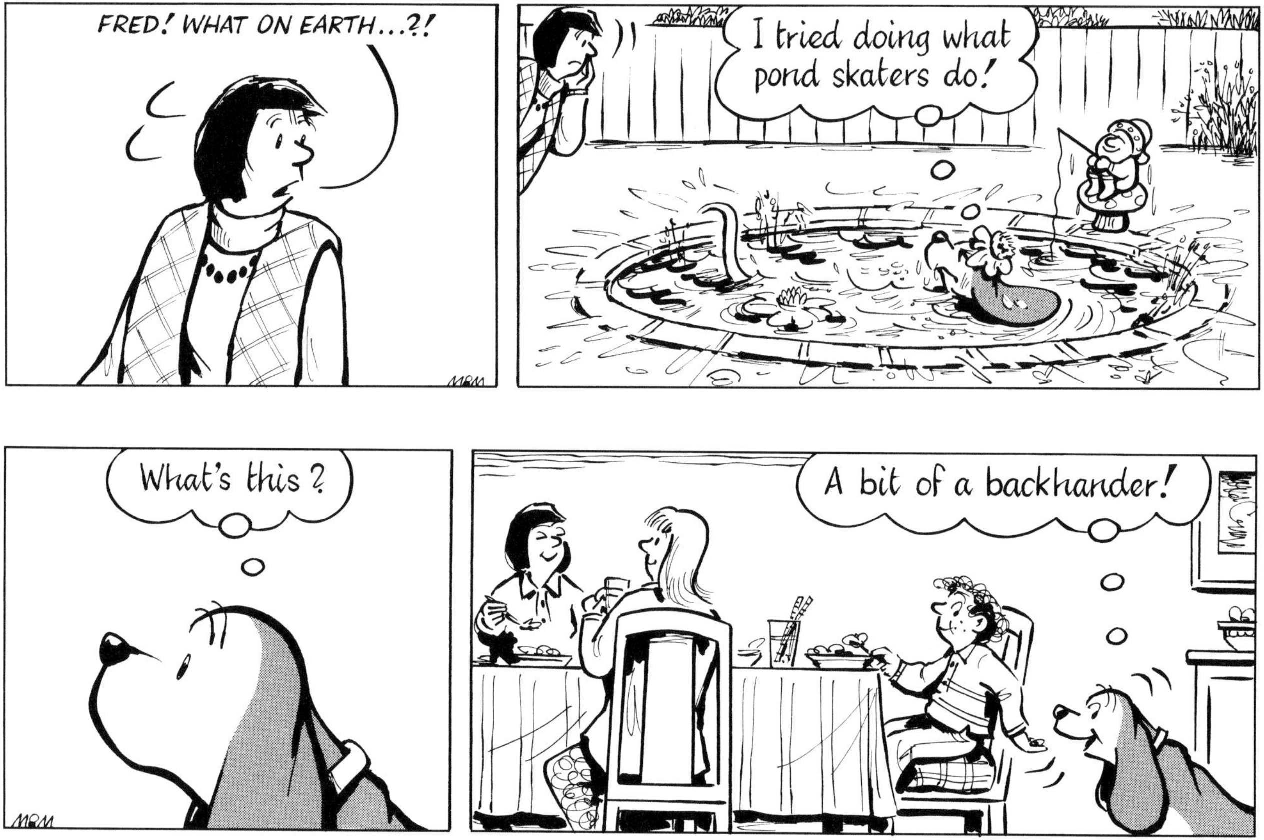

FRED! WHAT ON EARTH...?!
I tried doing what pond skaters do!
What's this?
A bit of a backhander!

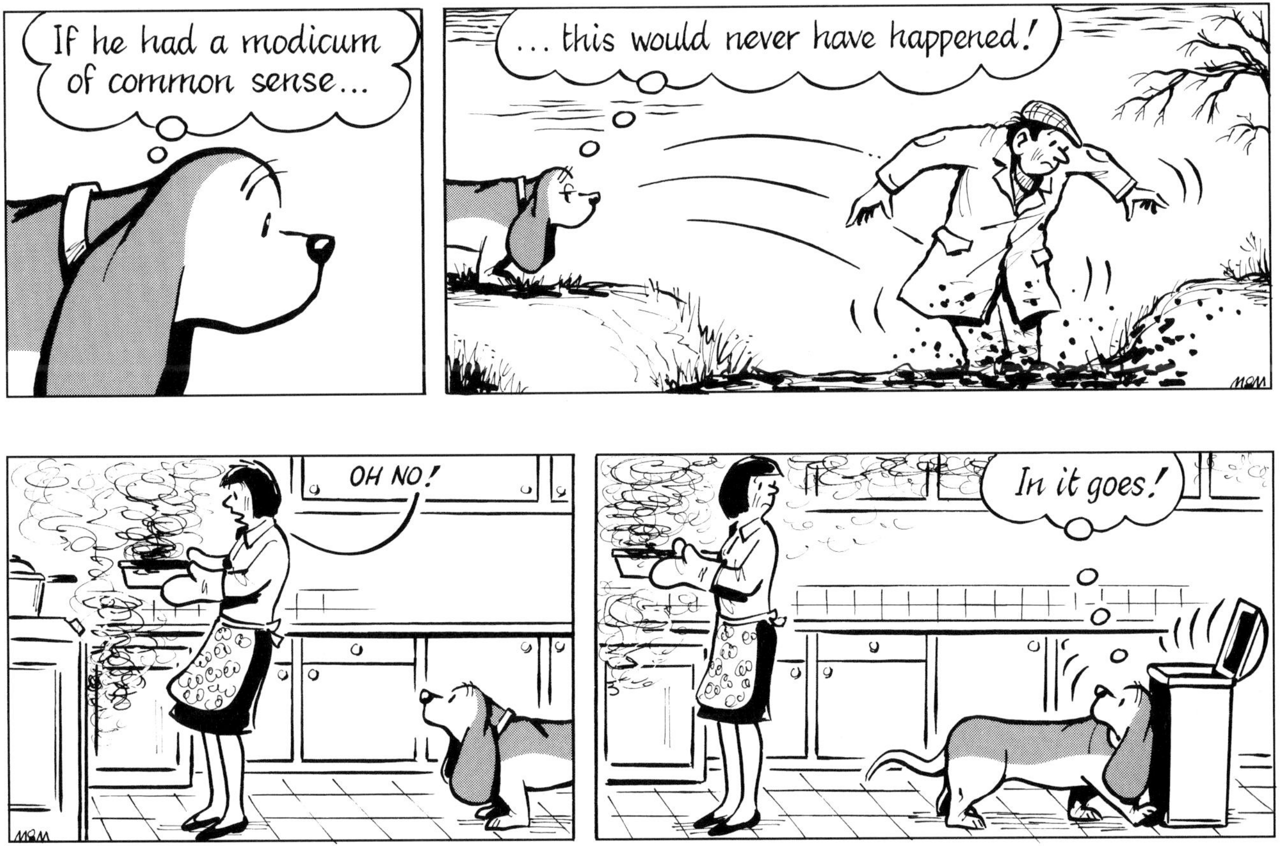
If he had a modicum of common sense...
... this would never have happened!
MSM
OH NO!
MSM
In it goes!

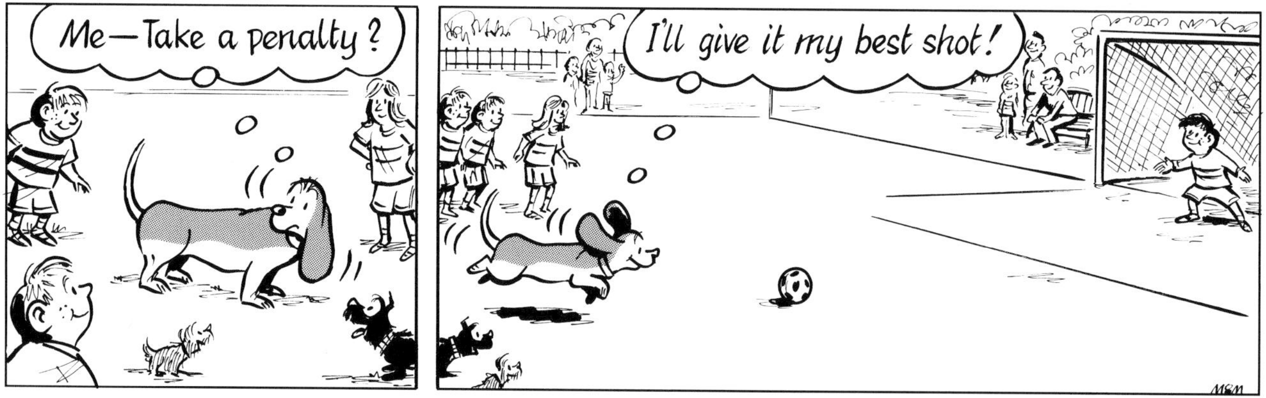
Me—Take a penalty?
I'll give it my best shot!
MSM

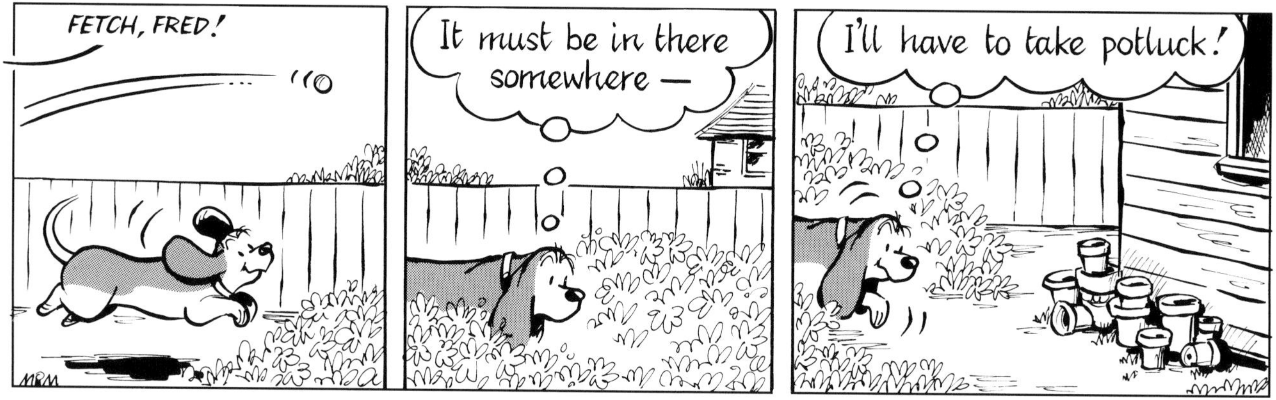
FETCH, FRED!
MSM
It must be in there somewhere—
I'll have to take potluck!

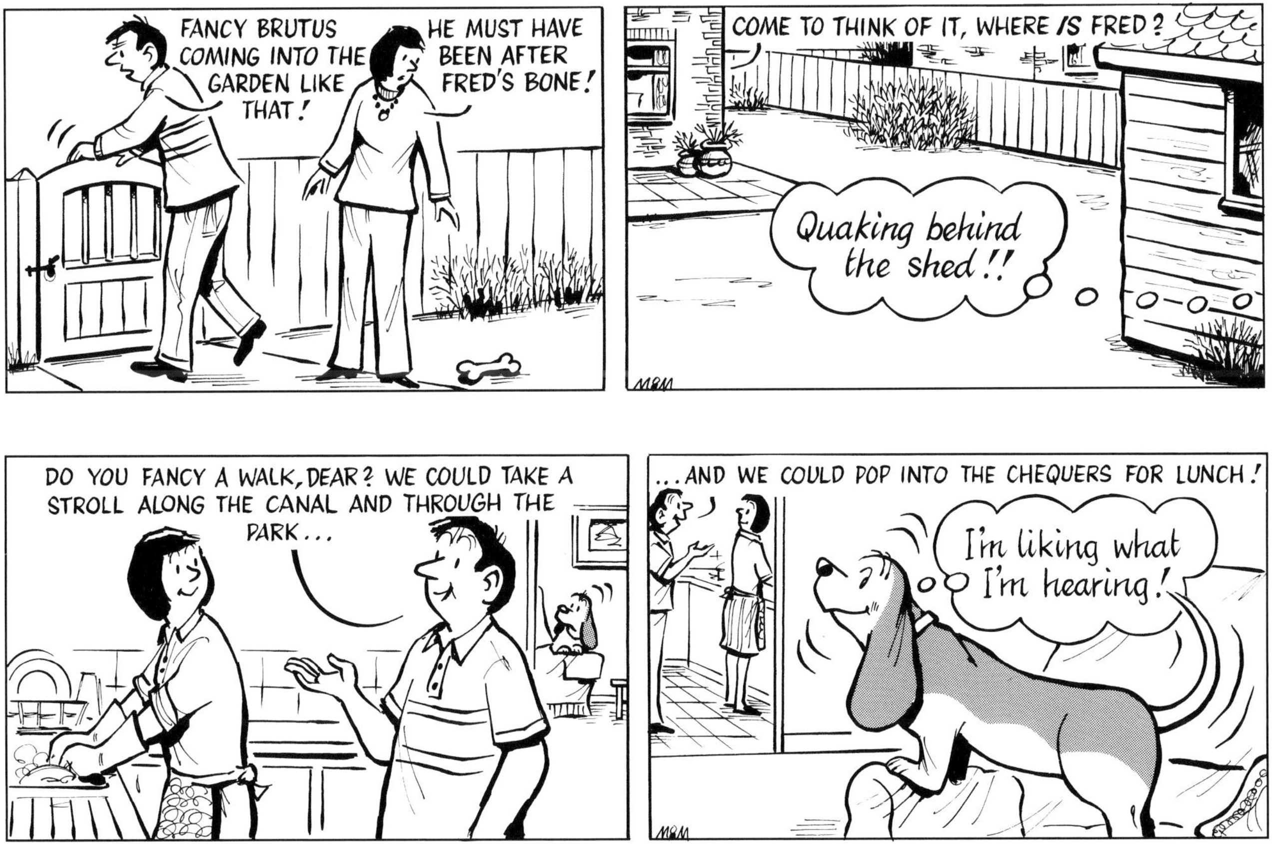
FANCY BRUTUS COMING INTO THE GARDEN LIKE THAT!
HE MUST HAVE BEEN AFTER FRED'S BONE!
COME TO THINK OF IT, WHERE IS FRED?
Quaking behind the shed!!
M&M
DO YOU FANCY A WALK, DEAR? WE COULD TAKE A STROLL ALONG THE CANAL AND THROUGH THE PARK...
...AND WE COULD POP INTO THE CHEQUERS FOR LUNCH!
I'm liking what I'm hearing!
M&M

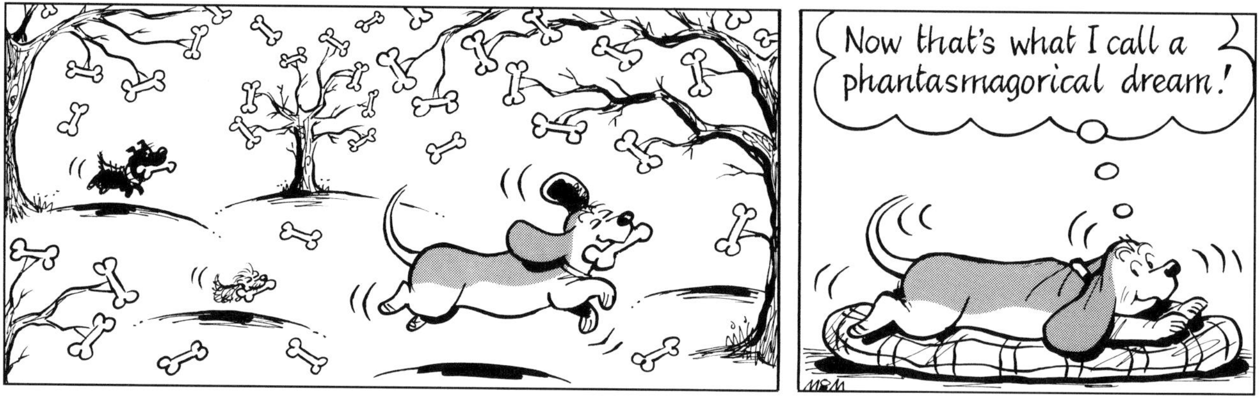
Now that's what I call a phantasmagorical dream!

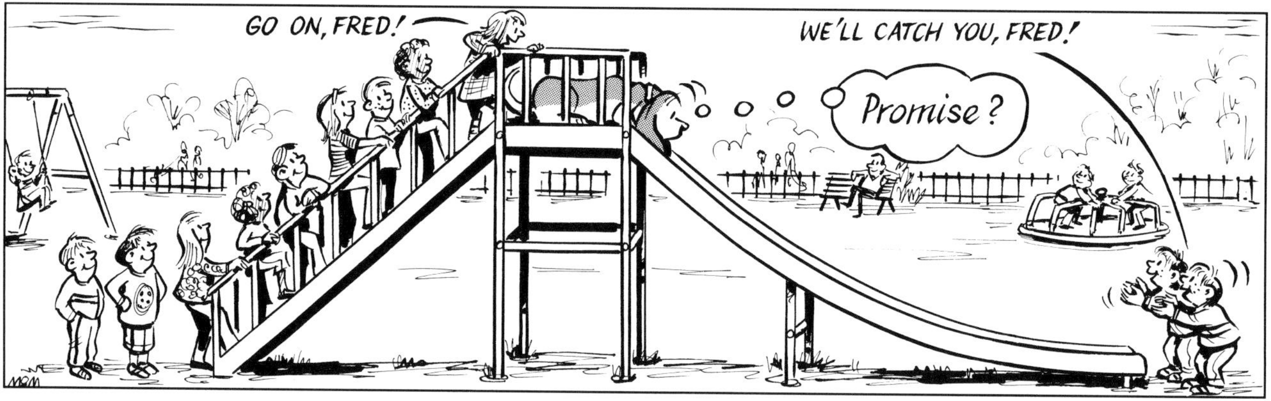
GO ON, FRED!
WE'LL CATCH YOU, FRED!
Promise?

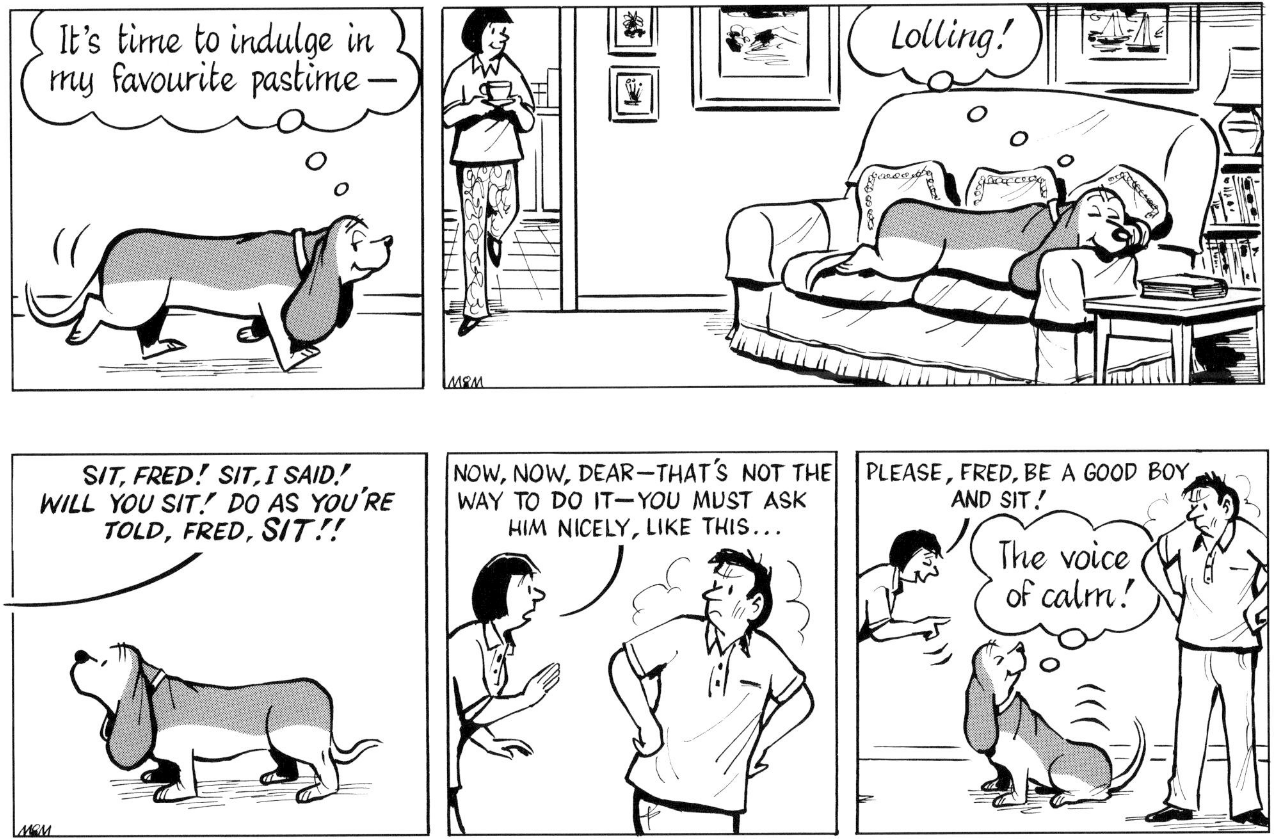
It's time to indulge in my favourite pastime —
Lolling!
M&M
SIT, FRED! SIT, I SAID! WILL YOU SIT! DO AS YOU'RE TOLD, FRED, SIT!!
NOW, NOW, DEAR—THAT'S NOT THE WAY TO DO IT—YOU MUST ASK HIM NICELY, LIKE THIS...
PLEASE, FRED, BE A GOOD BOY AND SIT!
The voice of calm!
M&M

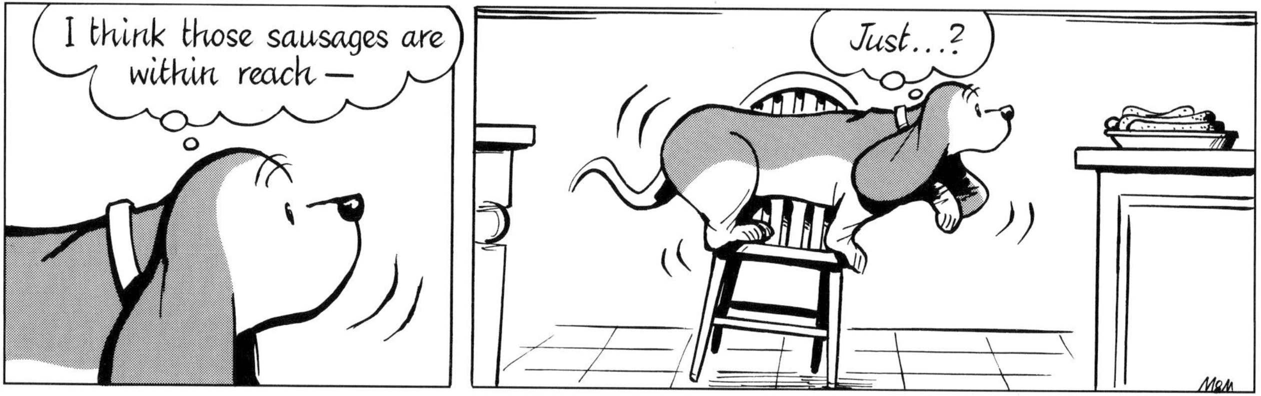
I think those sausages are within reach —
Just...?

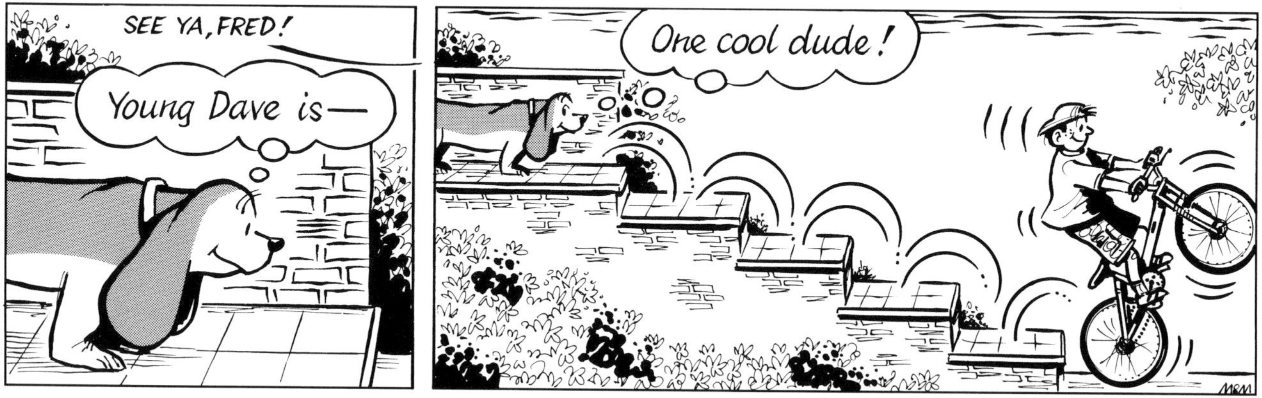
SEE YA, FRED!
Young Dave is —
One cool dude!

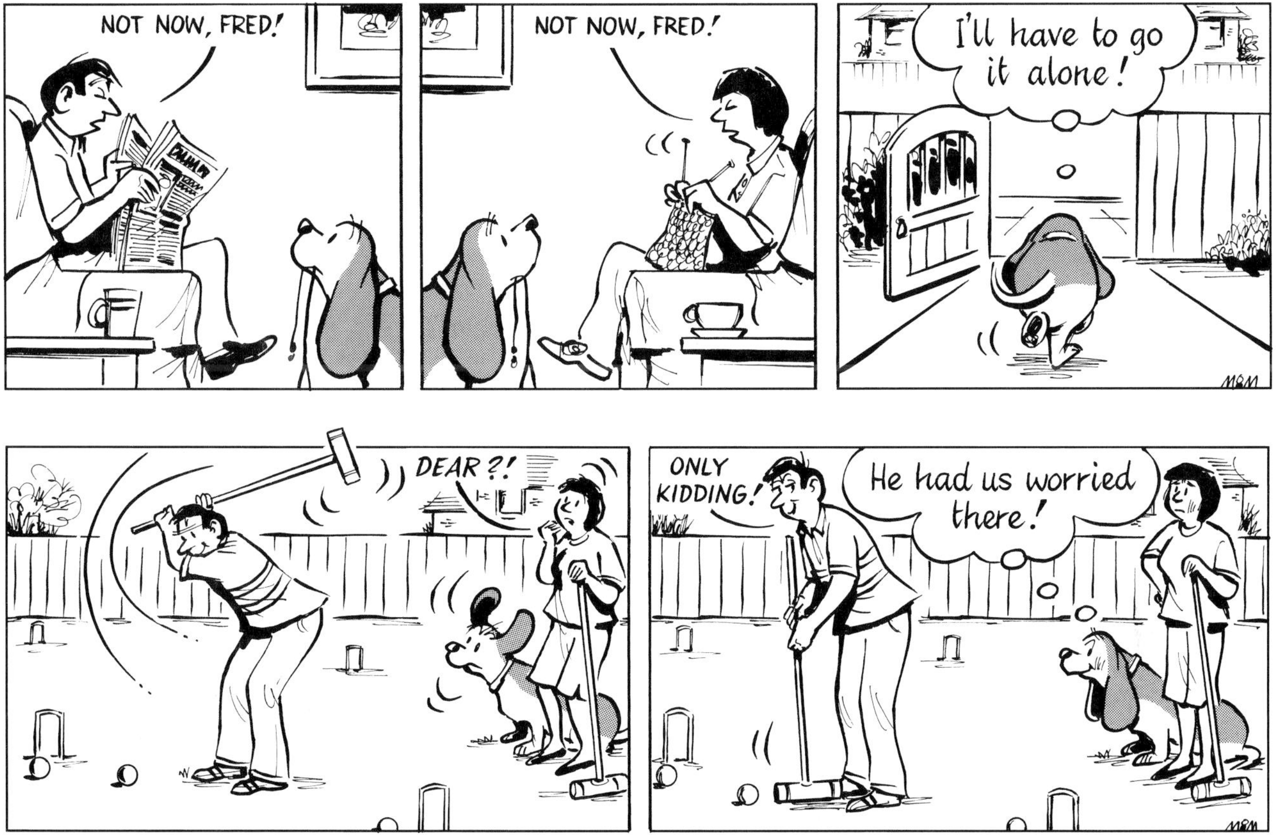

NOT NOW, FRED!
NOT NOW, FRED!
I'll have to go it alone!
M&M
DEAR?!
ONLY KIDDING!
He had us worried there!
M&M

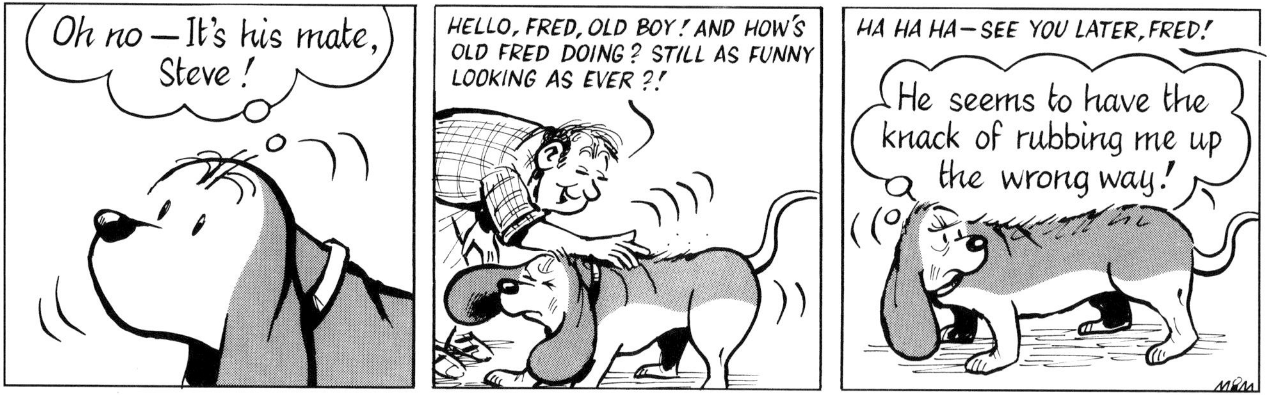
Oh no — It's his mate, Steve!
HELLO, FRED, OLD BOY! AND HOW'S OLD FRED DOING? STILL AS FUNNY LOOKING AS EVER?!
HA HA HA — SEE YOU LATER, FRED!
He seems to have the knack of rubbing me up the wrong way!

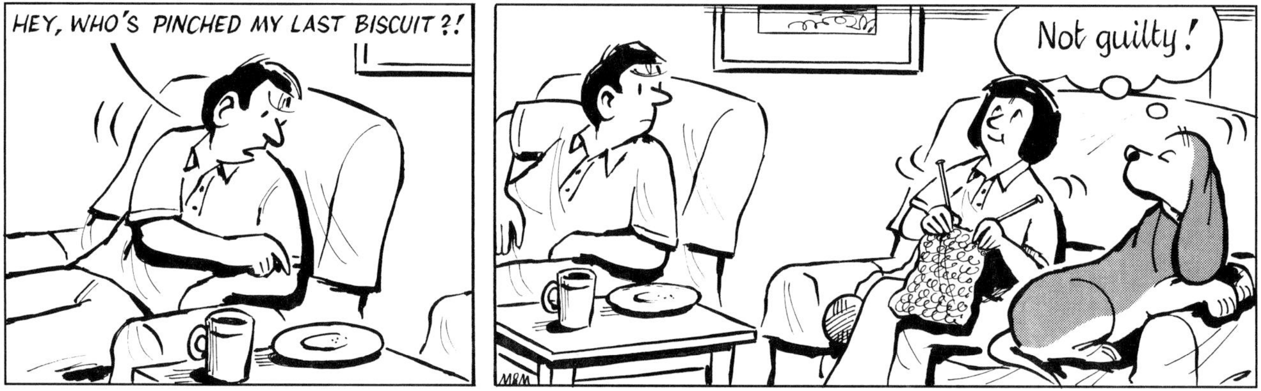
HEY, WHO'S PINCHED MY LAST BISCUIT?!
Not guilty!

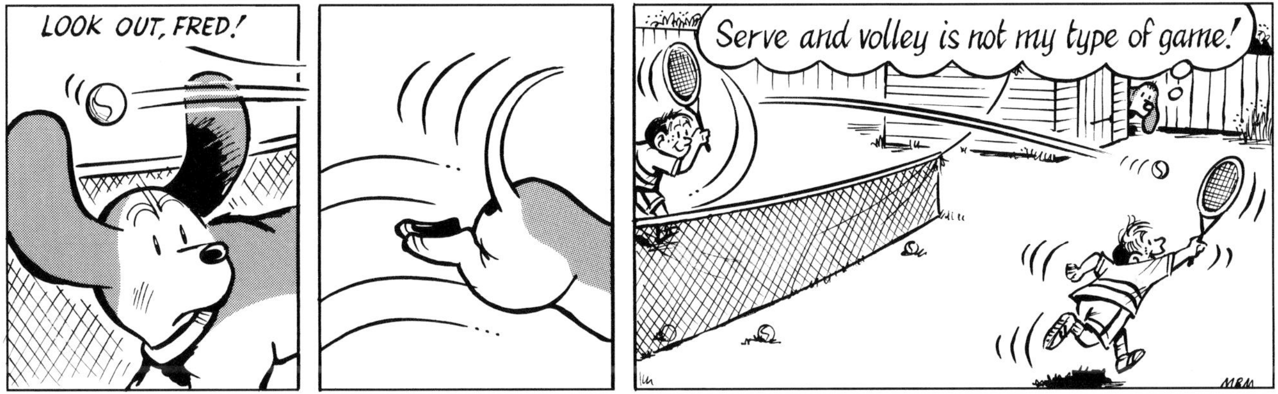
LOOK OUT, FRED!
Serve and volley is not my type of game!
MBM

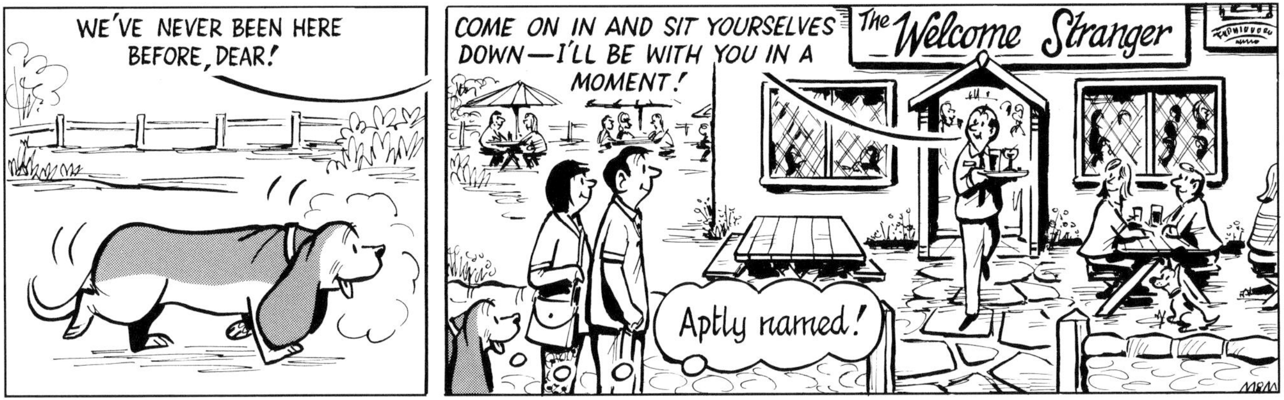
WE'VE NEVER BEEN HERE BEFORE, DEAR!
COME ON IN AND SIT YOURSELVES DOWN—I'LL BE WITH YOU IN A MOMENT!
The Welcome Stranger
Aptly named!
MBM

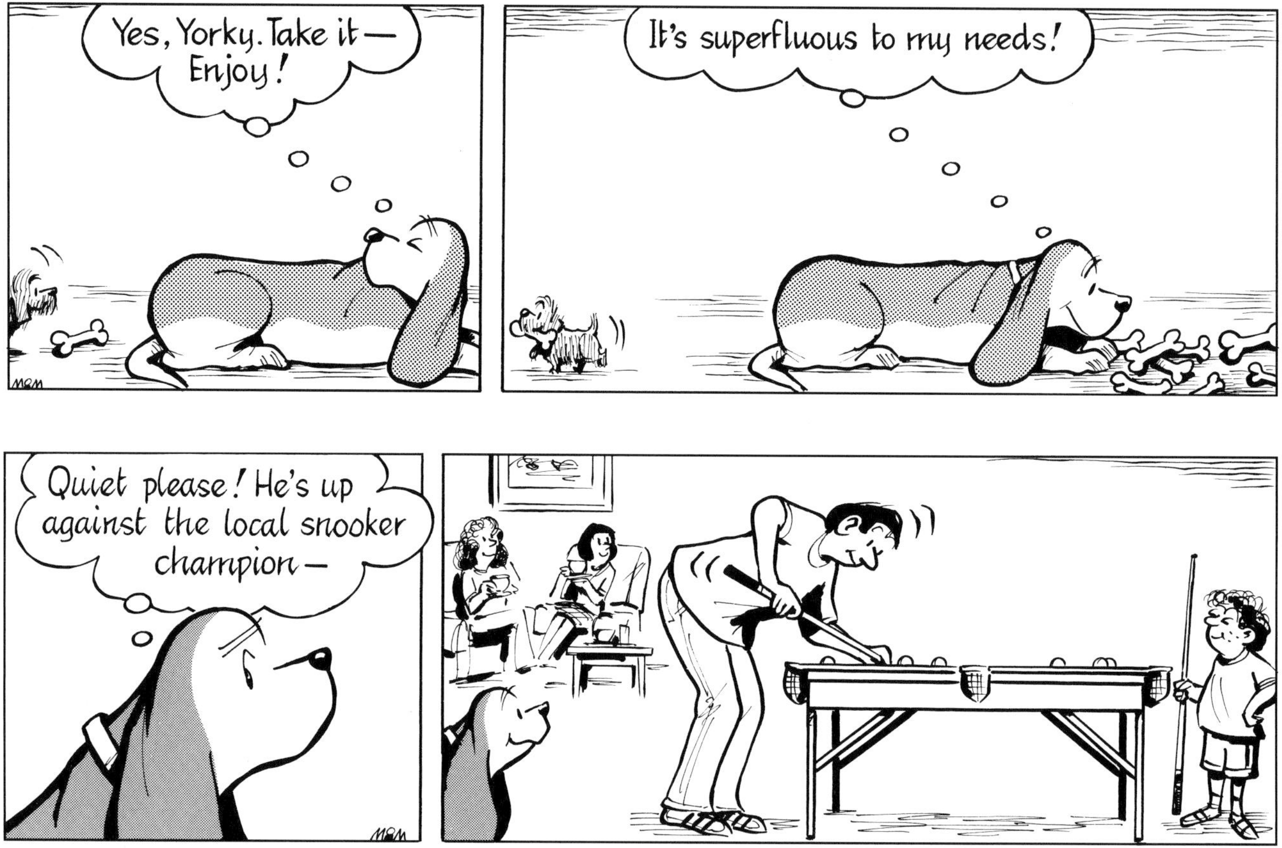

Yes, Yorky. Take it — Enjoy!
It's superfluous to my needs!
Quiet please! He's up against the local snooker champion —

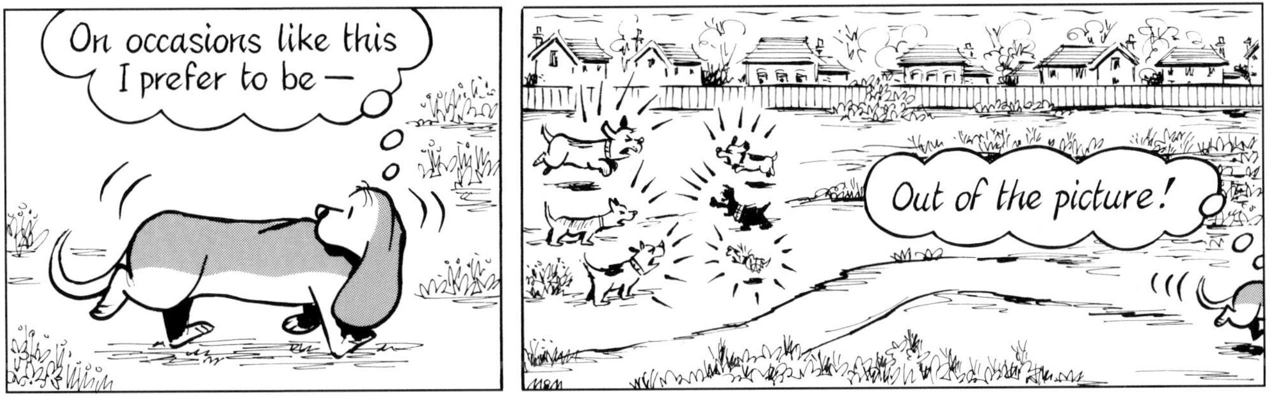
On occasions like this I prefer to be —
Out of the picture!

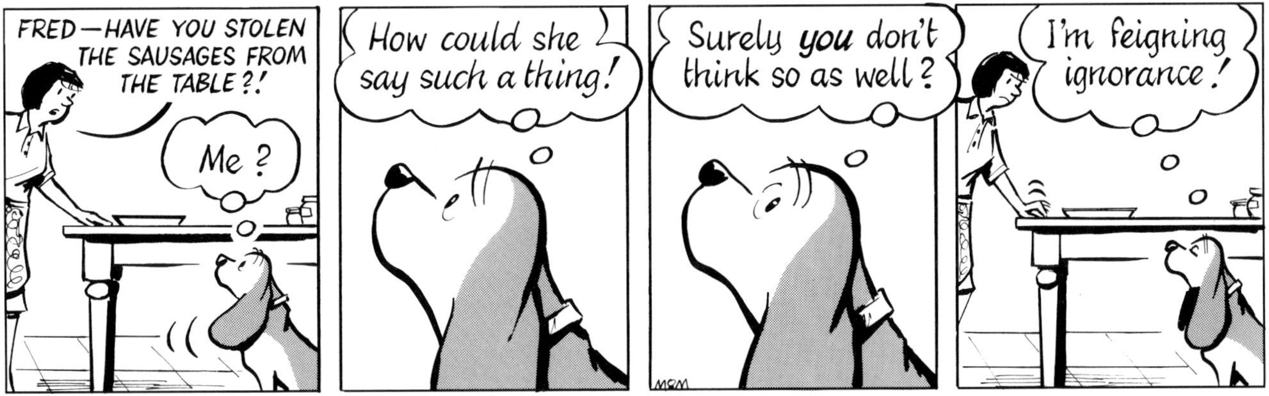
FRED — HAVE YOU STOLEN THE SAUSAGES FROM THE TABLE ?!
Me ?
How could she say such a thing!
Surely *you* don't think so as well ?
I'm feigning ignorance!

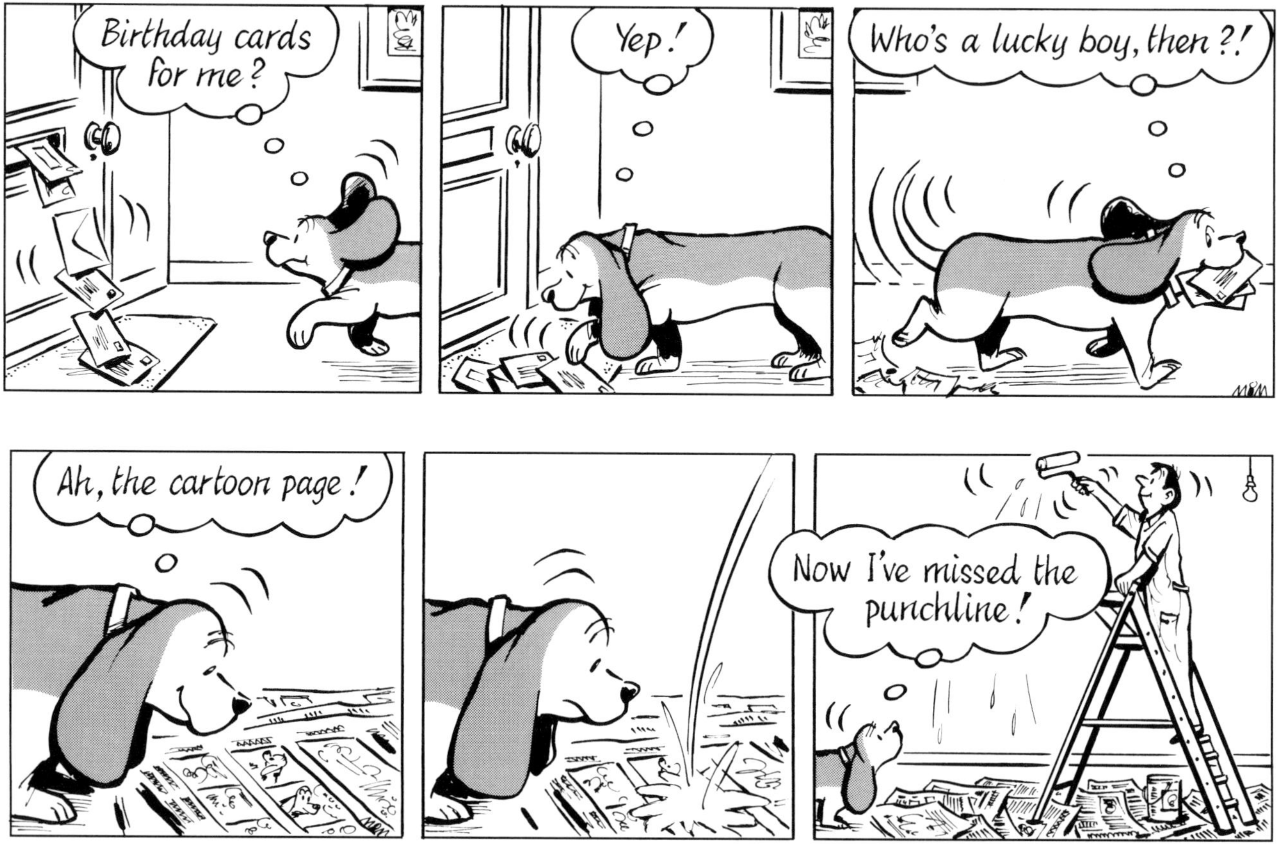
Birthday cards for me?
Yep!
Who's a lucky boy, then?!
Ah, the cartoon page!
Now I've missed the punchline!

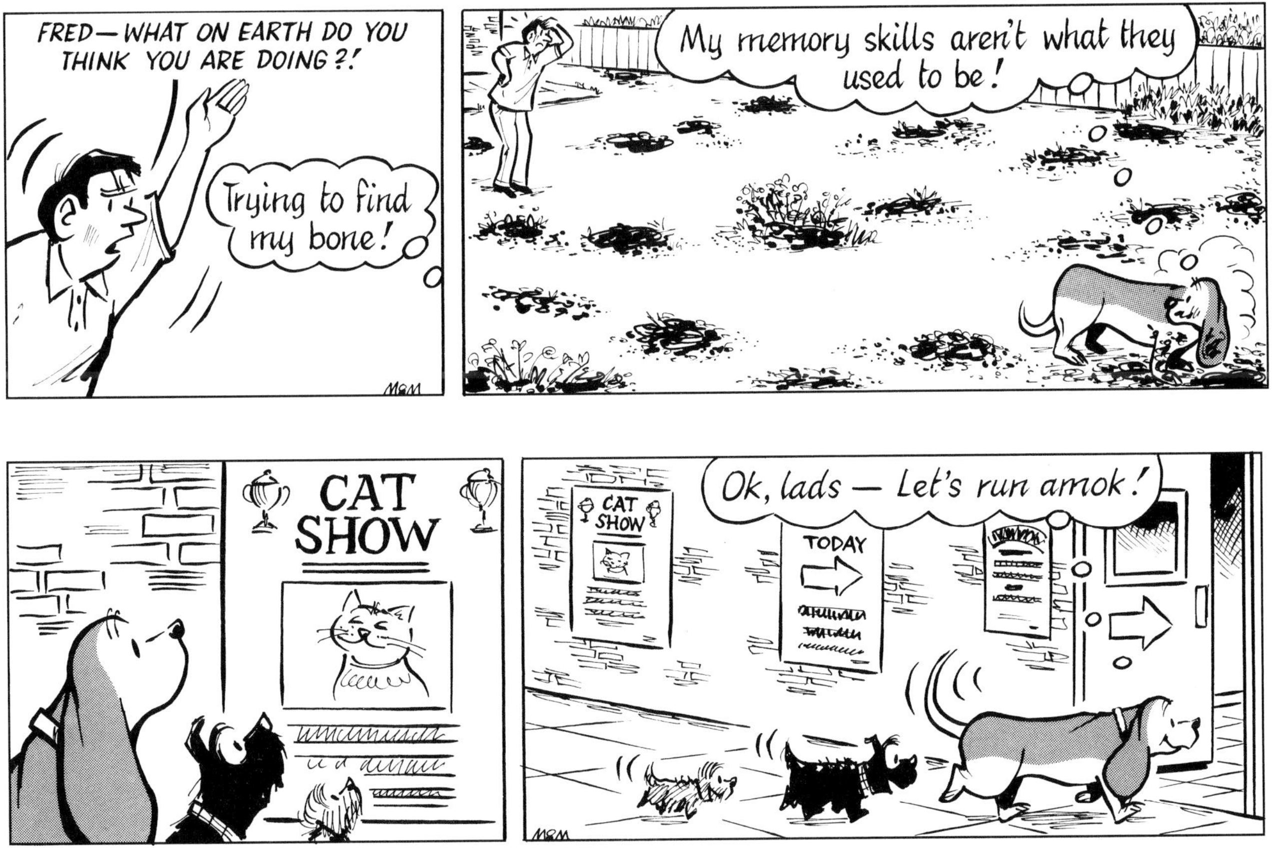
FRED—WHAT ON EARTH DO YOU THINK YOU ARE DOING?!
Trying to find my bone!
My memory skills aren't what they used to be!
CAT SHOW
CAT SHOW
TODAY
Ok, lads — Let's run amok!

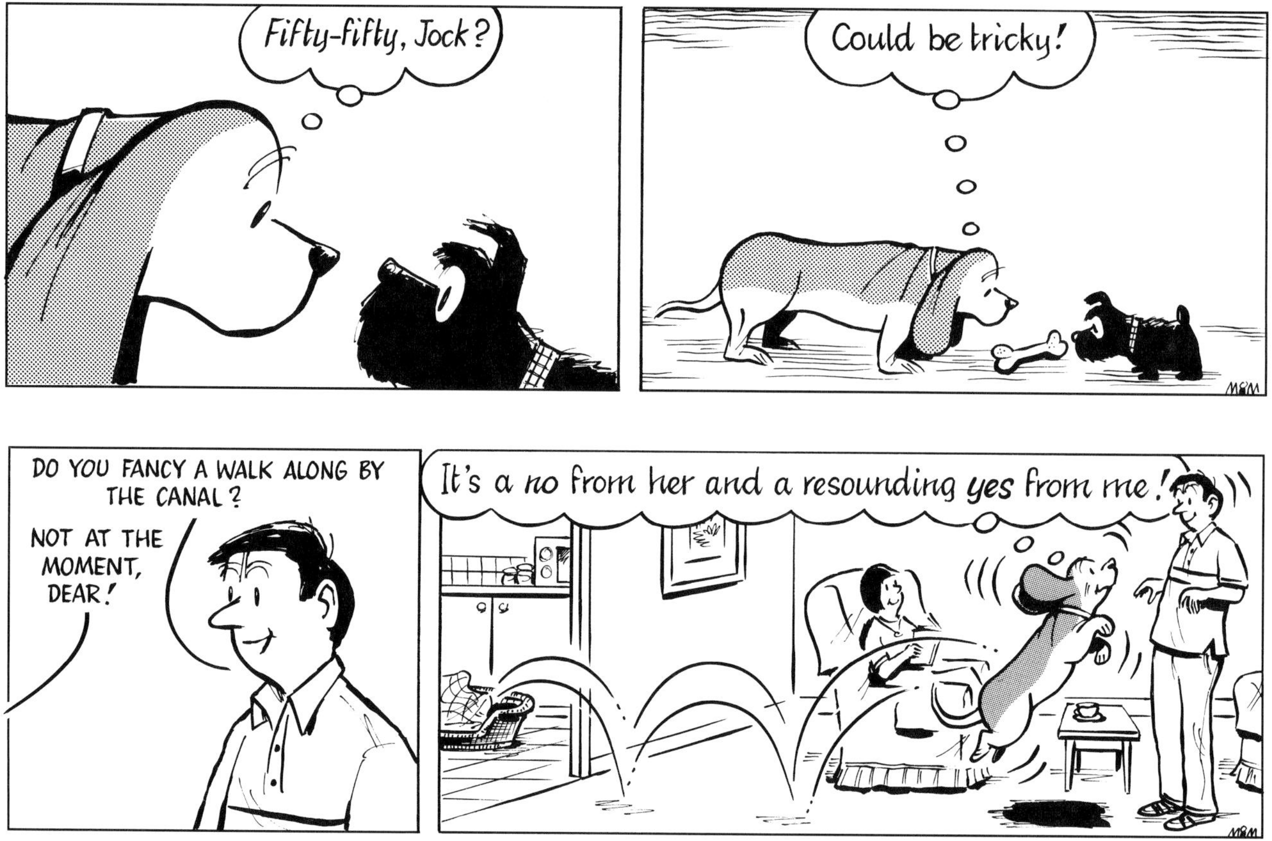

Fifty-fifty, Jock?
Could be tricky!
DO YOU FANCY A WALK ALONG BY THE CANAL?
NOT AT THE MOMENT, DEAR!
It's a no from her and a resounding yes from me!

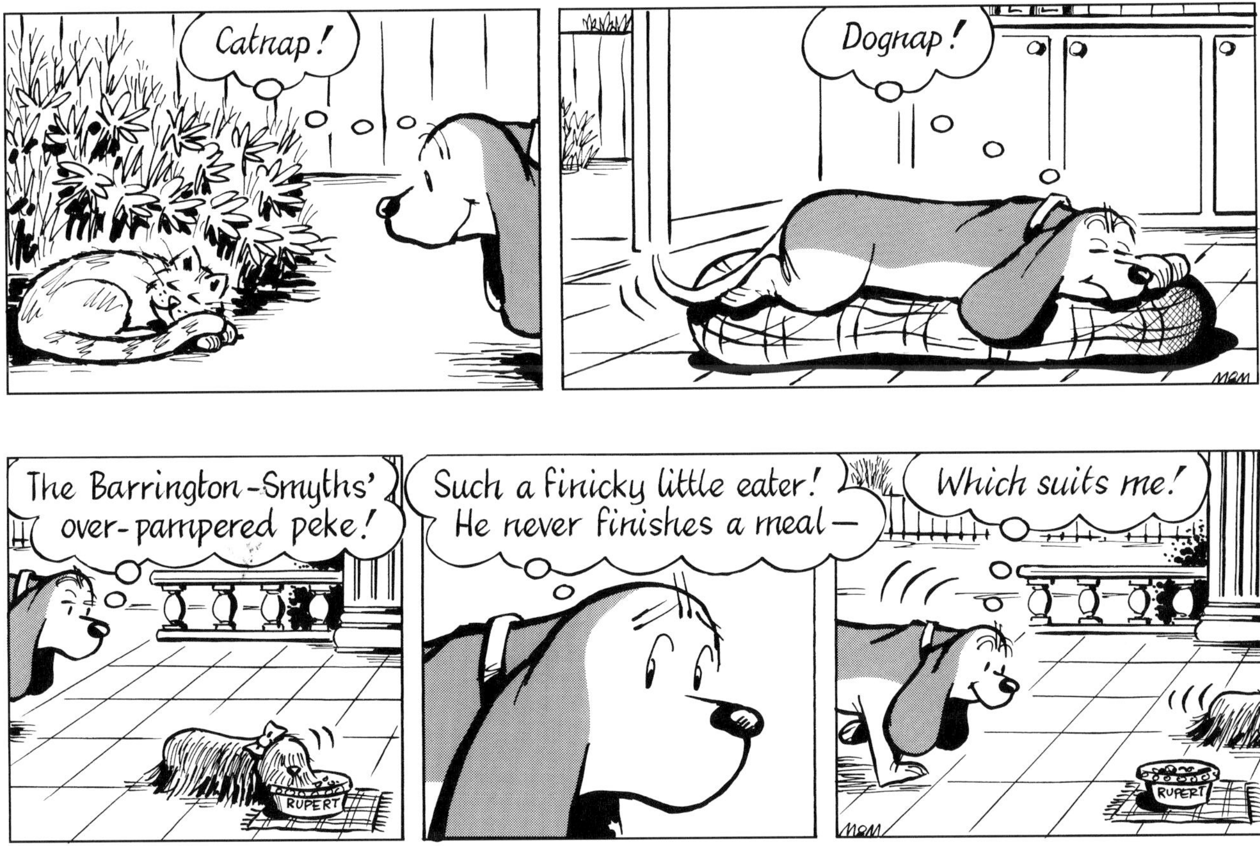
Catnap!
Dognap!
MSM
The Barrington-Smyths' over-pampered peke!
Such a finicky little eater! He never finishes a meal—
Which suits me!
RUPERT
RUPERT
MSM

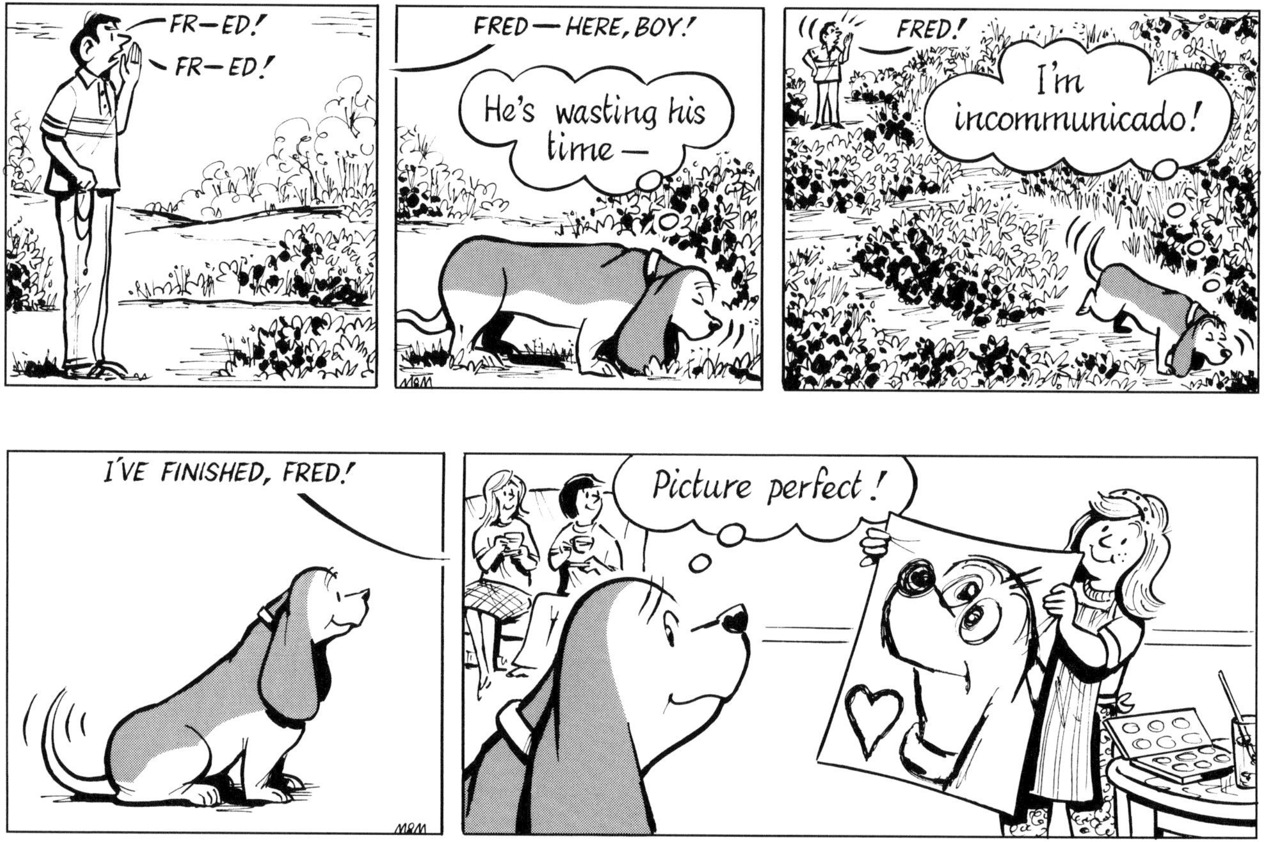
FR—ED!
FR—ED!
FRED—HERE, BOY!
He's wasting his time—
FRED!
I'm incommunicado!
I'VE FINISHED, FRED!
Picture perfect!

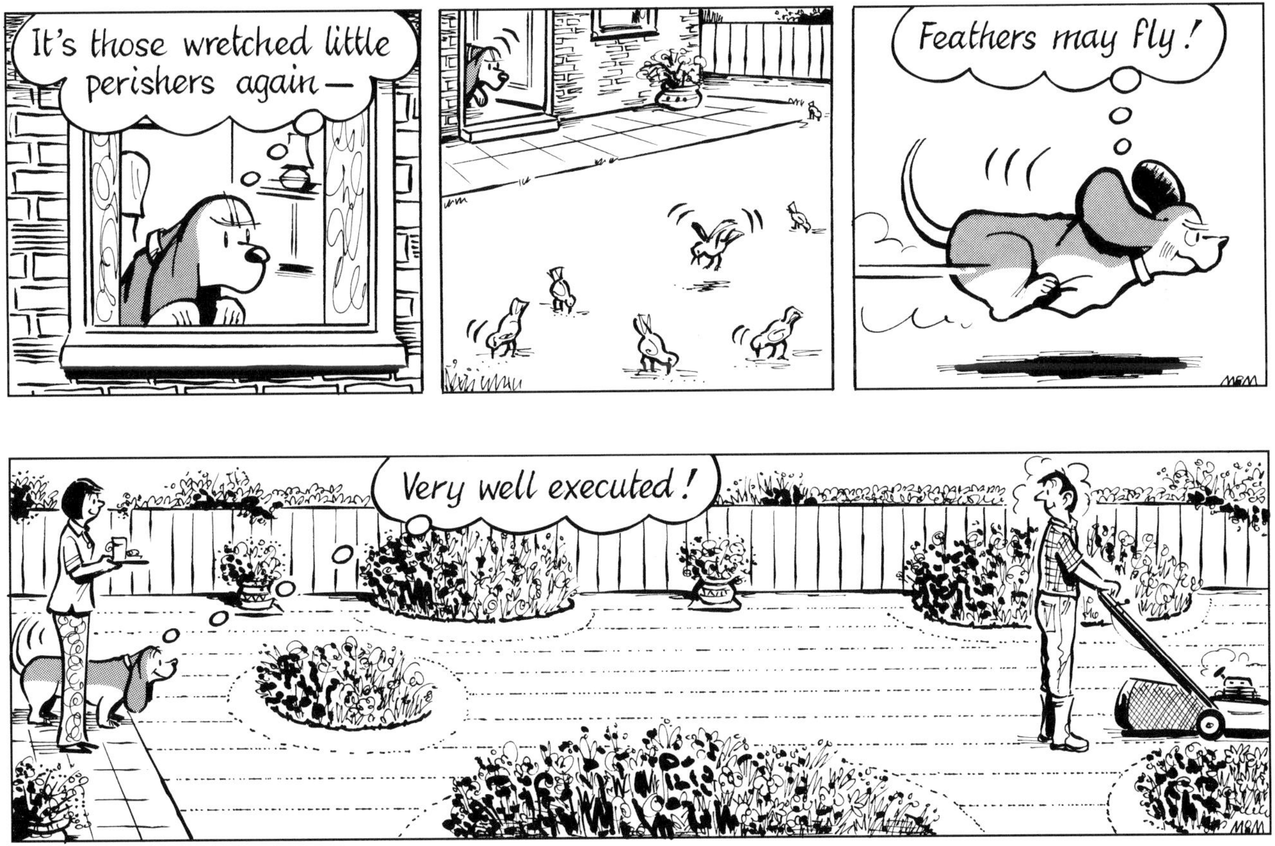
It's those wretched little perishers again—
Feathers may fly!
MGM
Very well executed!
MGM

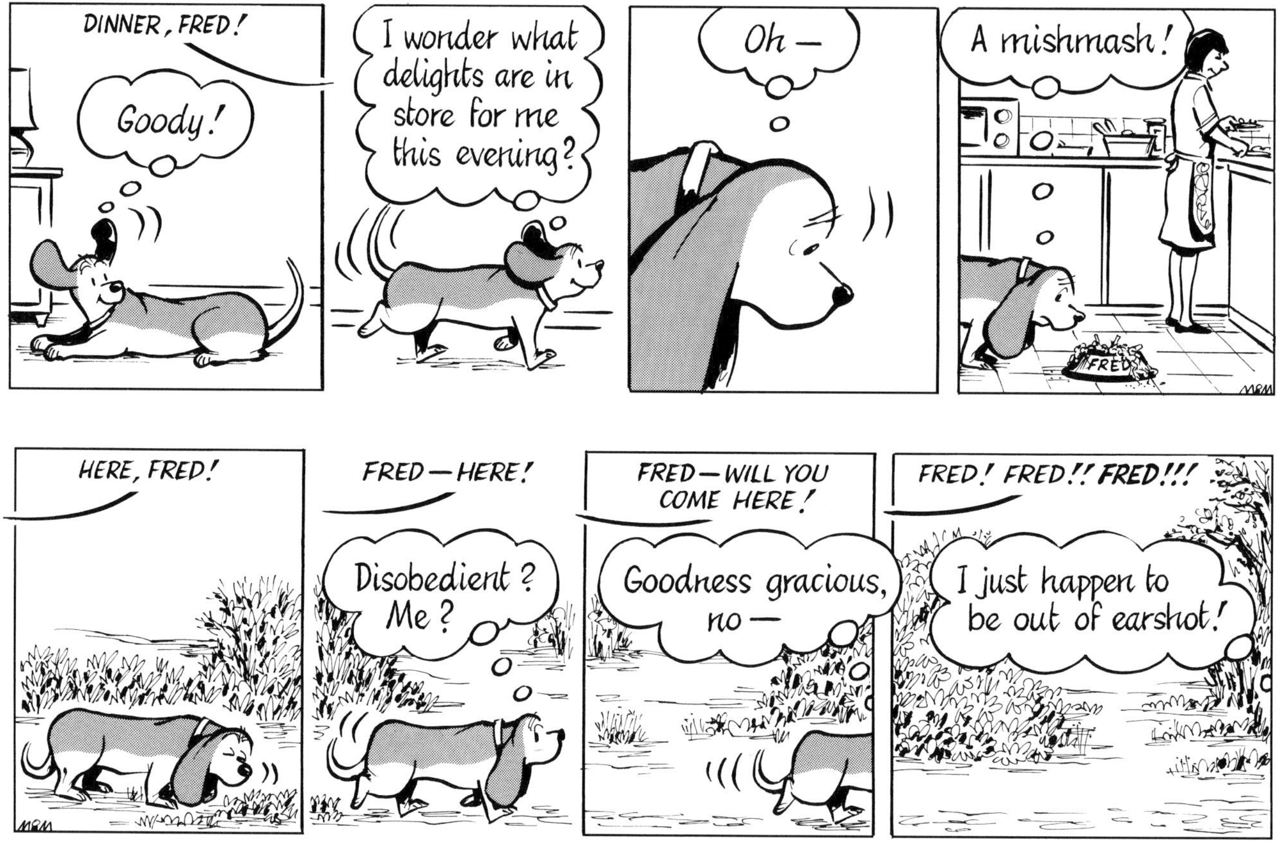
DINNER, FRED!
Goody!
I wonder what delights are in store for me this evening?
Oh —
A mishmash!
FRED
MSM
HERE, FRED!
FRED — HERE!
Disobedient? Me?
FRED — WILL YOU COME HERE!
Goodness gracious, no —
FRED! FRED!! FRED!!!
I just happen to be out of earshot!
MSM

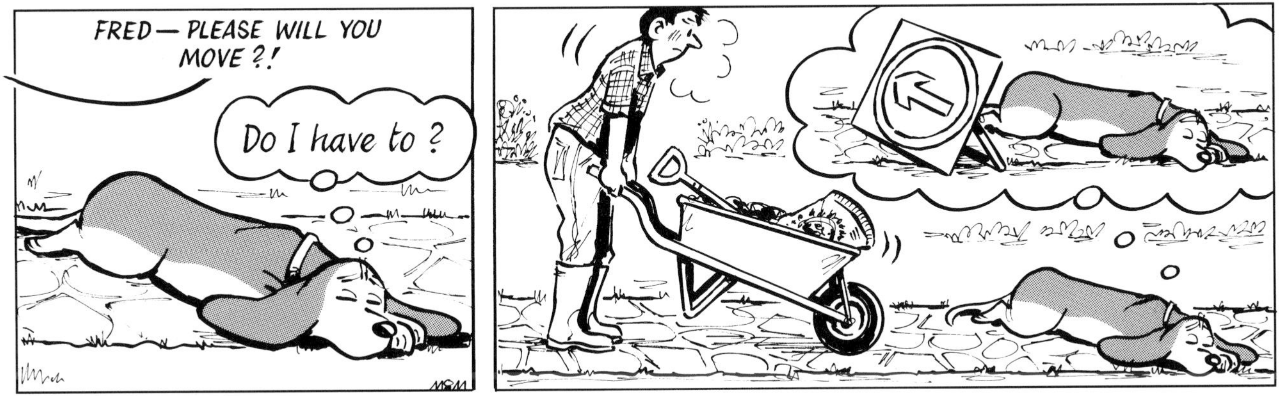
FRED — PLEASE WILL YOU MOVE ?!
Do I have to ?

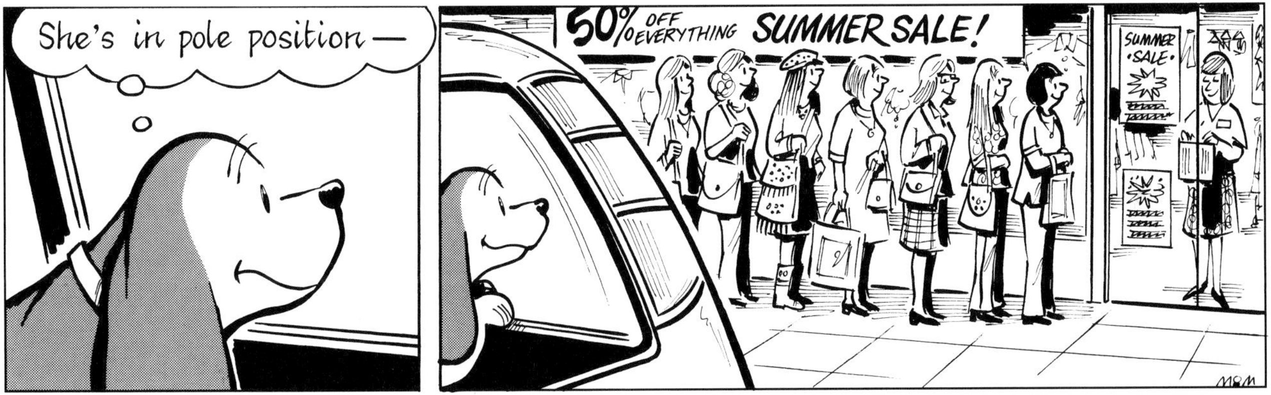
She's in pole position —
50% OFF EVERYTHING SUMMER SALE!
SUMMER •SALE•

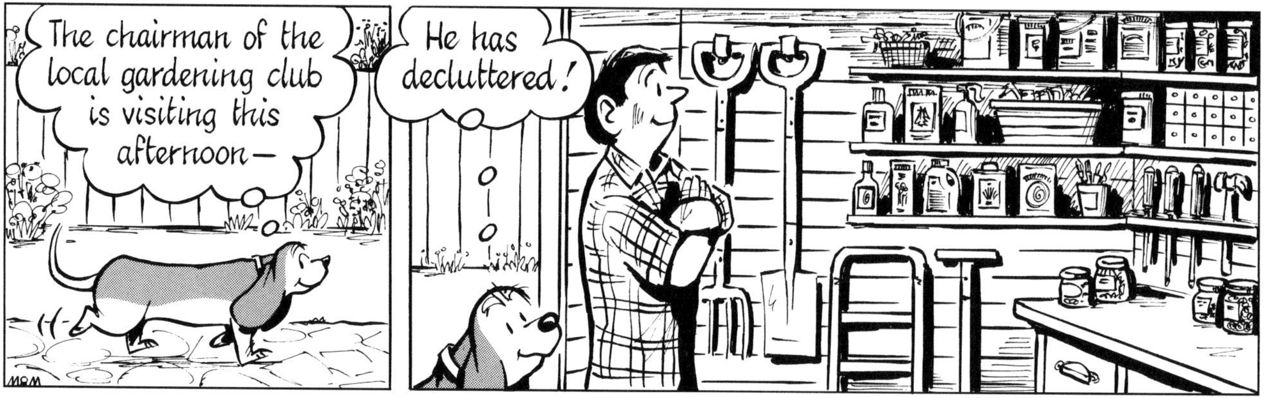
The chairman of the local gardening club is visiting this afternoon—
He has decluttered!

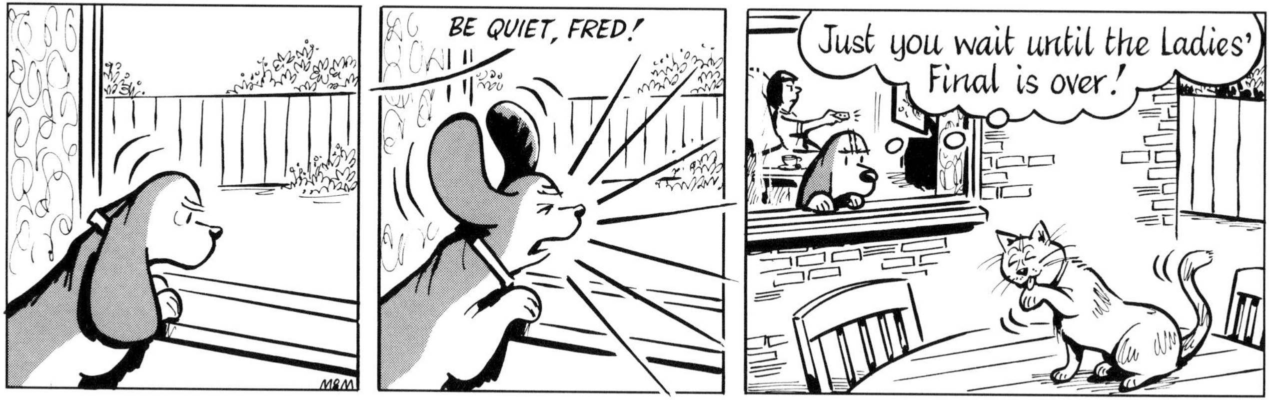
BE QUIET, FRED!
Just you wait until the Ladies' Final is over!

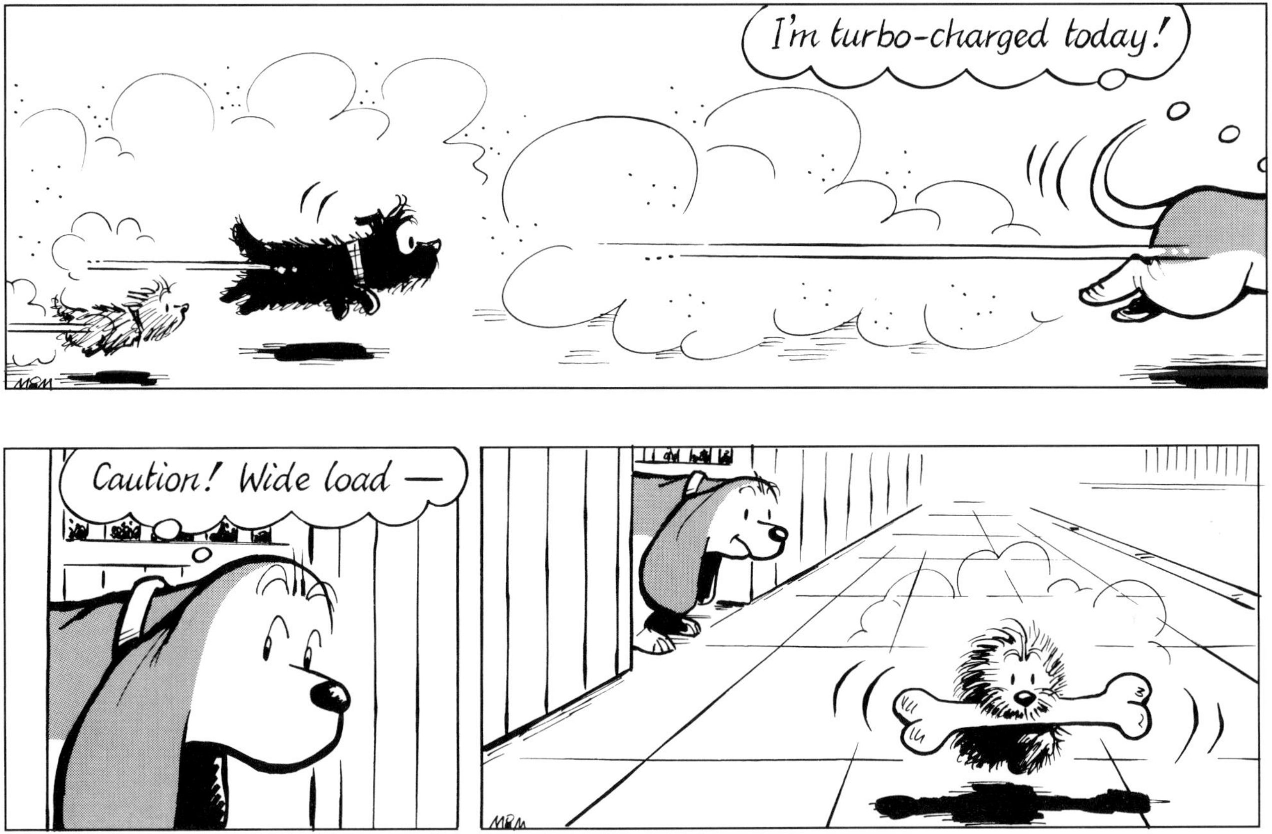
I'm turbo-charged today!
MRM
Caution! Wide load —
MRM

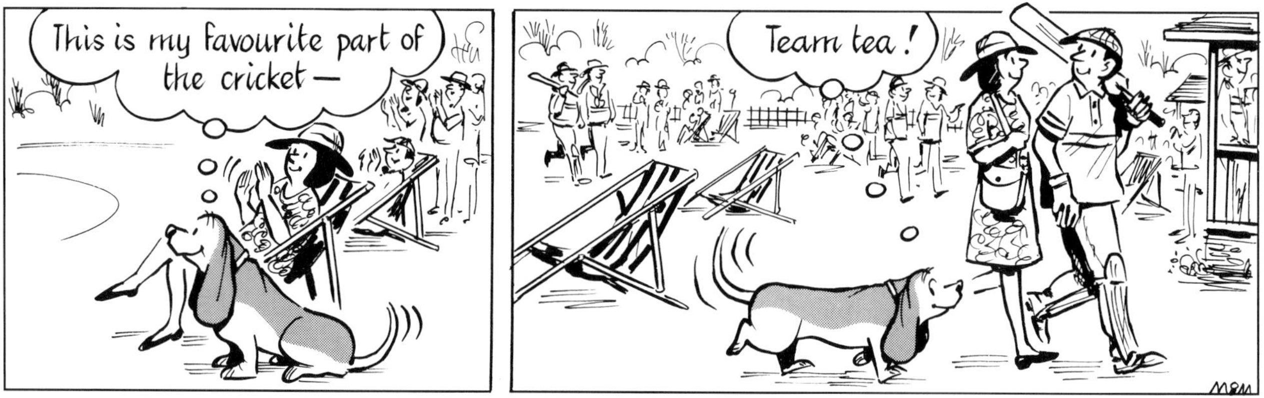
This is my favourite part of the cricket —
Team tea !

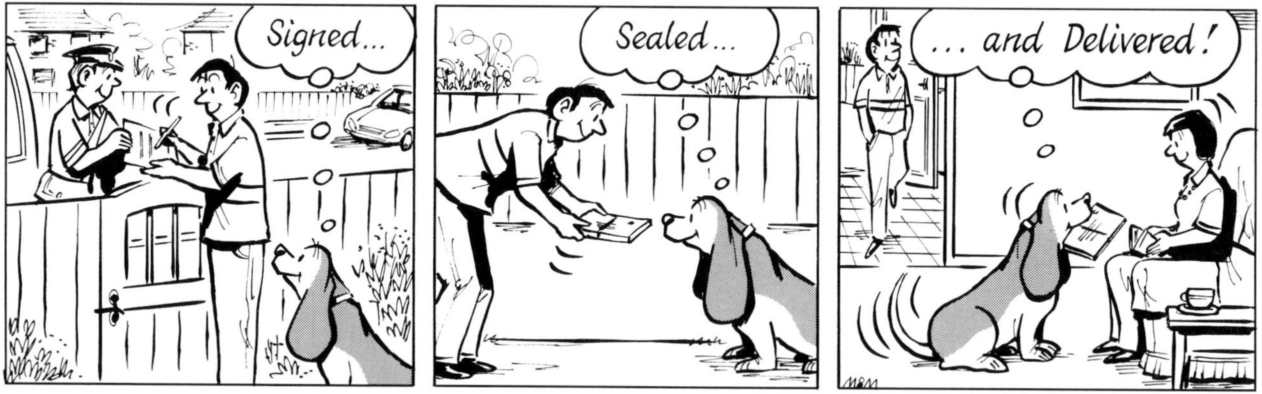
Signed ...
Sealed ...
... and Delivered !

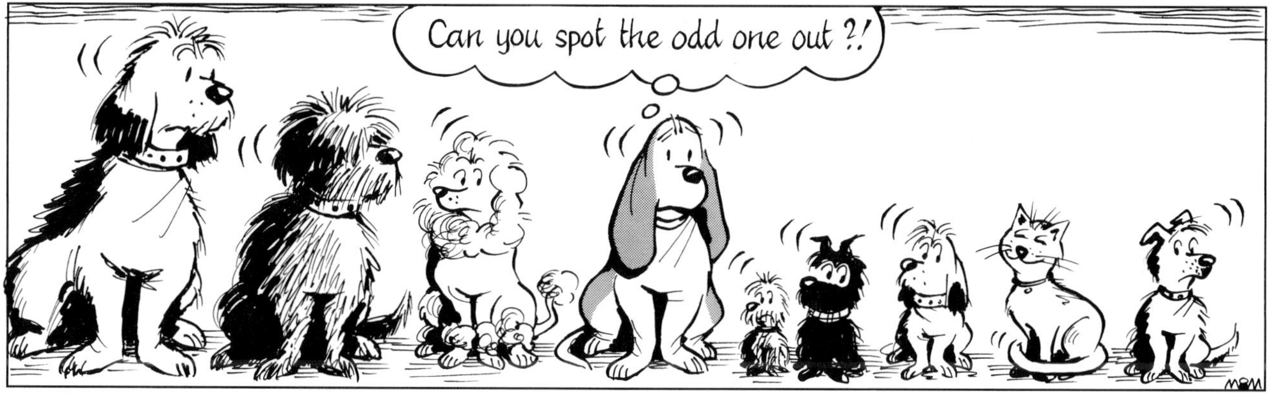
Can you spot the odd one out ?!

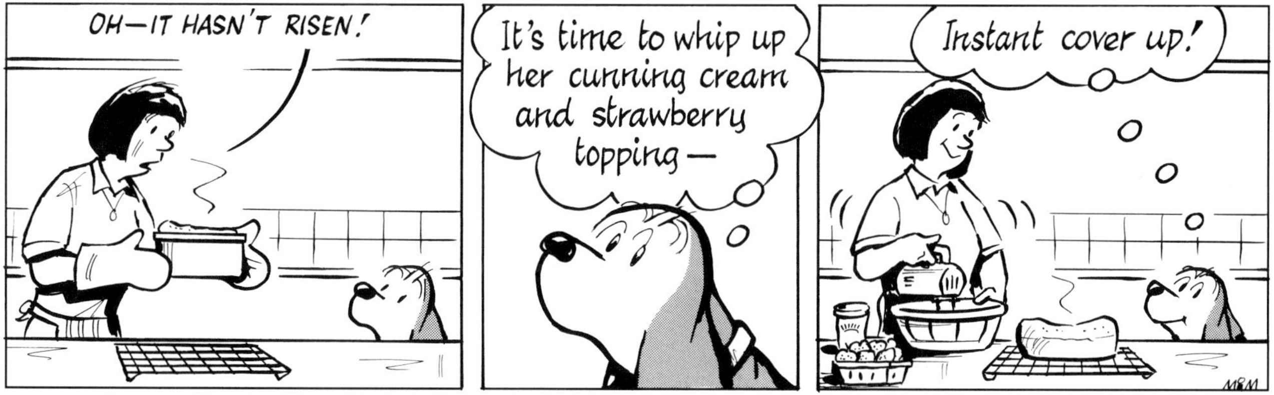
OH—IT HASN'T RISEN!
It's time to whip up her cunning cream and strawberry topping—
Instant cover up!

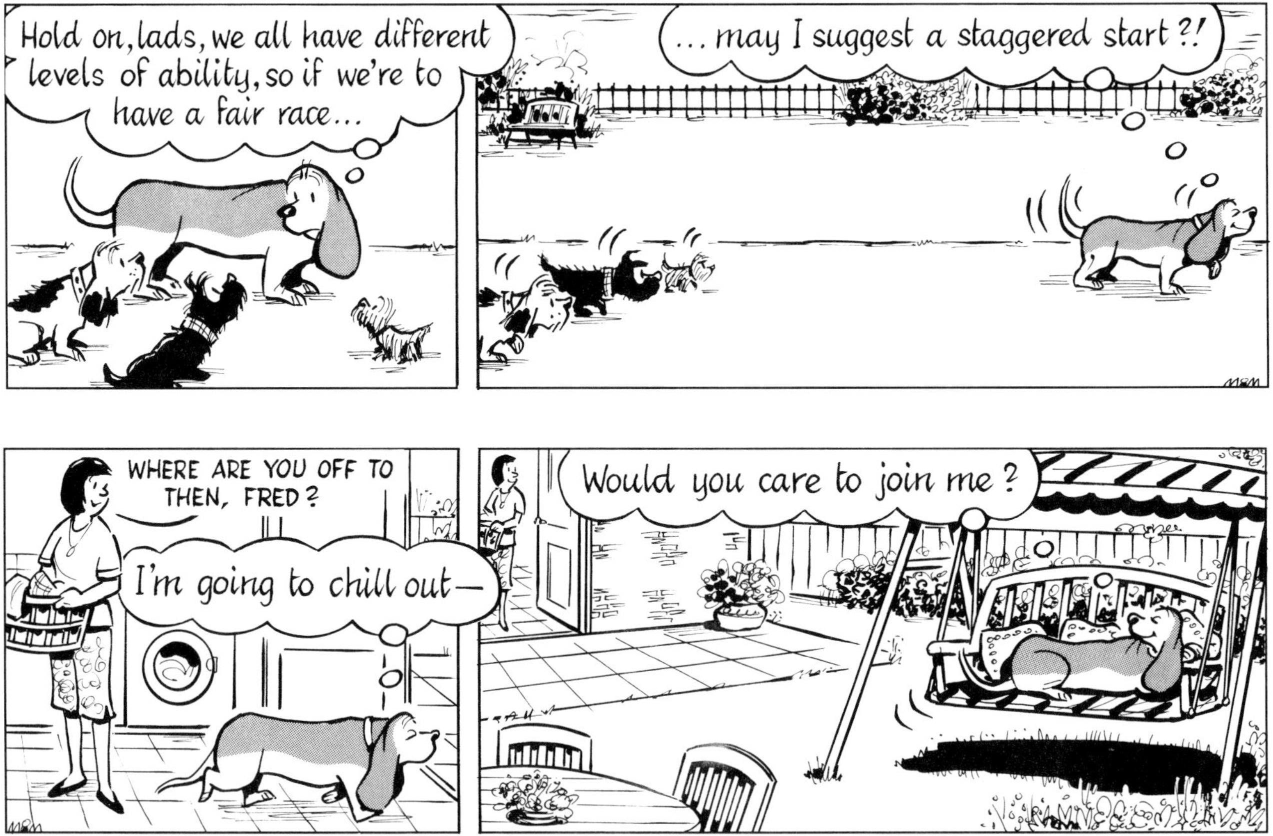

Hold on, lads, we all have different levels of ability, so if we're to have a fair race...
... may I suggest a staggered start ?!
WHERE ARE YOU OFF TO THEN, FRED ?
I'm going to chill out—
Would you care to join me ?

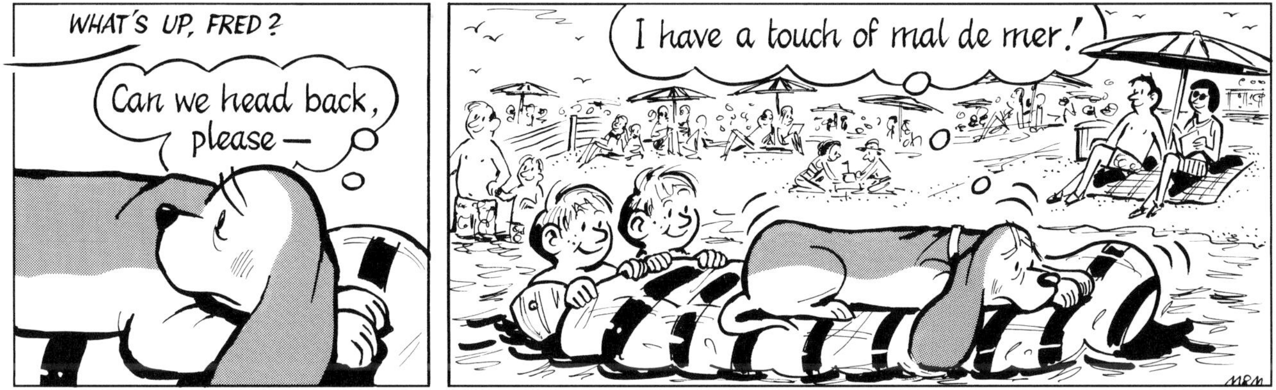
WHAT'S UP, FRED?
Can we head back, please—
I have a touch of mal de mer!

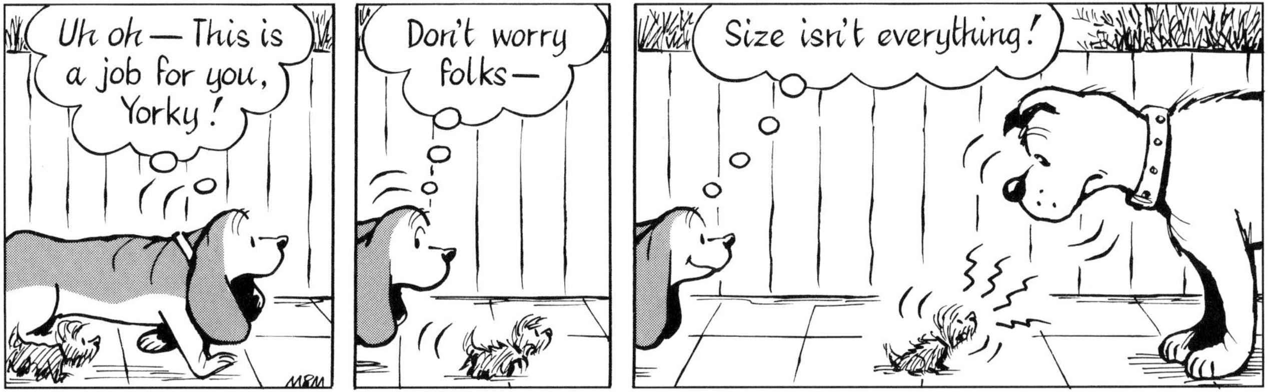
Uh oh — This is a job for you, Yorky!
Don't worry folks—
Size isn't everything!

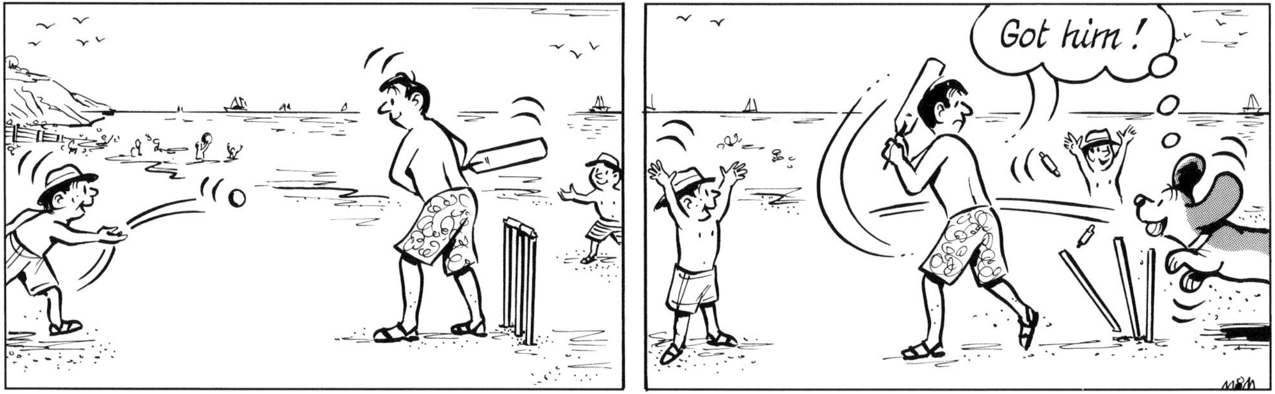
Got him !

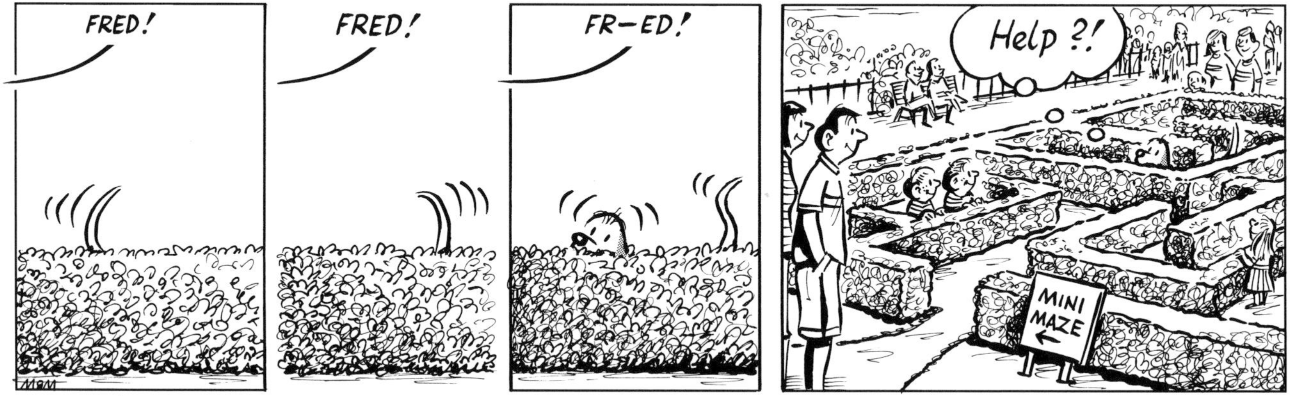
FRED!
FRED!
FR—ED!
Help ?!
MINI MAZE

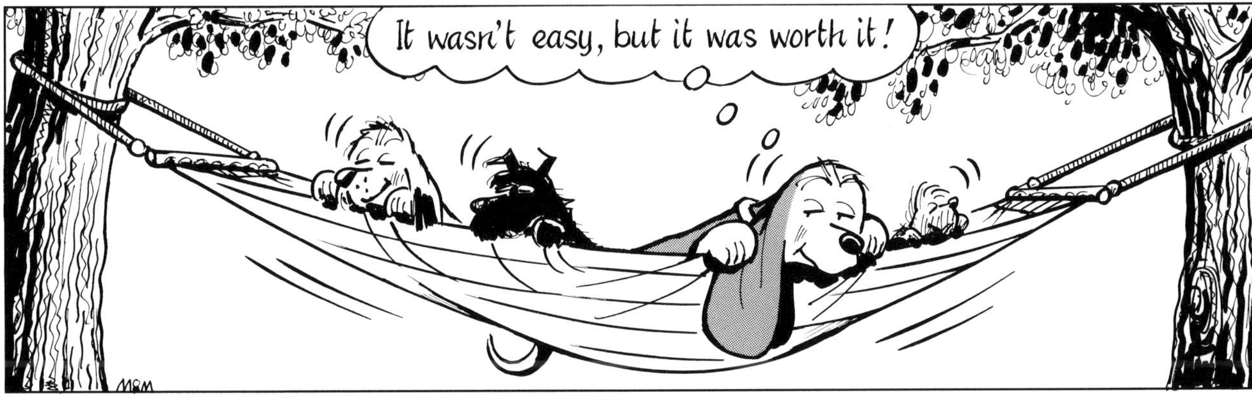
It wasn't easy, but it was worth it!
M&M

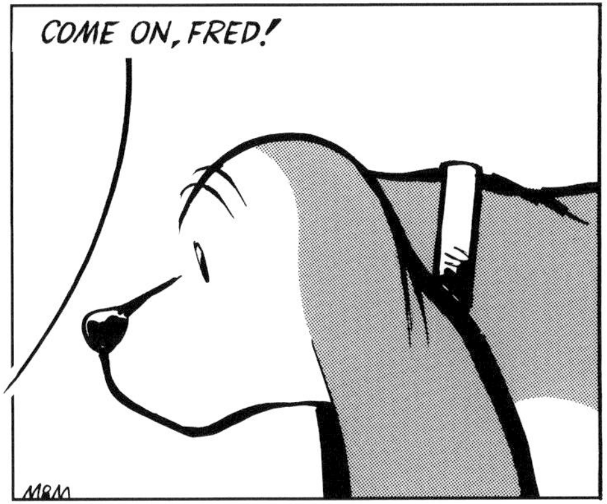
COME ON, FRED!
M&M

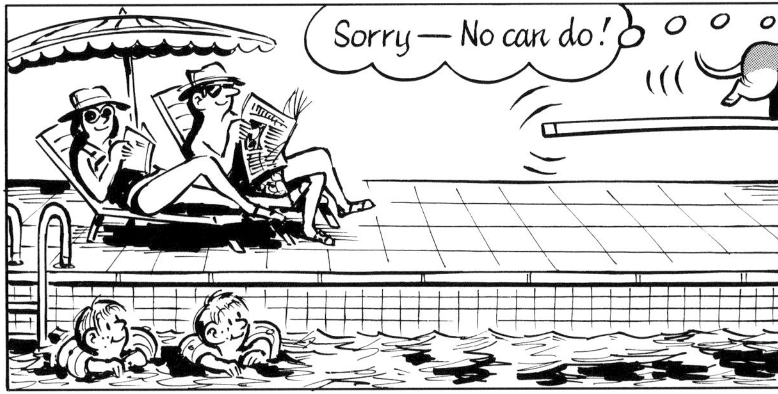
Sorry — No can do!

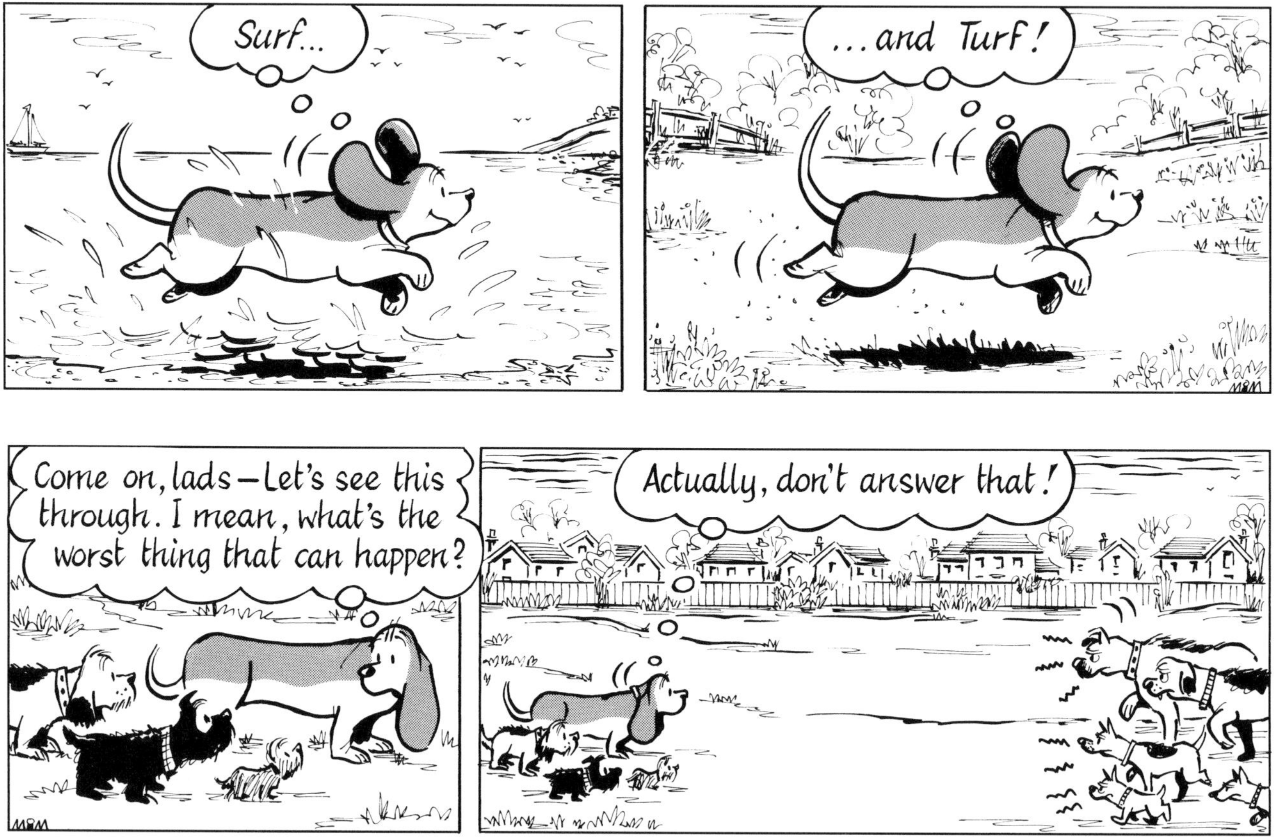
Surf...
...and Turf!
Come on, lads—Let's see this through. I mean, what's the worst thing that can happen?
Actually, don't answer that!

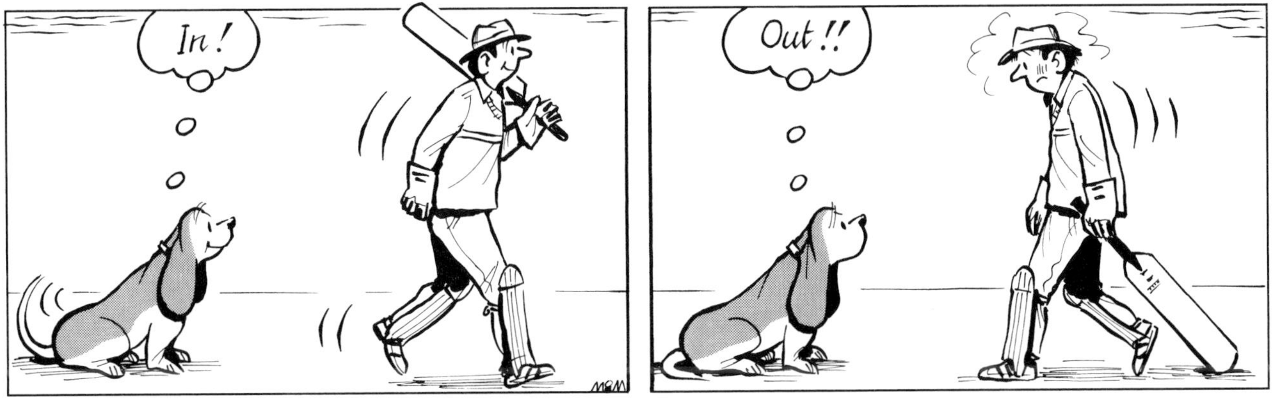
In!
Out!!
M&M

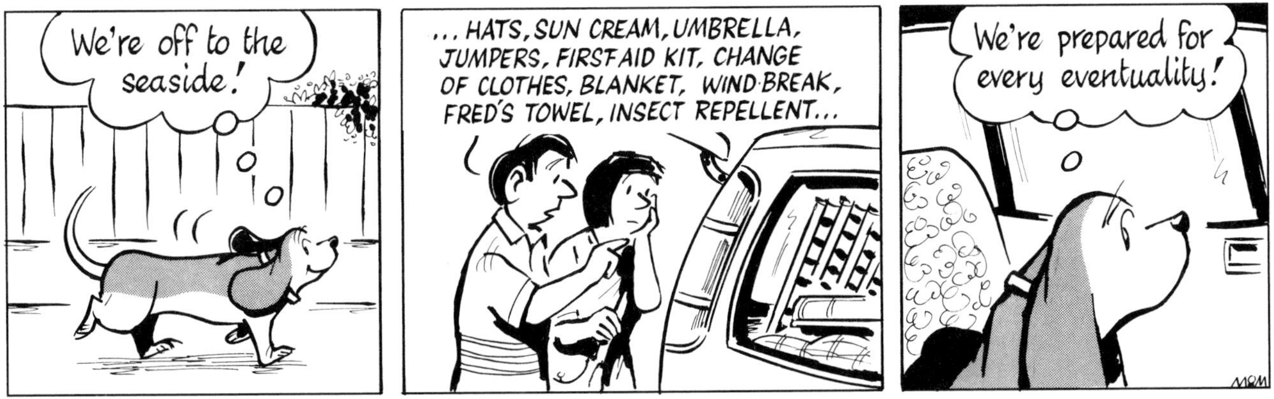
We're off to the seaside!
... HATS, SUN CREAM, UMBRELLA, JUMPERS, FIRST AID KIT, CHANGE OF CLOTHES, BLANKET, WIND BREAK, FRED'S TOWEL, INSECT REPELLENT...
We're prepared for every eventuality!
M&M

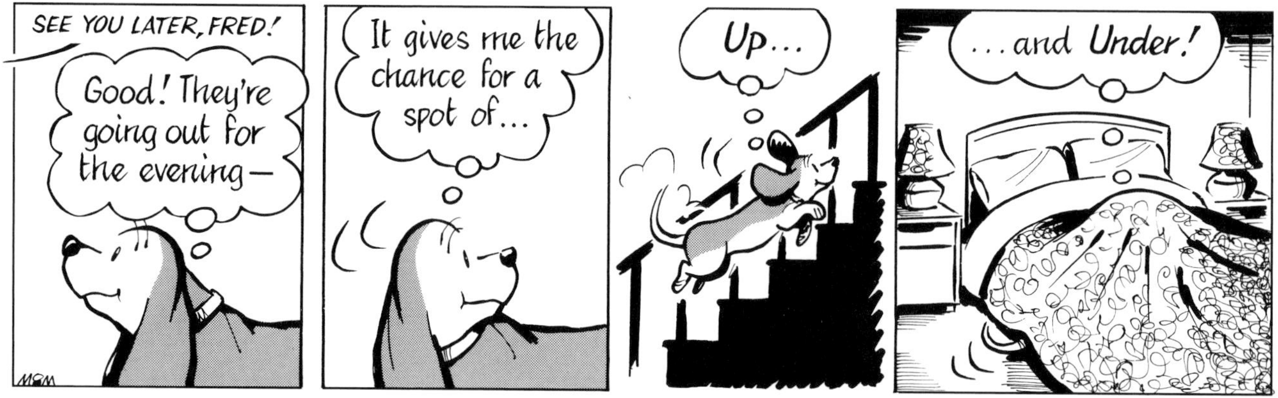
SEE YOU LATER, FRED!
Good! They're going out for the evening—
It gives me the chance for a spot of...
Up...
...and Under!

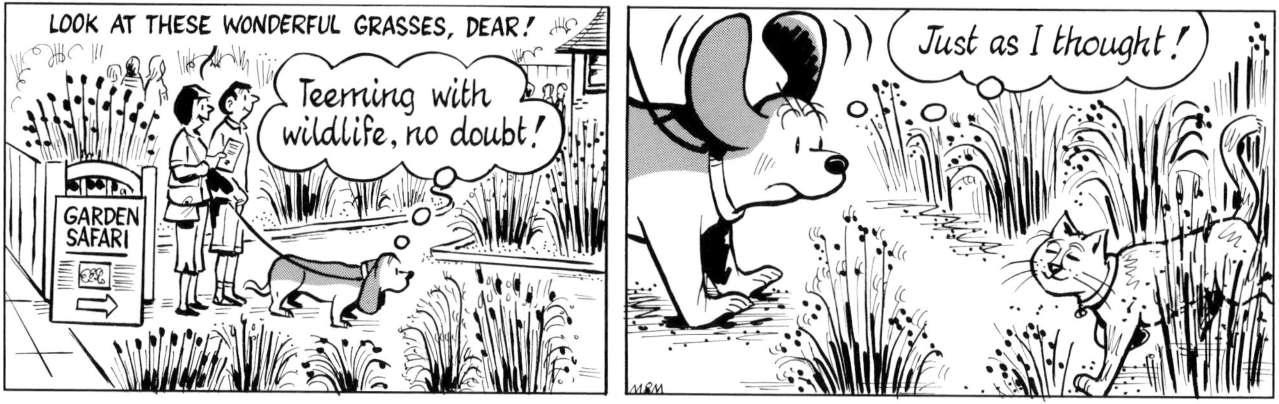
LOOK AT THESE WONDERFUL GRASSES, DEAR!
Teeming with wildlife, no doubt!
GARDEN SAFARI
Just as I thought!

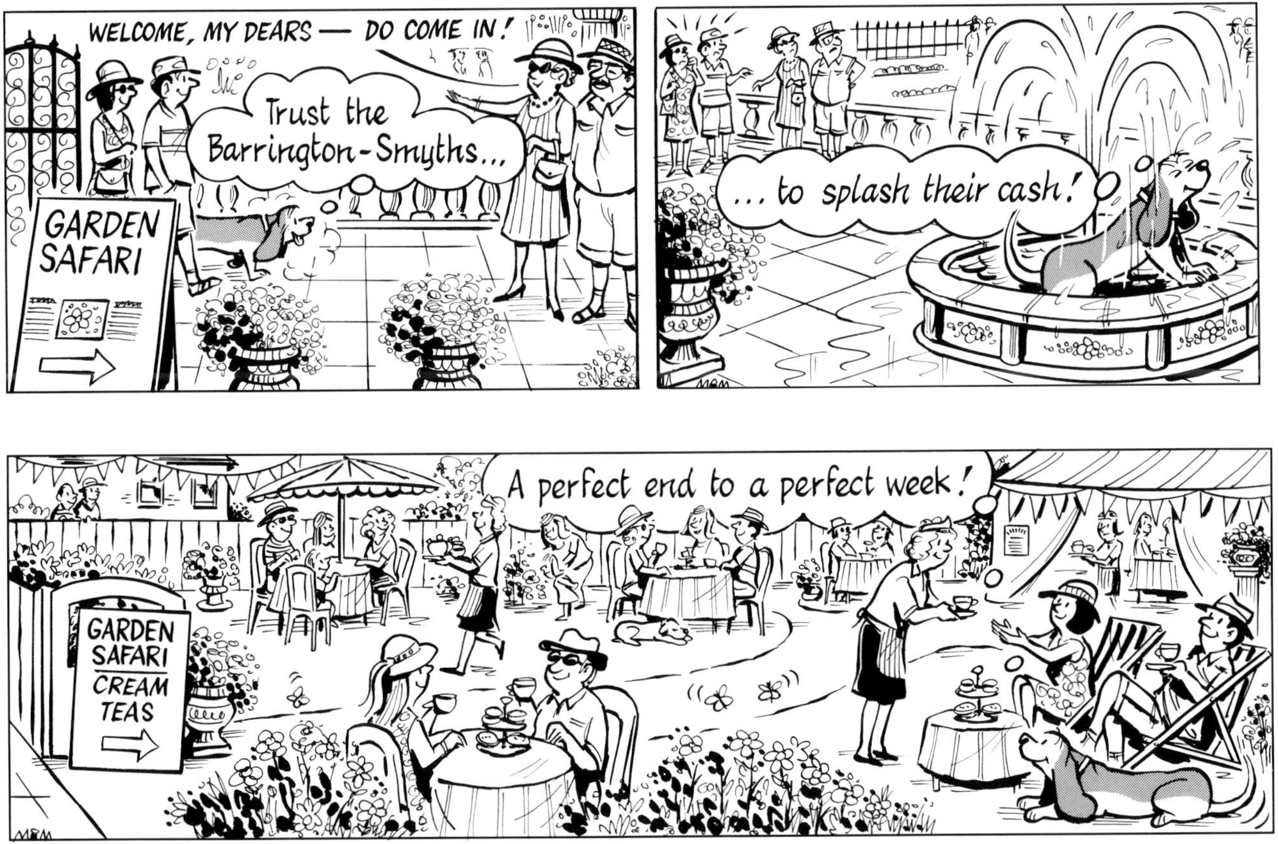
WELCOME, MY DEARS — DO COME IN!
Trust the Barrington-Smyths...
GARDEN SAFARI
... to splash their cash!
A perfect end to a perfect week!
GARDEN SAFARI
CREAM TEAS

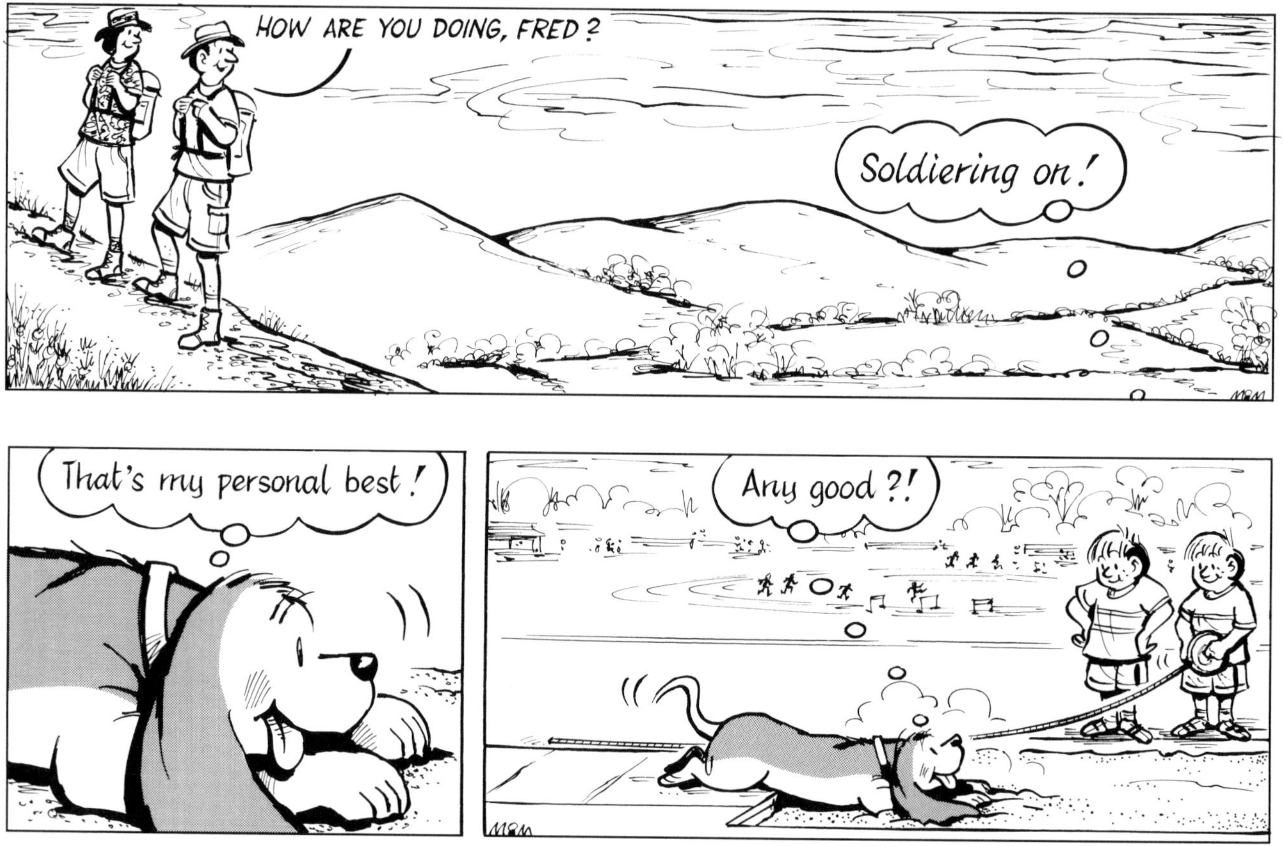
HOW ARE YOU DOING, FRED?
Soldiering on!
That's my personal best!
Any good?!

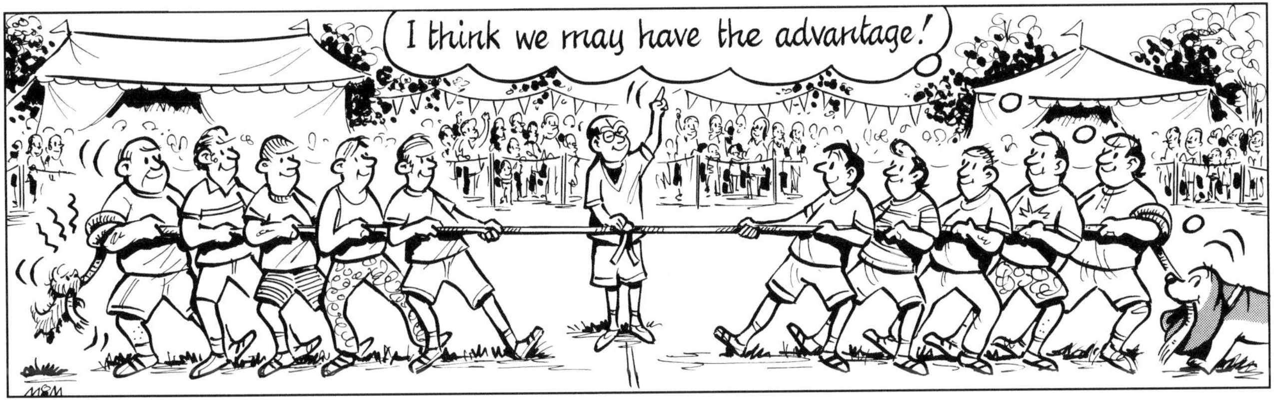
I think we may have the advantage!
MQM

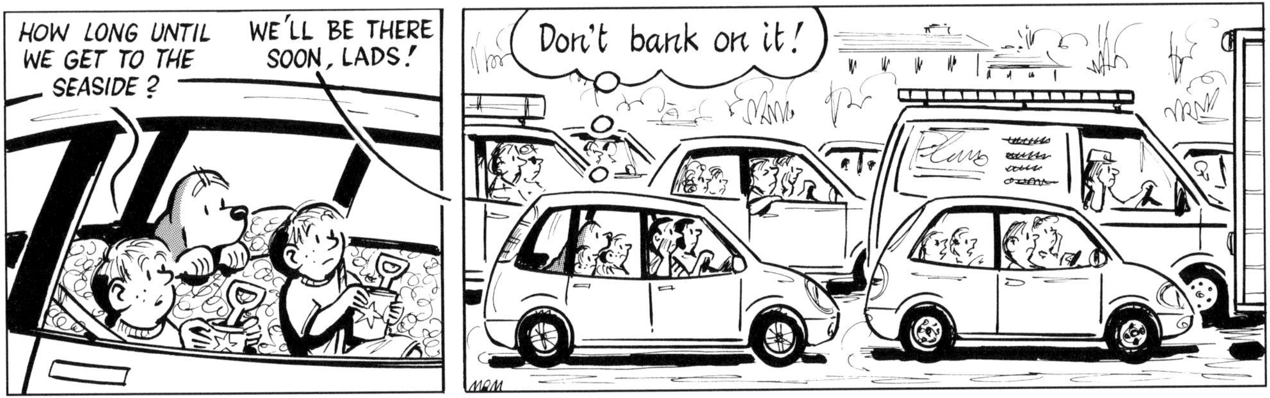
HOW LONG UNTIL WE GET TO THE SEASIDE?
WE'LL BE THERE SOON, LADS!
Don't bank on it!
MQM

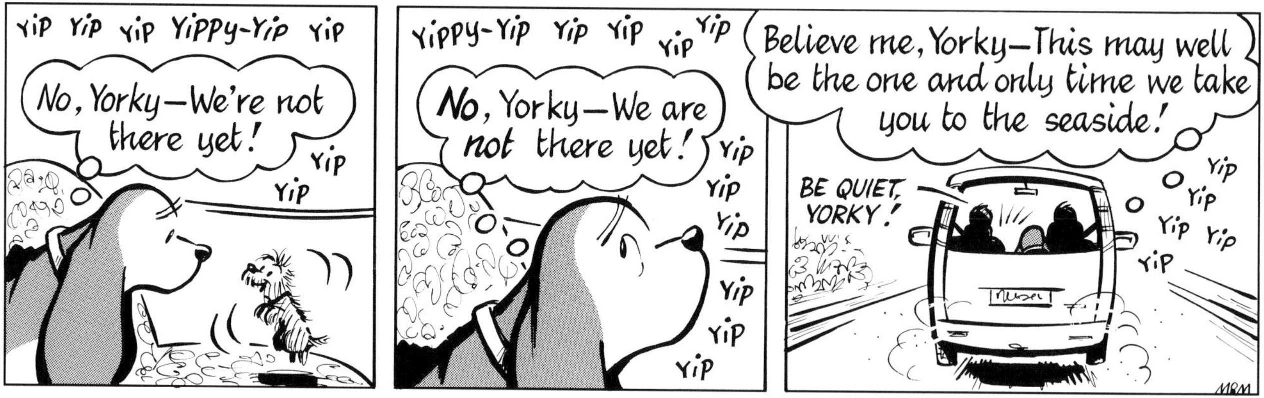
YIP YIP YIP YIPPY-YIP YIP
No, Yorky—We're not there yet!
YIP
YIP
YIPPY-YIP YIP YIP YIP YIP
No, Yorky—We are not there yet!
YIP
YIP
YIP
YIP
YIP
YIP
Believe me, Yorky—This may well be the one and only time we take you to the seaside!
BE QUIET, YORKY!
YIP
YIP
YIP YIP
YIP
MRM

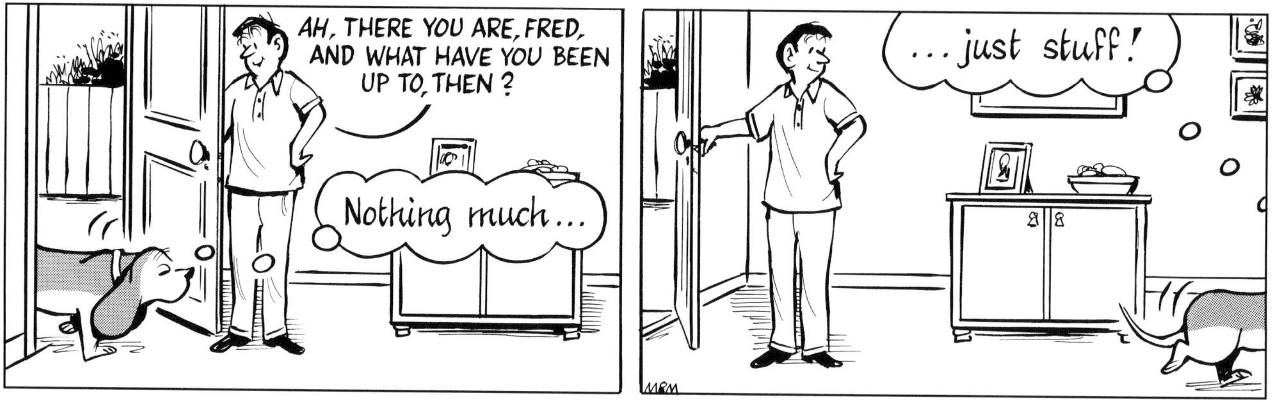
AH, THERE YOU ARE, FRED, AND WHAT HAVE YOU BEEN UP TO, THEN?
Nothing much...
MRM
...just stuff!

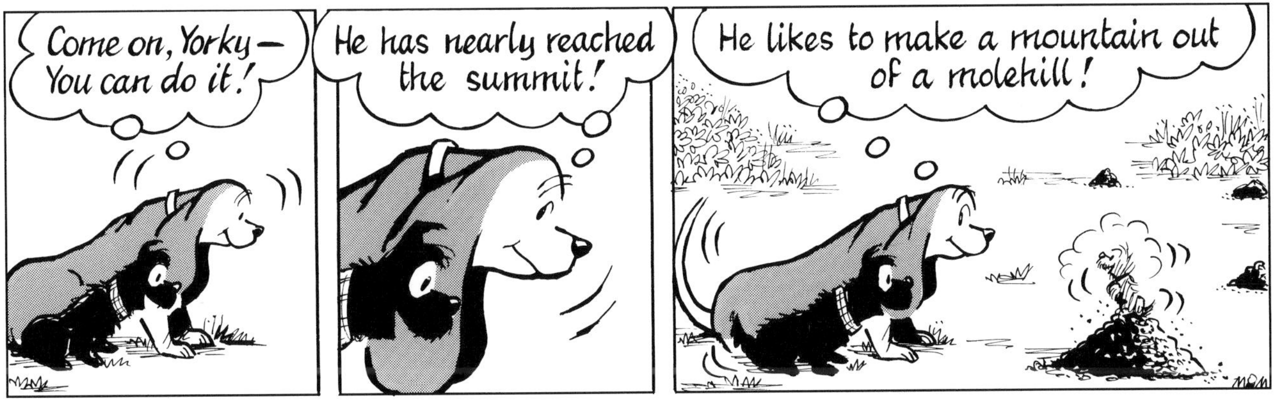
Come on, Yorky—
You can do it!
He has nearly reached the summit!
He likes to make a mountain out of a molehill!
MBM

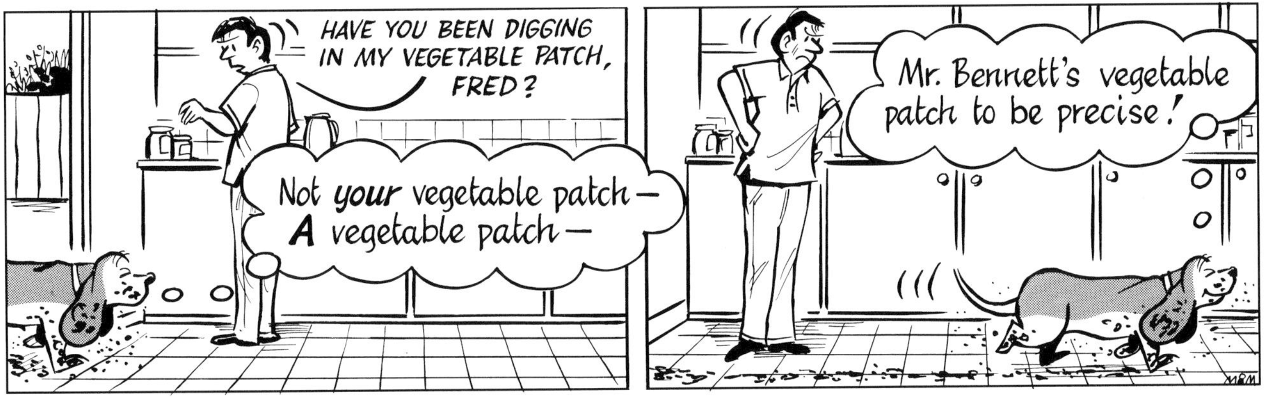
HAVE YOU BEEN DIGGING IN MY VEGETABLE PATCH, FRED?
Not your vegetable patch—
A vegetable patch—
Mr. Bennett's vegetable patch to be precise!
MBM

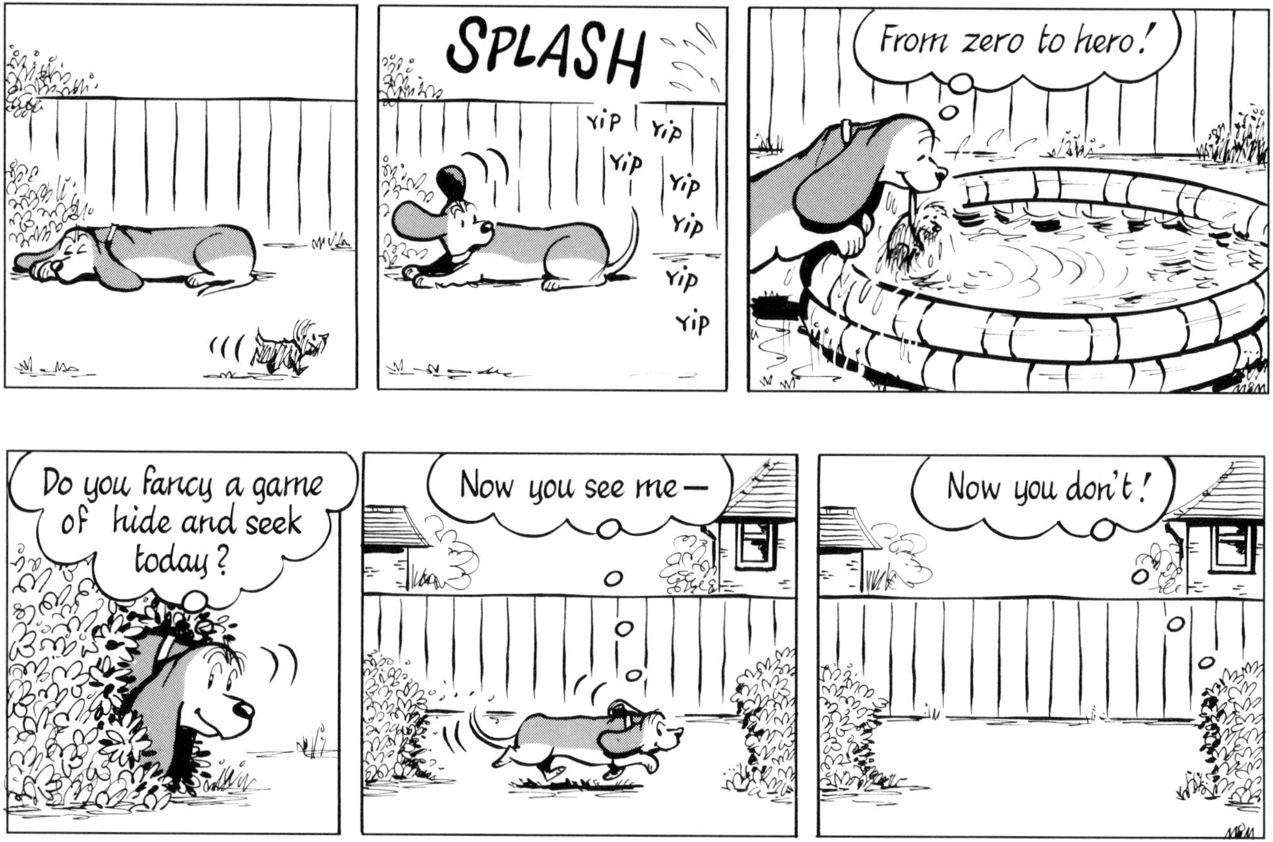

SPLASH
YIP YIP YIP YIP YIP YIP YIP
From zero to hero!
Do you fancy a game of hide and seek today?
Now you see me—
Now you don't!

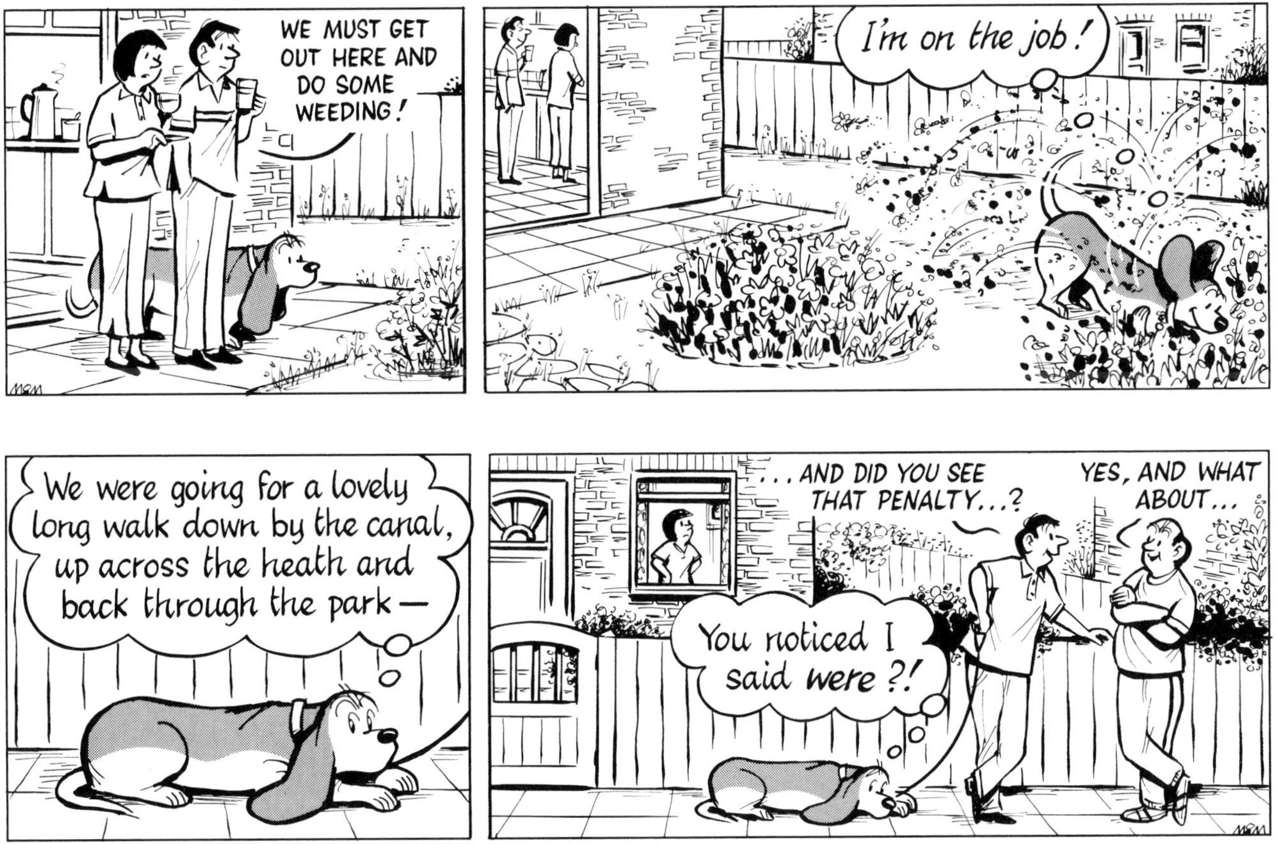
WE MUST GET OUT HERE AND DO SOME WEEDING!
I'm on the job!
We were going for a lovely long walk down by the canal, up across the heath and back through the park —
...AND DID YOU SEE THAT PENALTY...?
YES, AND WHAT ABOUT...
You noticed I said were?!

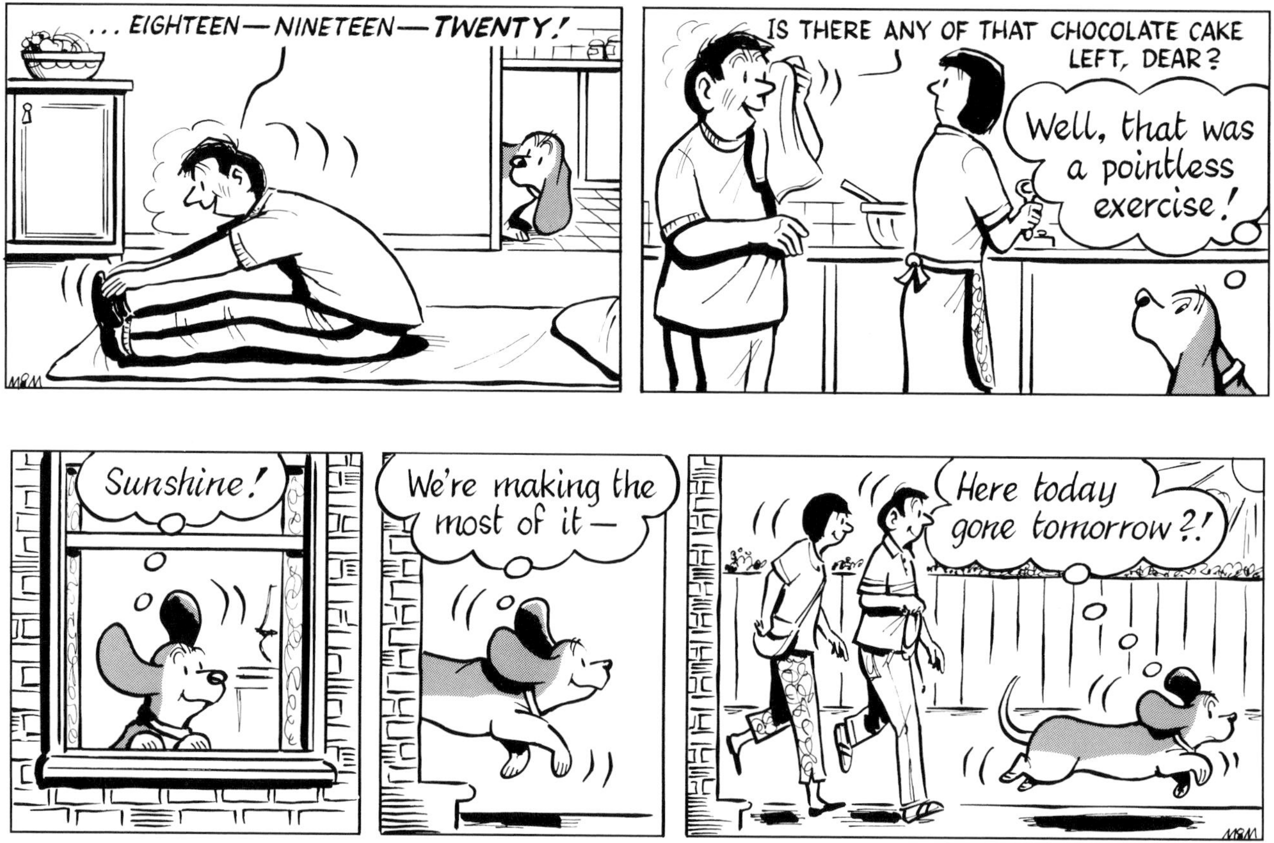
... EIGHTEEN — NINETEEN — TWENTY!
IS THERE ANY OF THAT CHOCOLATE CAKE LEFT, DEAR?
Well, that was a pointless exercise!
Sunshine!
We're making the most of it —
Here today gone tomorrow?!

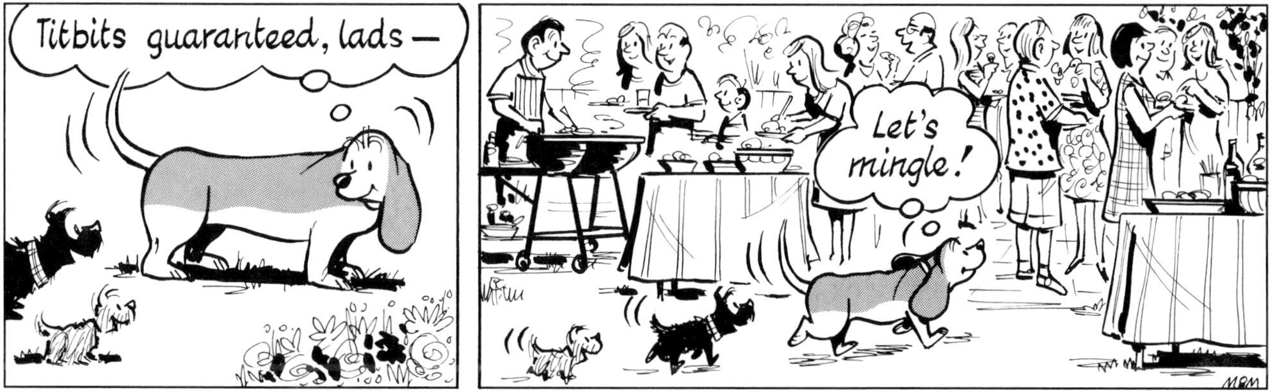
Titbits guaranteed, lads —
Let's mingle!
MBM

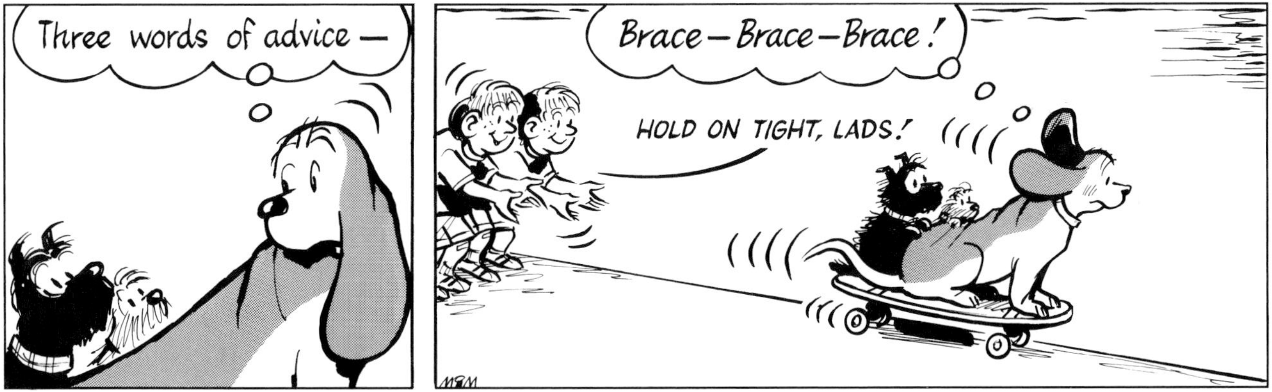
Three words of advice —
Brace — Brace — Brace!
HOLD ON TIGHT, LADS!
MBM

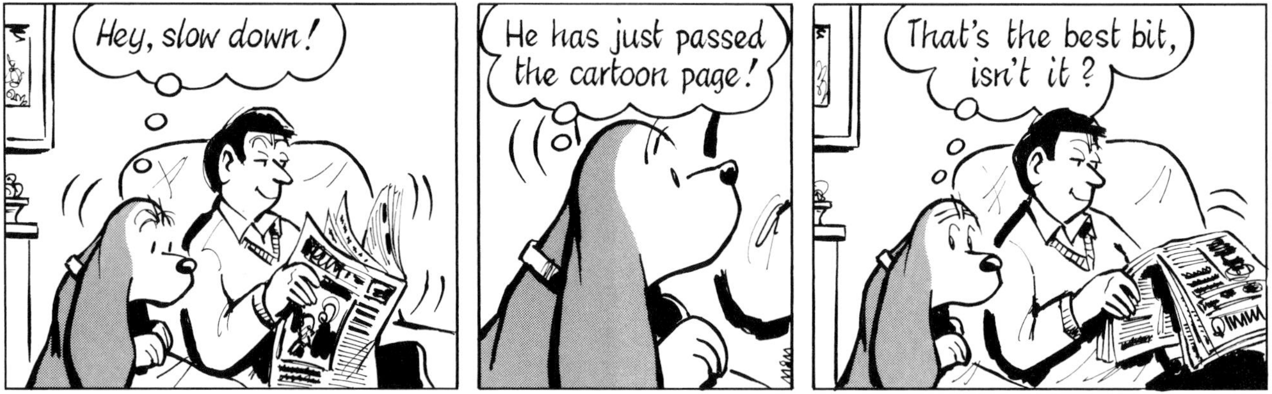
Hey, slow down!
He has just passed the cartoon page!
That's the best bit, isn't it?

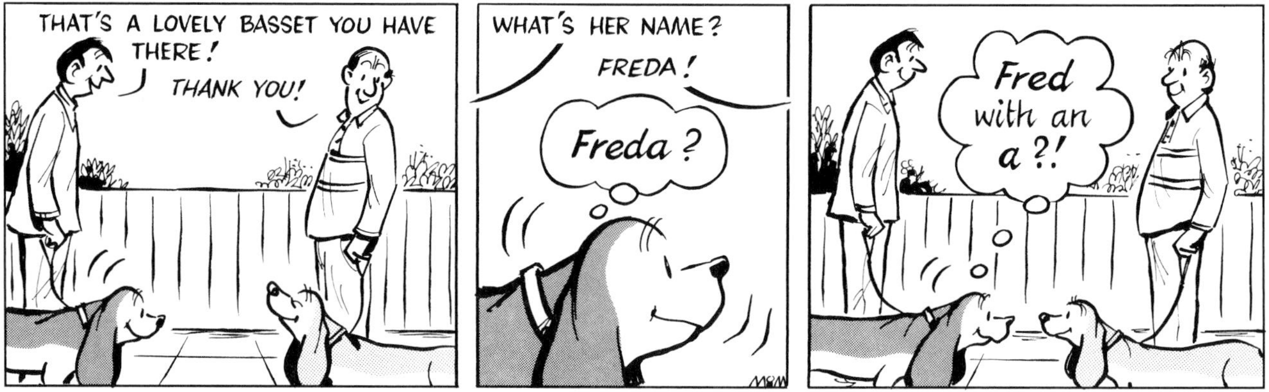
THAT'S A LOVELY BASSET YOU HAVE THERE!
THANK YOU!
WHAT'S HER NAME?
FREDA!
Freda?
Fred with an a?!

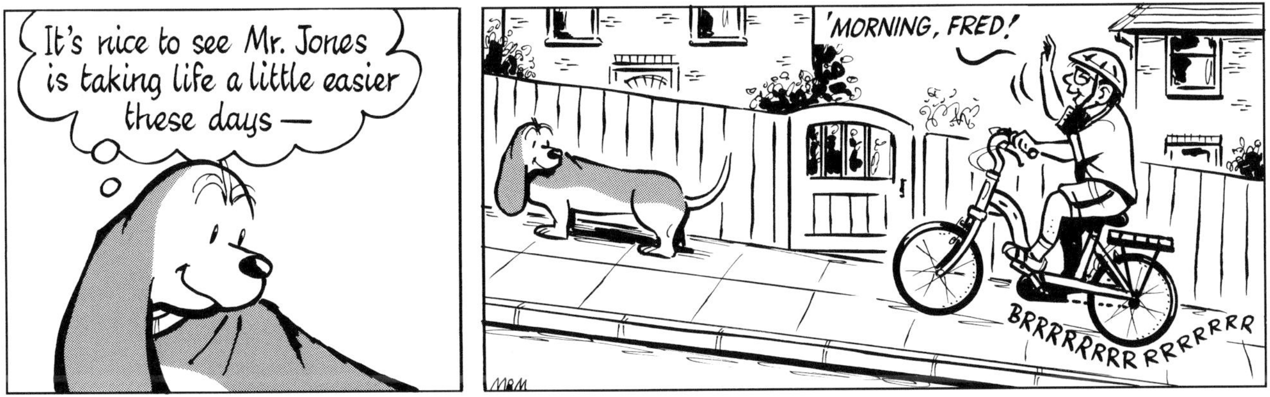
It's nice to see Mr. Jones is taking life a little easier these days —
'MORNING, FRED!
BRRRRRRRRR RRRRRRR
MSM

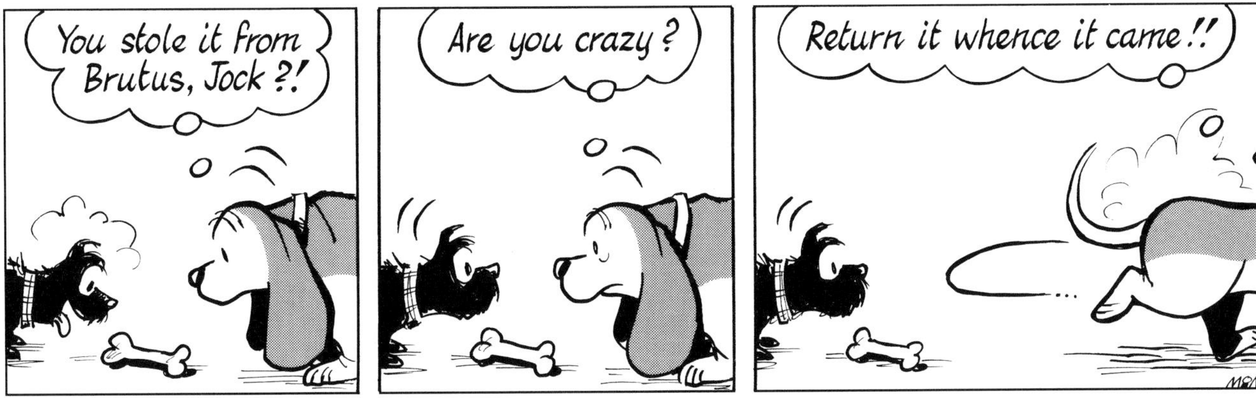
You stole it from Brutus, Jock ?!
Are you crazy ?
Return it whence it came !!
MSM

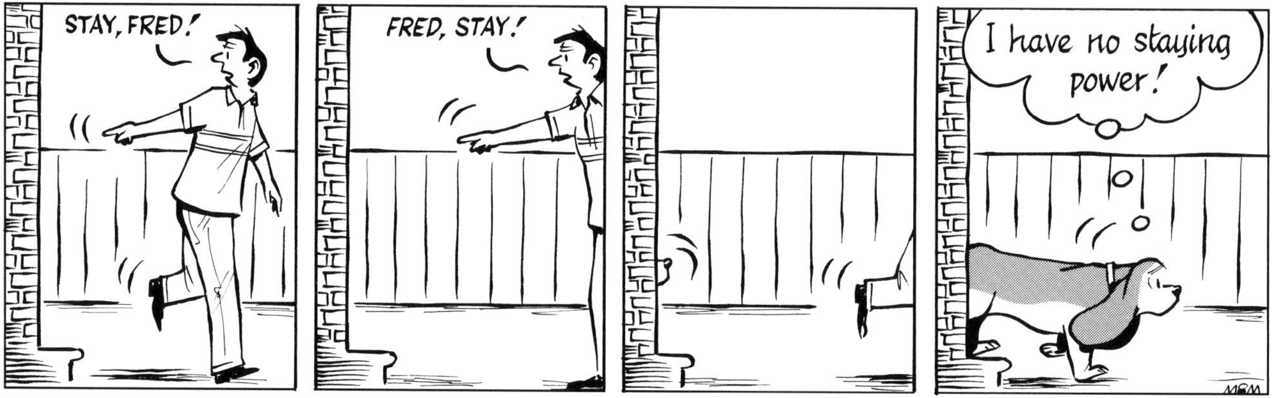
STAY, FRED!
FRED, STAY!
I have no staying power!
M&M

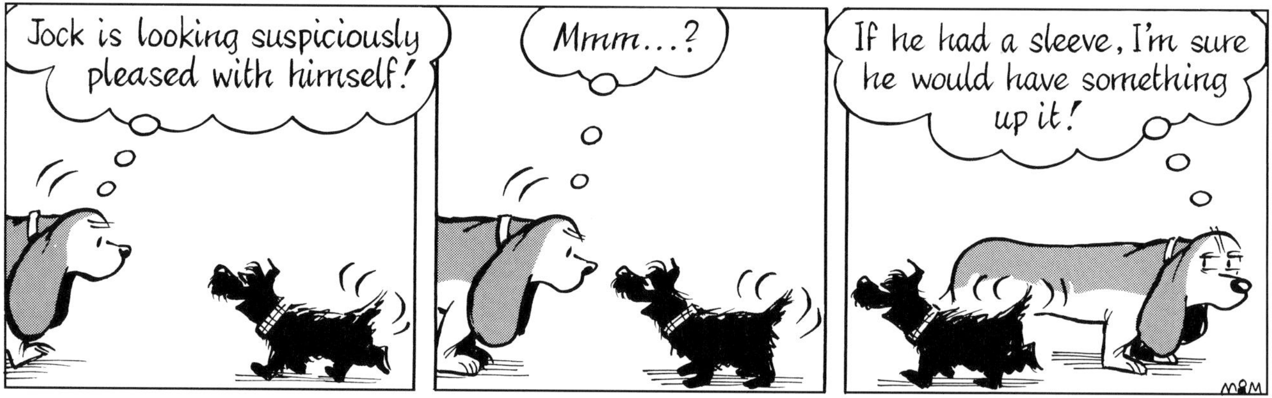
Jock is looking suspiciously pleased with himself!
Mmm...?
If he had a sleeve, I'm sure he would have something up it!
M&M

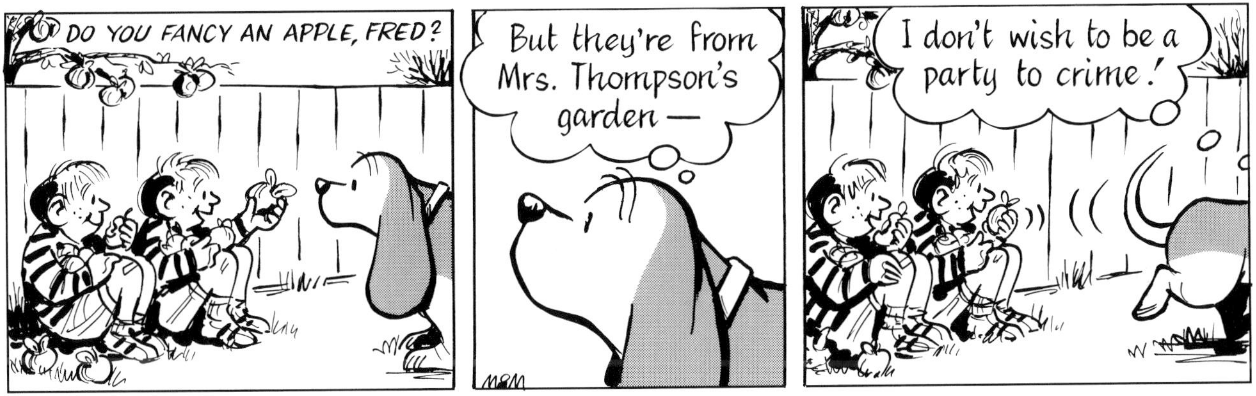
DO YOU FANCY AN APPLE, FRED?
But they're from Mrs. Thompson's garden —
I don't wish to be a party to crime!

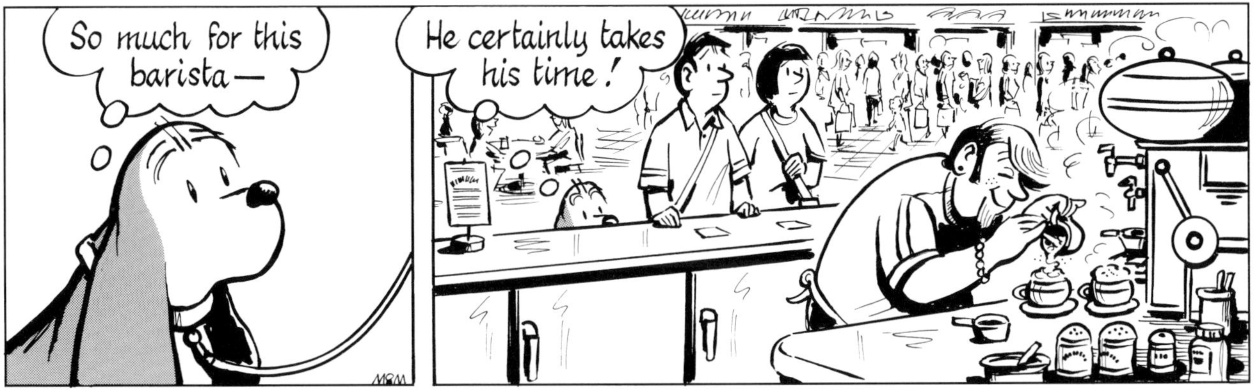
So much for this barista —
He certainly takes his time!

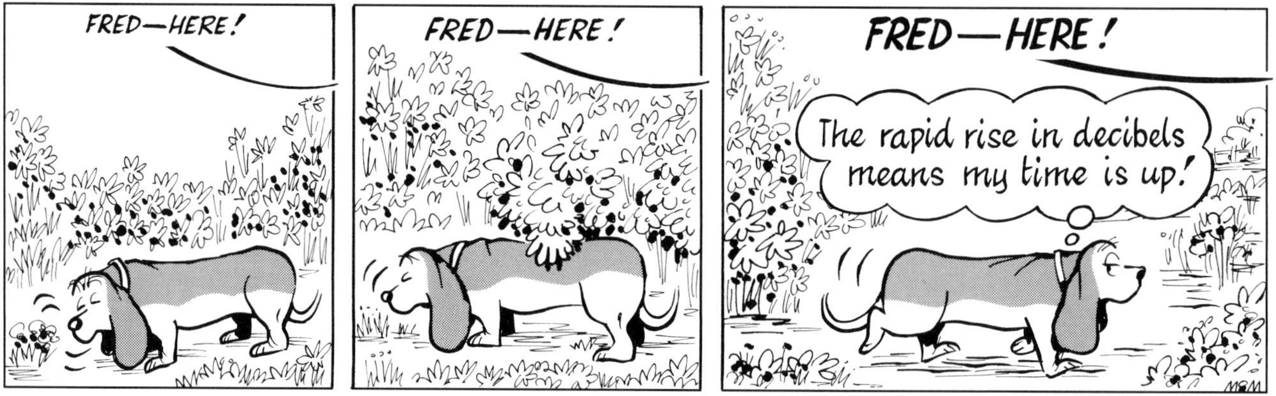
FRED—HERE!
FRED—HERE!
FRED—HERE!
The rapid rise in decibels means my time is up!

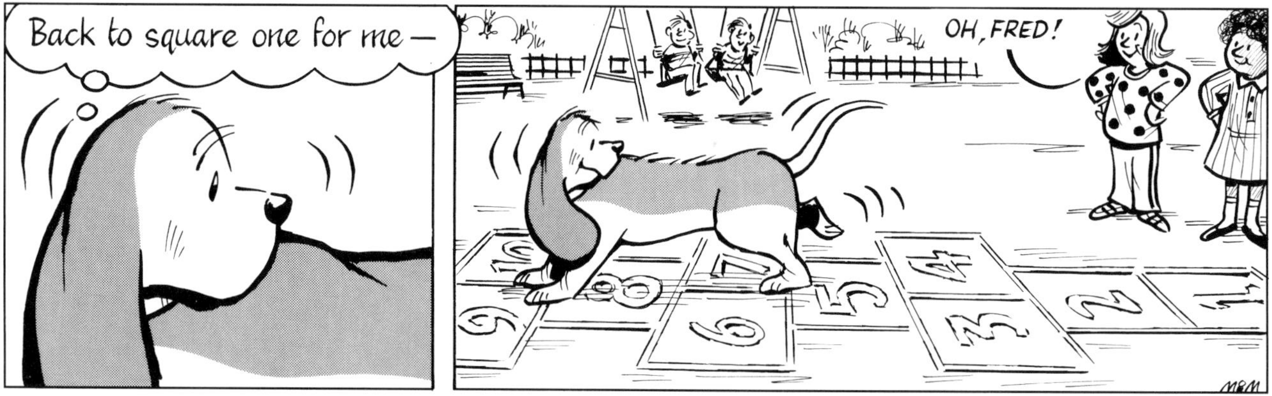
Back to square one for me —
OH, FRED!

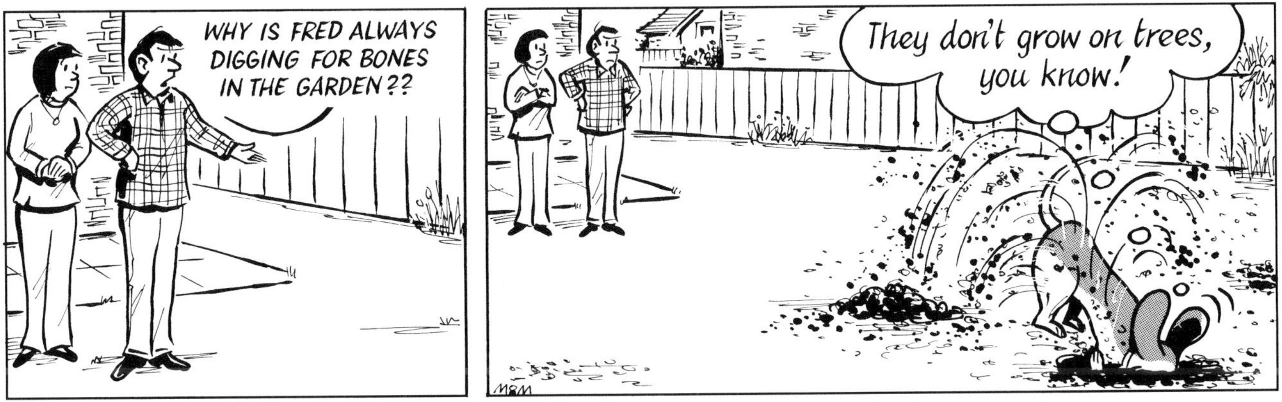
WHY IS FRED ALWAYS DIGGING FOR BONES IN THE GARDEN??
They don't grow on trees, you know!
M&M

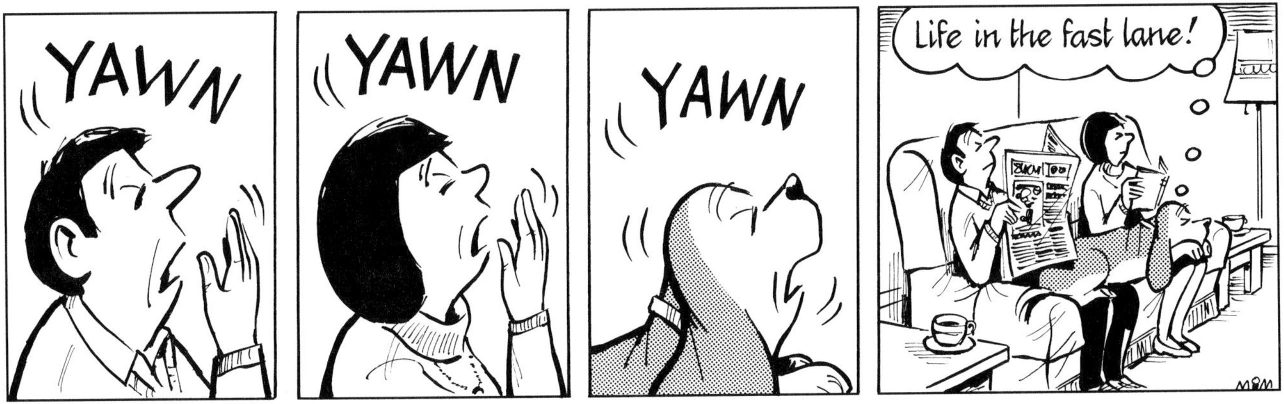
YAWN
YAWN
YAWN
Life in the fast lane!
M&M

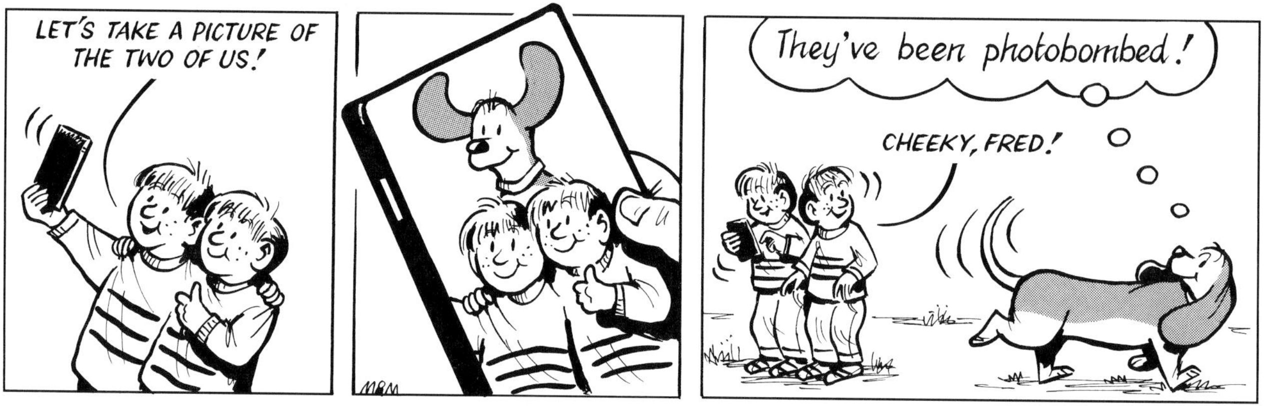
LET'S TAKE A PICTURE OF THE TWO OF US!
They've been photobombed!
CHEEKY, FRED!

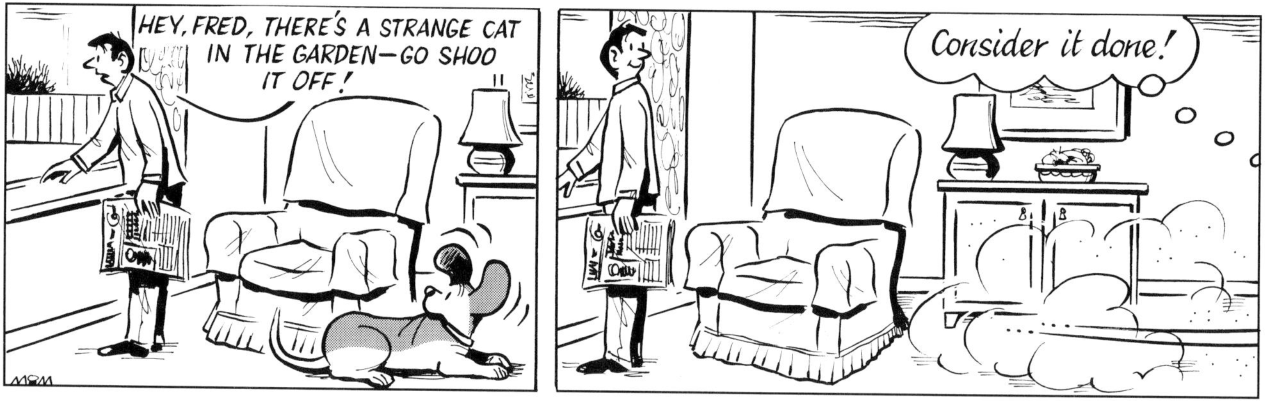
HEY, FRED, THERE'S A STRANGE CAT IN THE GARDEN—GO SHOO IT OFF!
Consider it done!

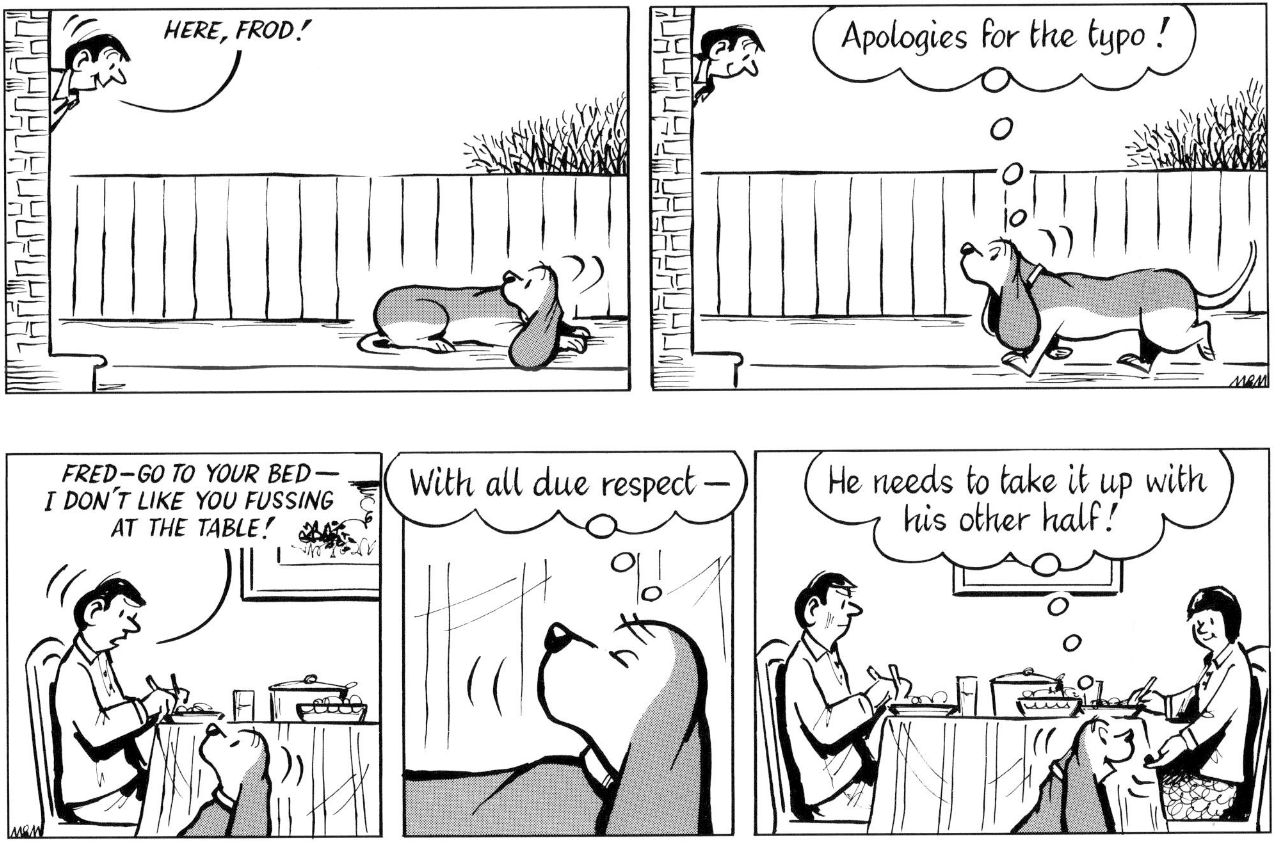
HERE, FROD!
Apologies for the typo!
FRED—GO TO YOUR BED—
I DON'T LIKE YOU FUSSING
AT THE TABLE!
With all due respect—
He needs to take it up with his other half!

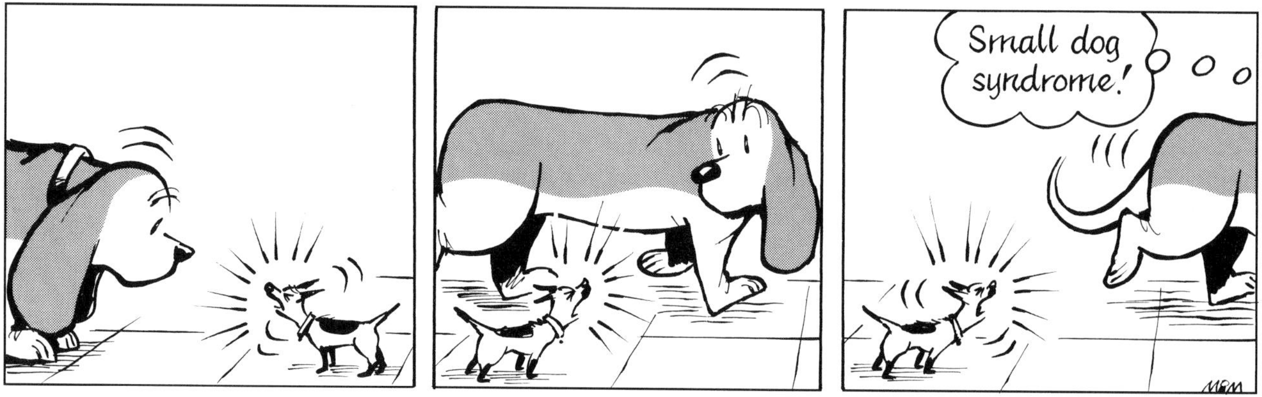
Small dog syndrome!

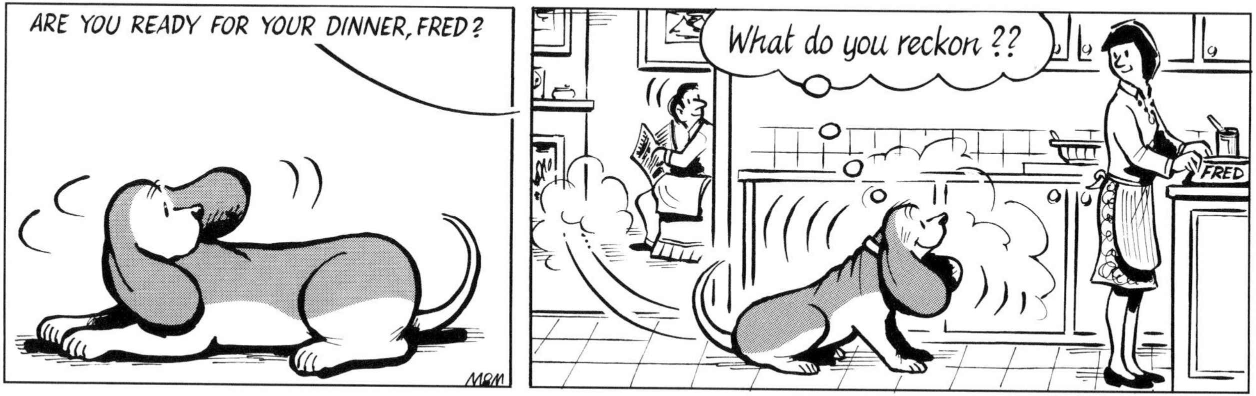
ARE YOU READY FOR YOUR DINNER, FRED?
What do you reckon??
FRED

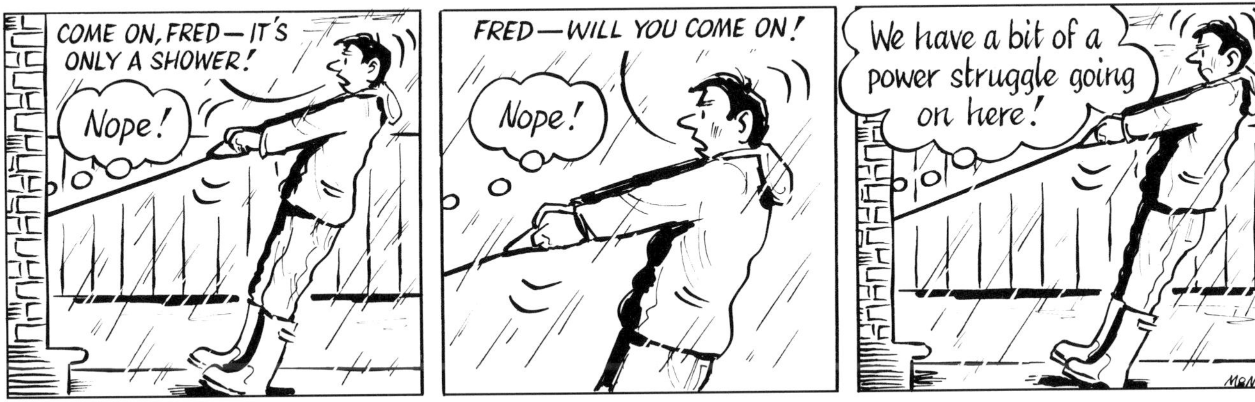
COME ON, FRED—IT'S ONLY A SHOWER!
Nope!
FRED—WILL YOU COME ON!
Nope!
We have a bit of a power struggle going on here!

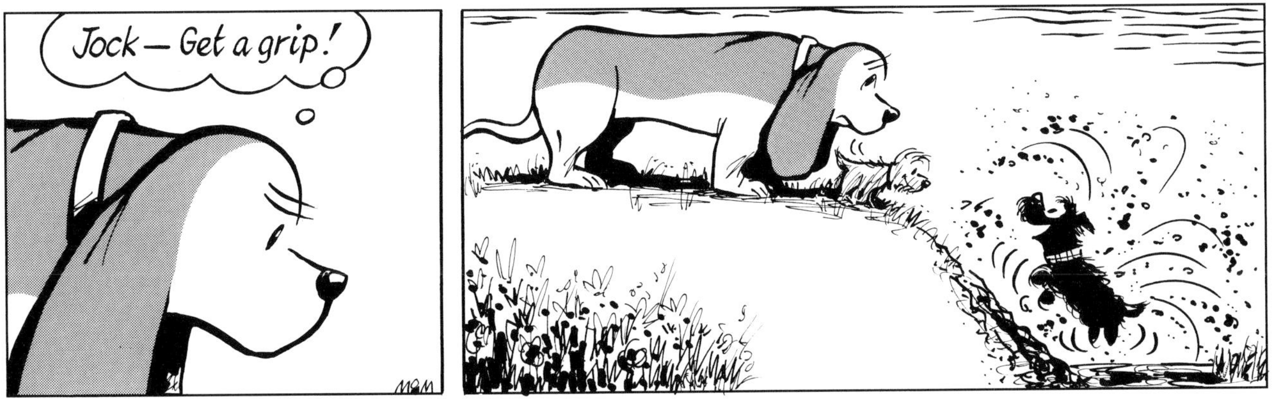
Jock—Get a grip!

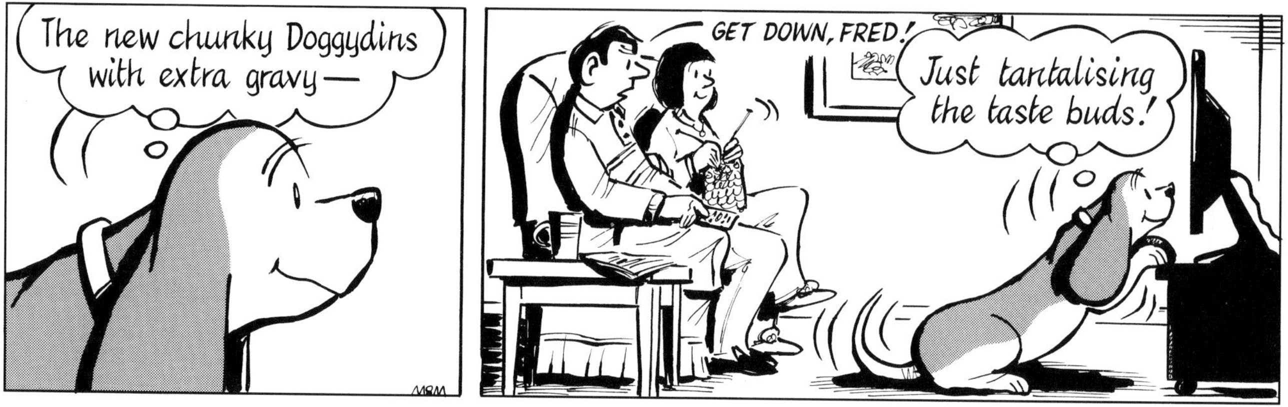
The new chunky Doggydins with extra gravy—
GET DOWN, FRED!
Just tantalising the taste buds!

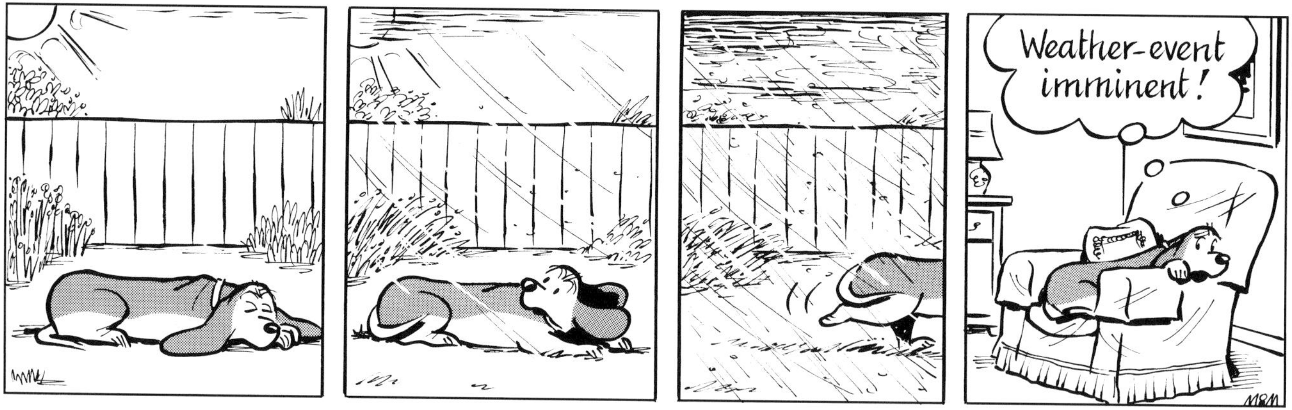
Weather-event imminent!

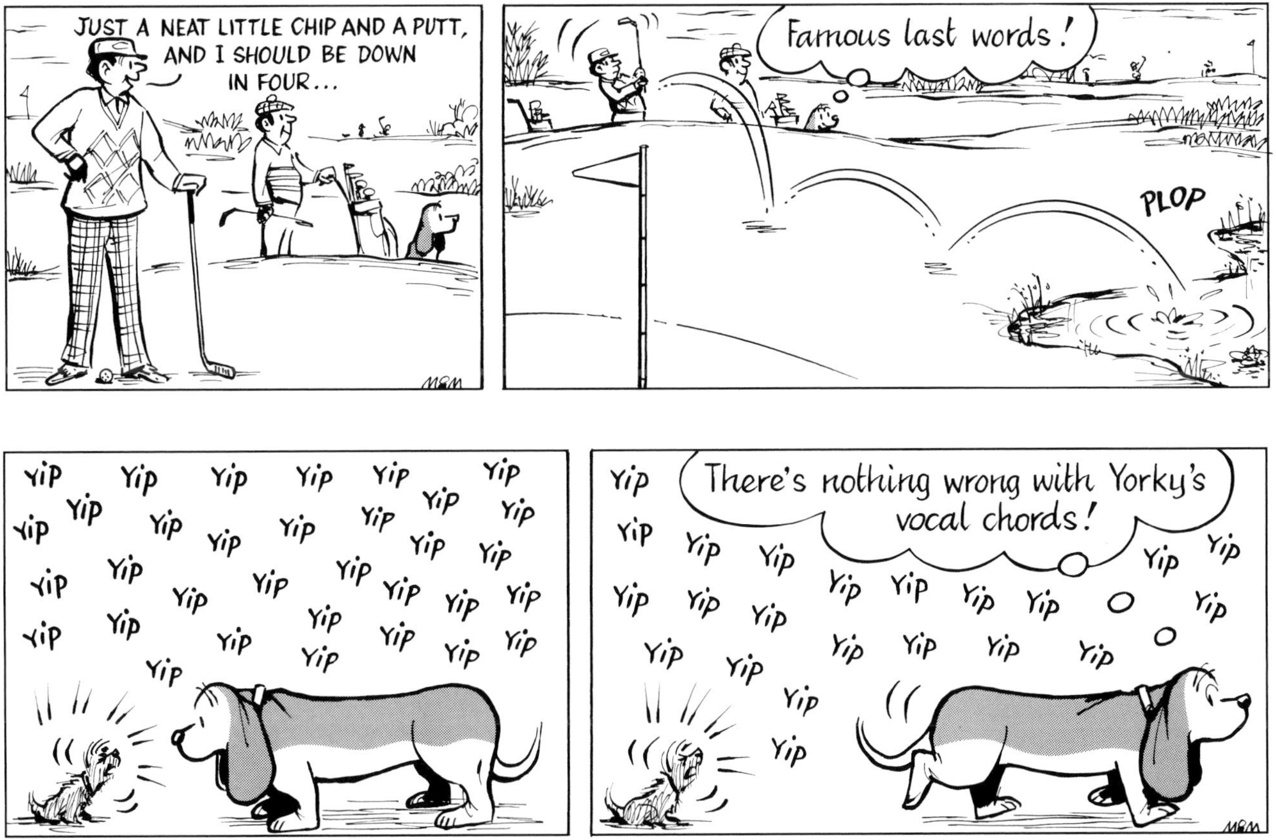
JUST A NEAT LITTLE CHIP AND A PUTT, AND I SHOULD BE DOWN IN FOUR...
Famous last words!
PLOP
Yip Yip Yip Yip Yip Yip Yip Yip Yip Yip Yip Yip Yip Yip Yip Yip Yip Yip Yip Yip Yip Yip Yip Yip Yip Yip Yip Yip Yip Yip Yip Yip Yip
Yip Yip Yip Yip Yip Yip Yip Yip Yip Yip Yip Yip Yip Yip Yip Yip Yip Yip Yip Yip Yip Yip
There's nothing wrong with Yorky's vocal chords!
MBM

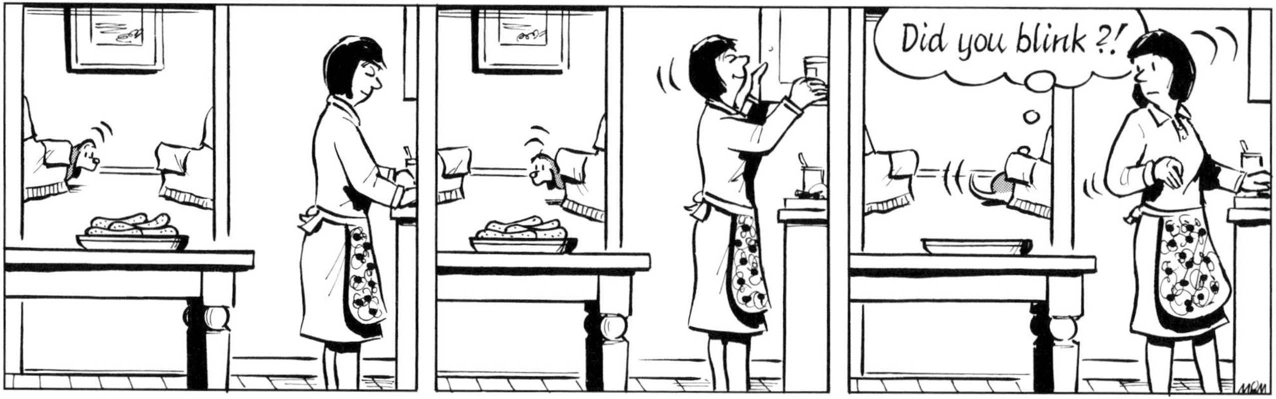
Did you blink ?!

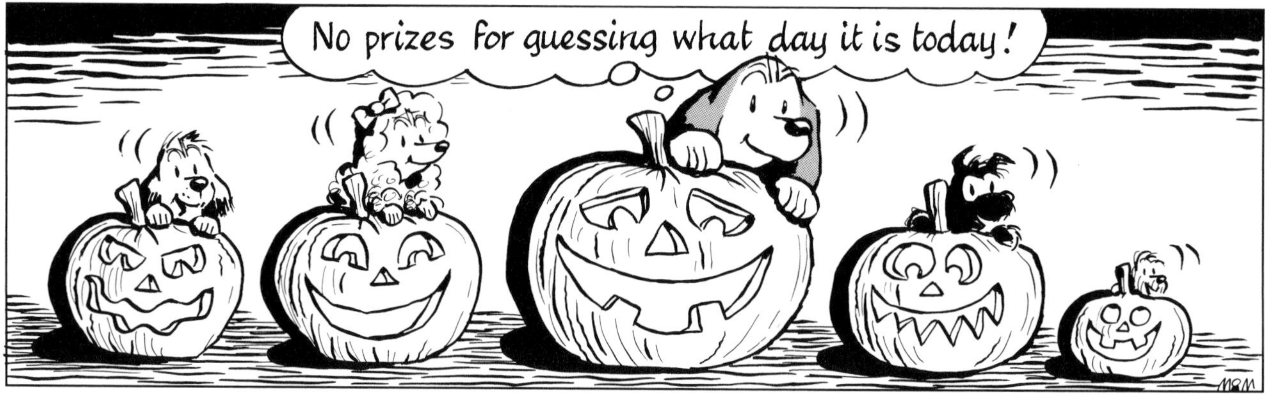
No prizes for guessing what day it is today!

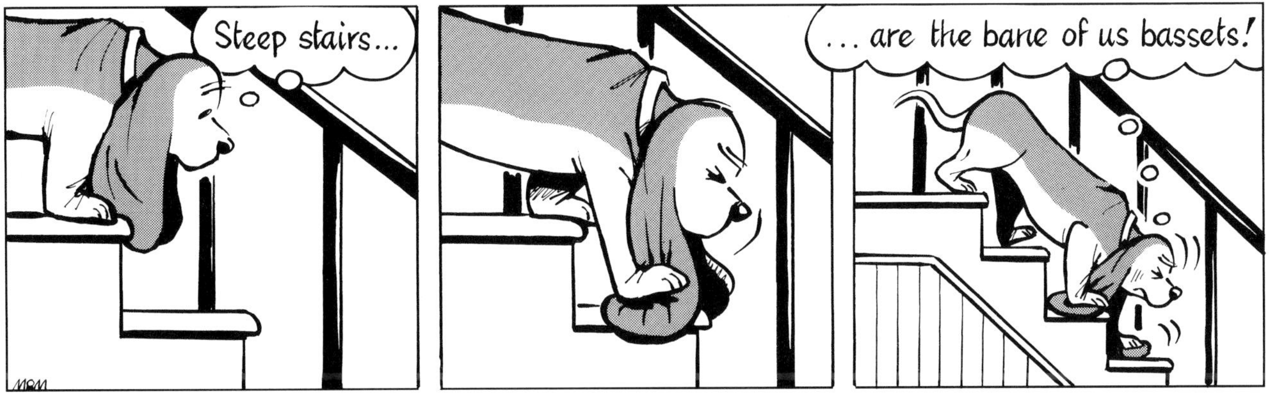
Steep stairs...
... are the bane of us bassets!

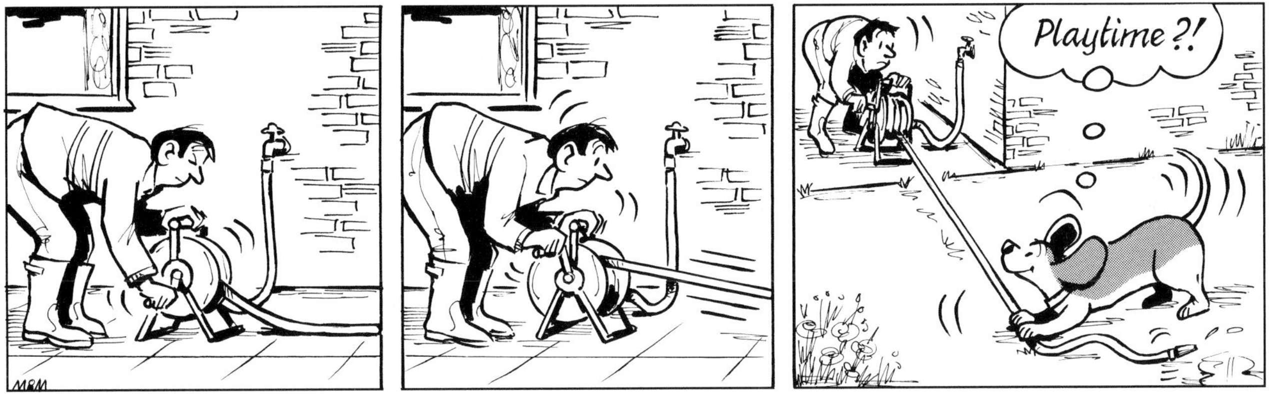
Playtime?!

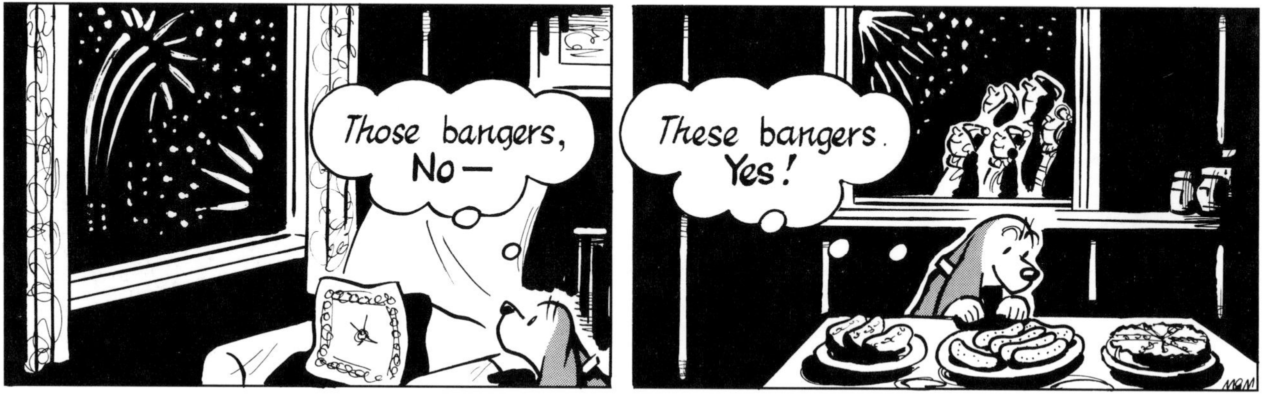
Those bangers,
No—
These bangers.
Yes!
M&M

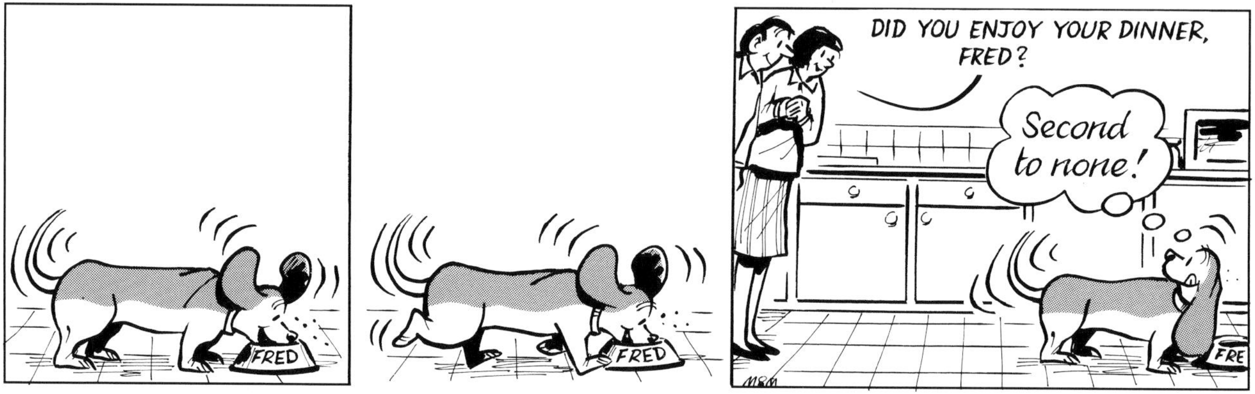
FRED
FRED
DID YOU ENJOY YOUR DINNER, FRED?
Second to none!
FRE
M&M

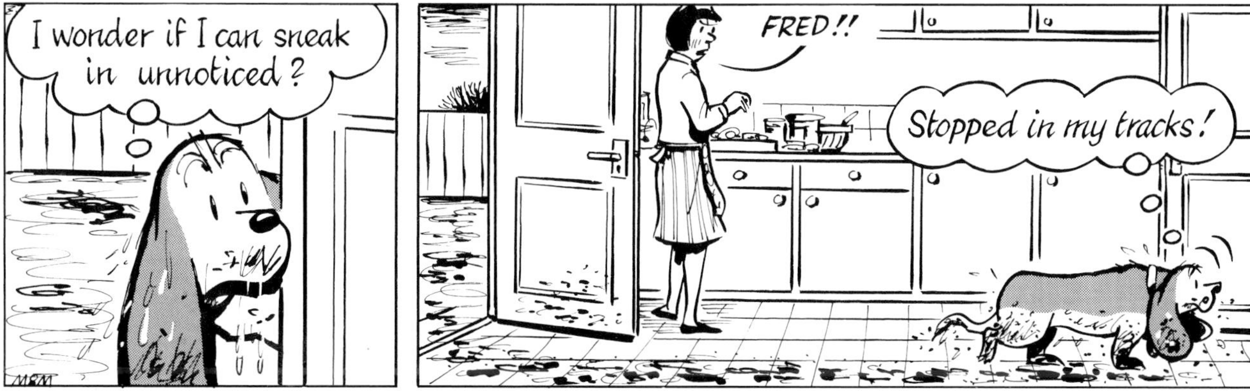
I wonder if I can sneak in unnoticed?
FRED!!
Stopped in my tracks!

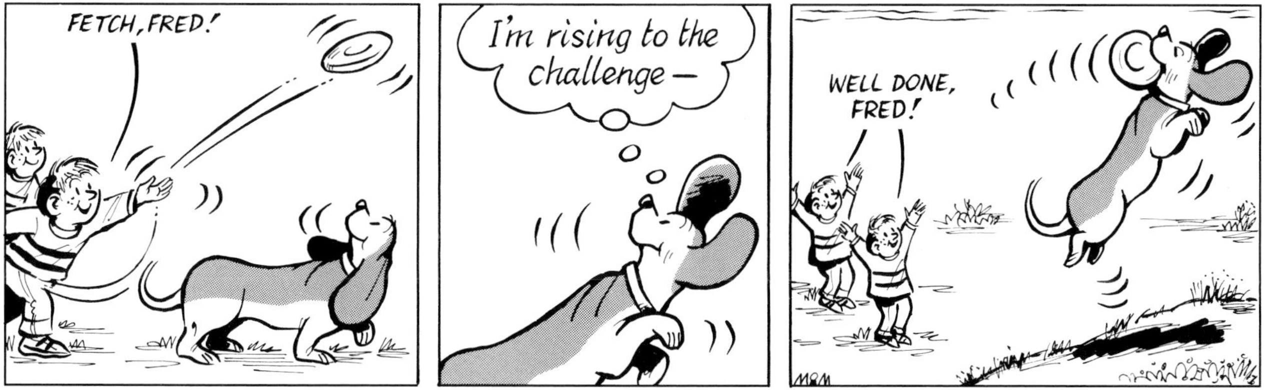
FETCH, FRED!
I'm rising to the challenge –
WELL DONE, FRED!

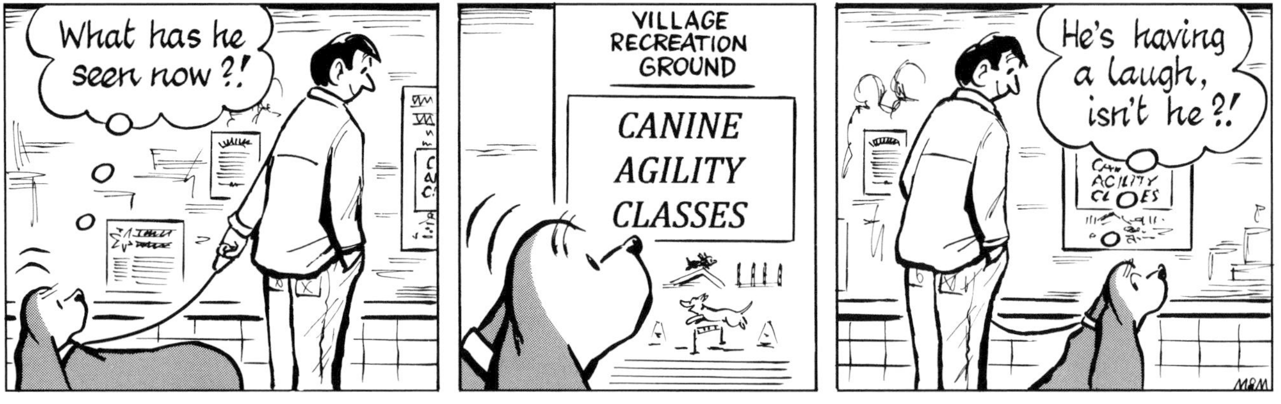
What has he seen now?!
VILLAGE RECREATION GROUND
CANINE AGILITY CLASSES
He's having a laugh, isn't he?!

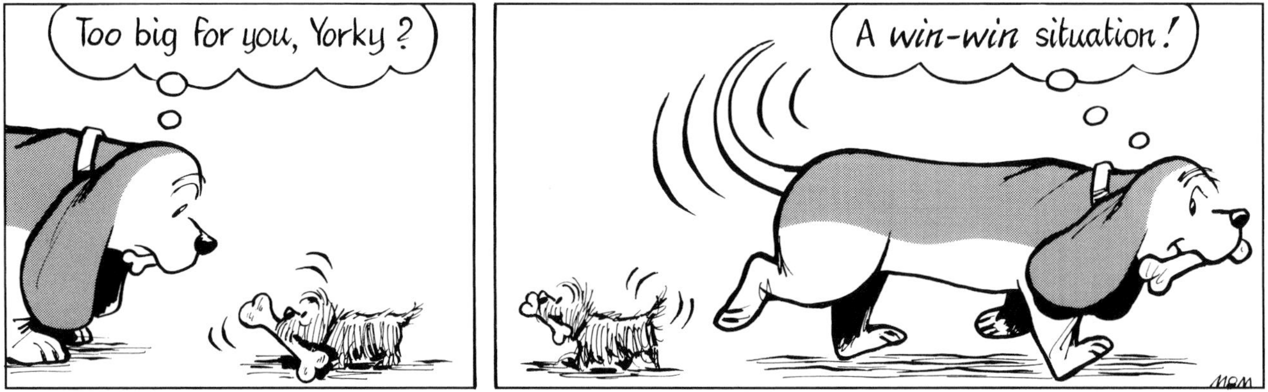
Too big for you, Yorky?
A *win-win* situation!

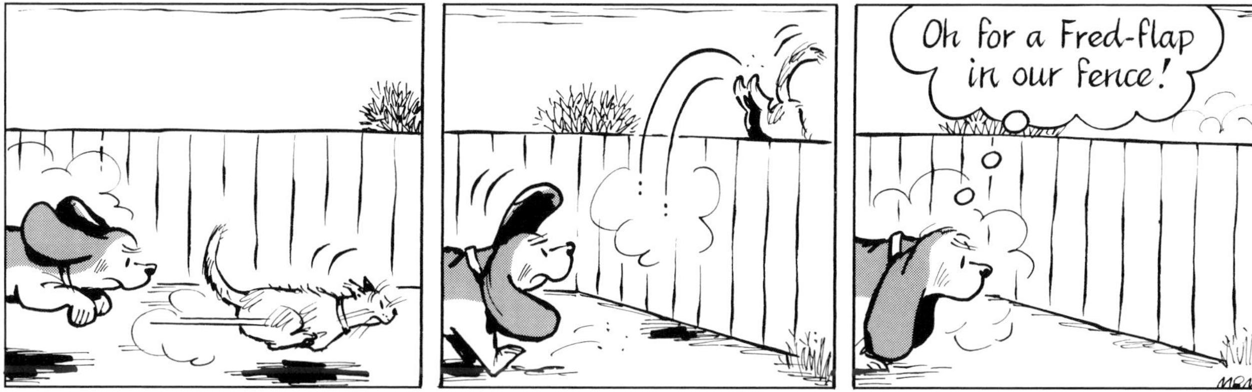
Oh for a Fred-flap in our fence!

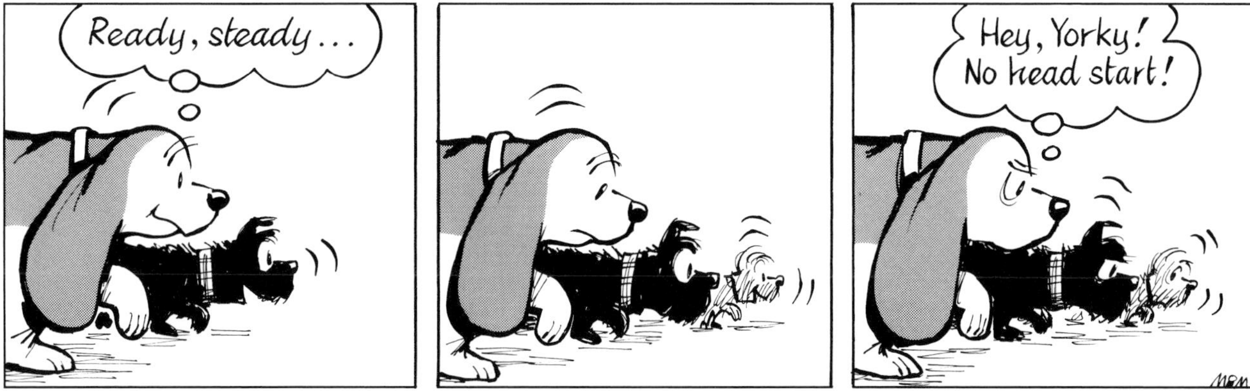
Ready, steady . . .
Hey, Yorky! No head start!

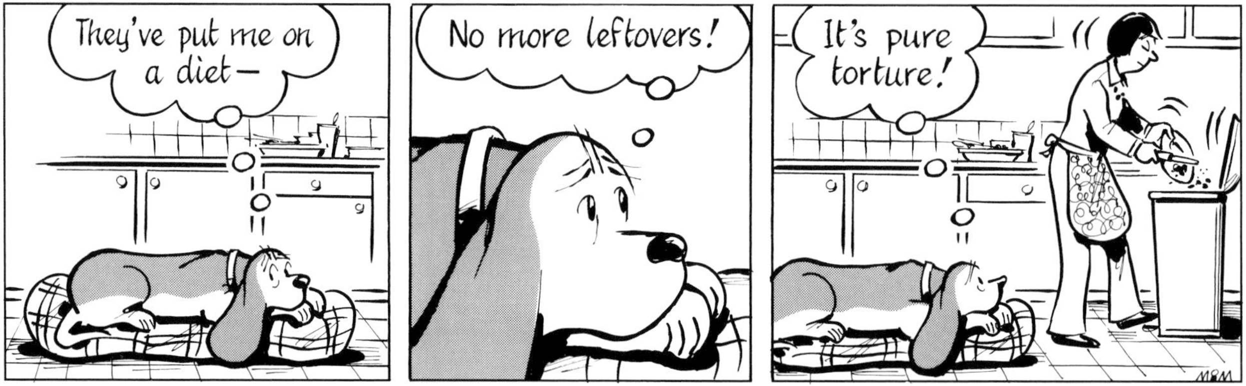
They've put me on a diet—
No more leftovers!
It's pure torture!

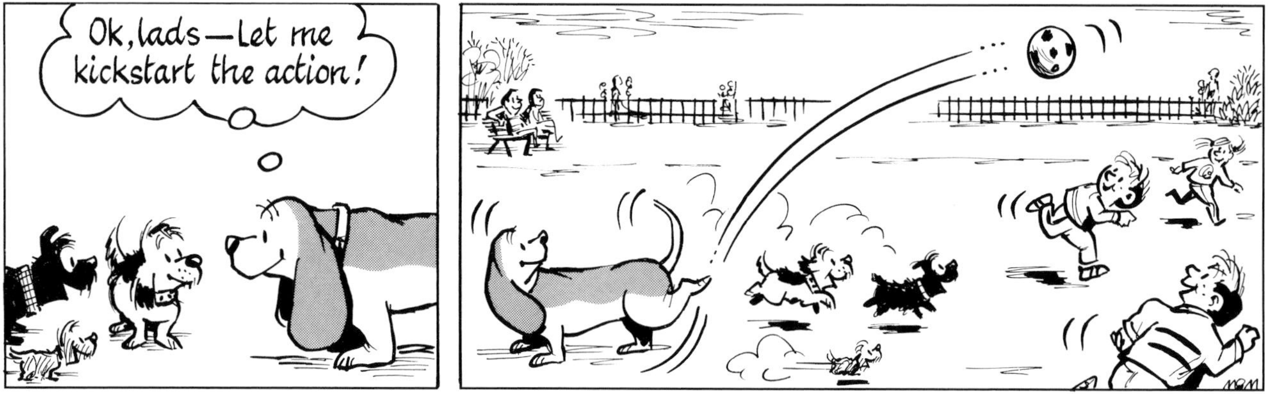
Ok, lads—Let me kickstart the action!

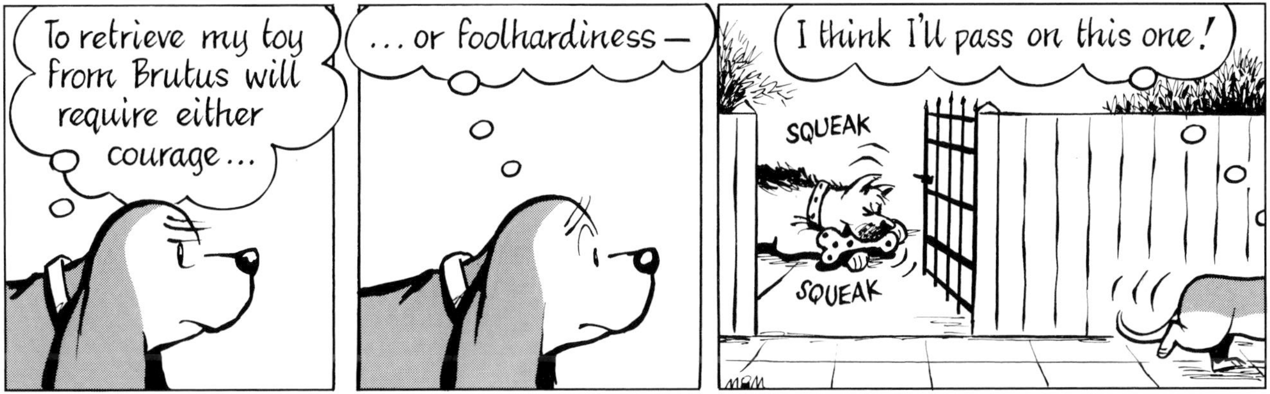
To retrieve my toy from Brutus will require either courage...
... or foolhardiness —
I think I'll pass on this one!
SQUEAK
SQUEAK

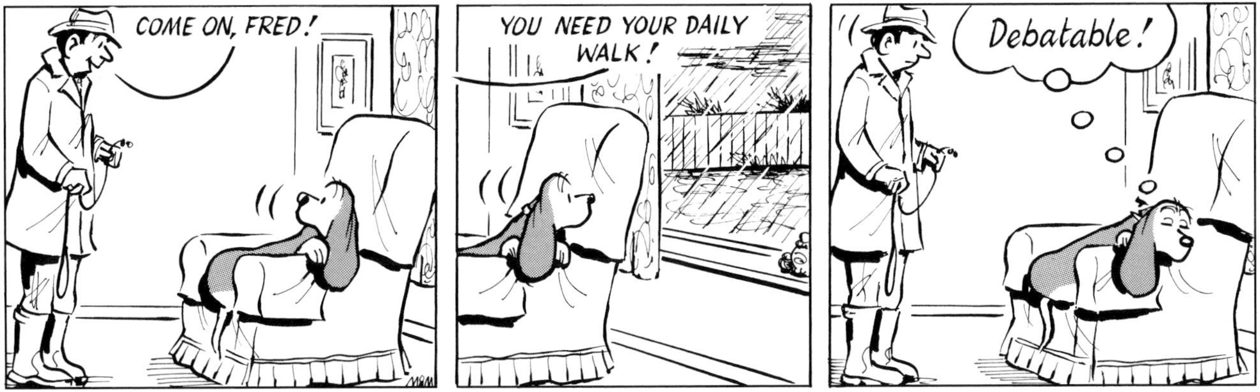
COME ON, FRED!
YOU NEED YOUR DAILY WALK!
Debatable!

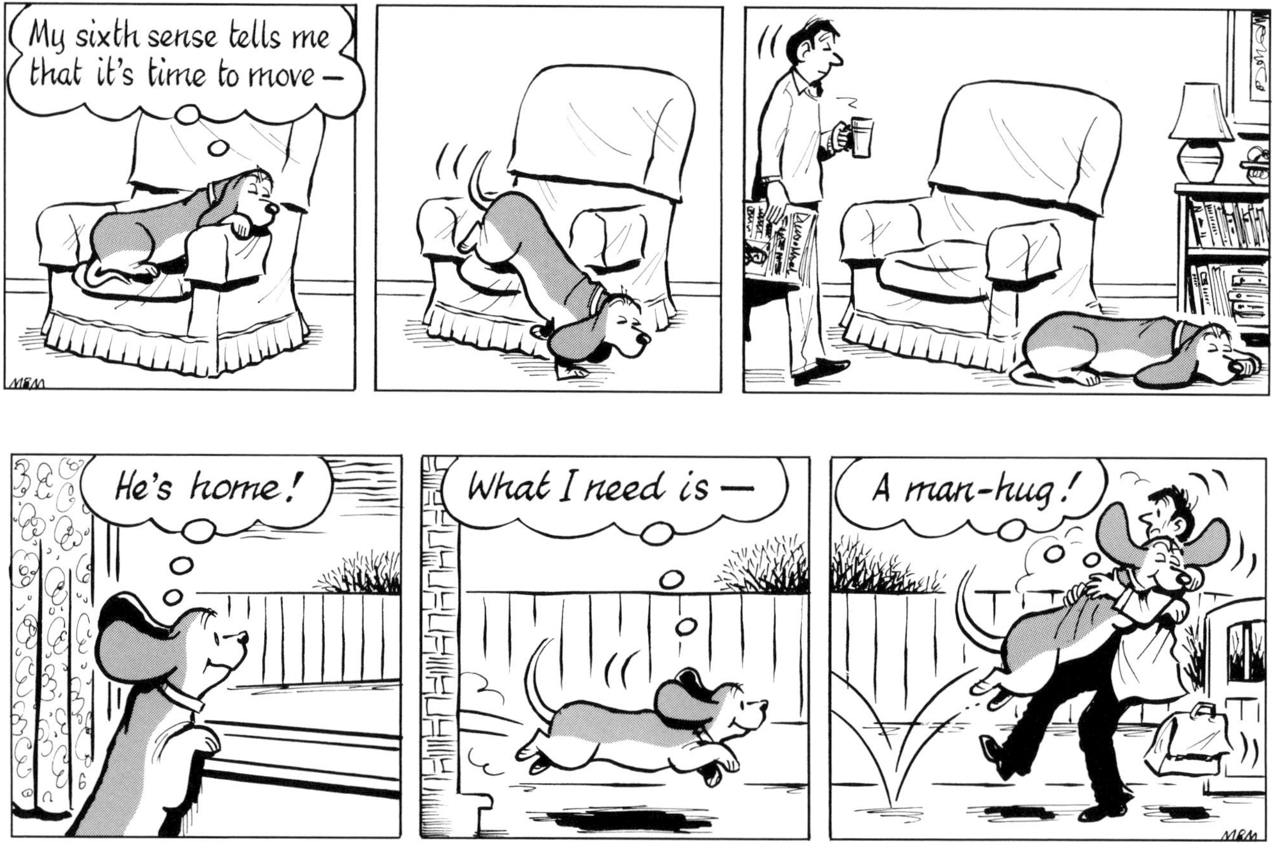
My sixth sense tells me that it's time to move –
He's home!
What I need is –
A man-hug!

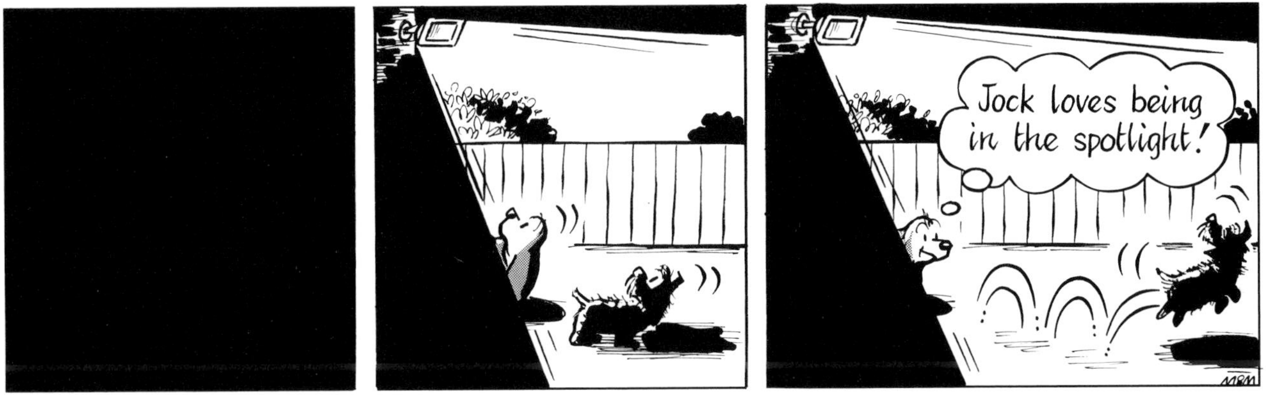
Jock loves being in the spotlight!

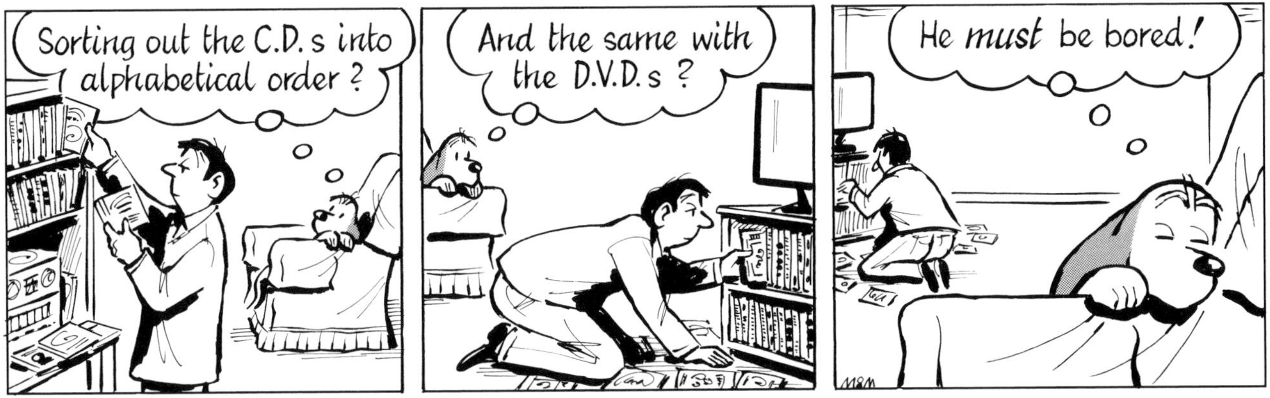
Sorting out the C.D.s into alphabetical order?
And the same with the D.V.D.s?
He *must* be bored!

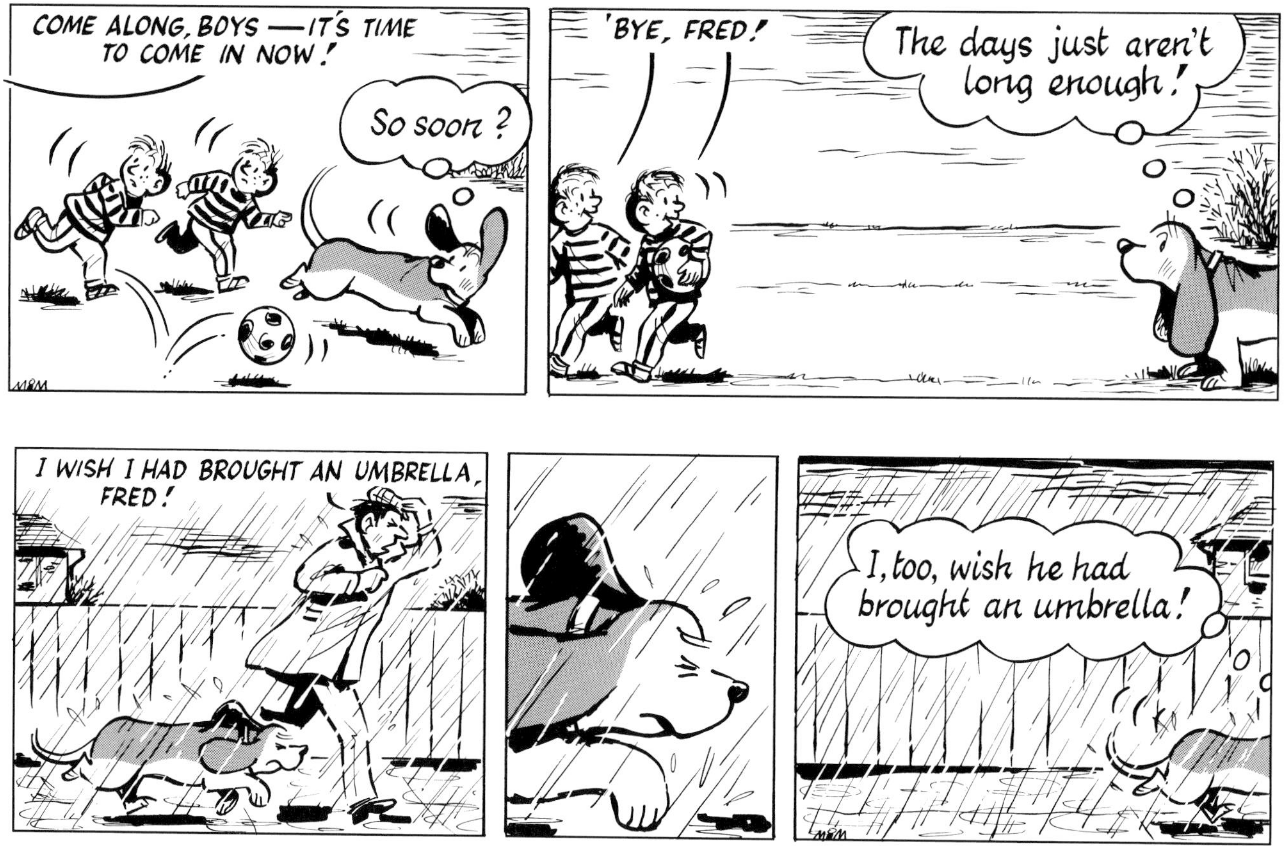

COME ALONG, BOYS —IT'S TIME TO COME IN NOW!
So soon ?
'BYE, FRED!
The days just aren't long enough!
I WISH I HAD BROUGHT AN UMBRELLA, FRED!
I, too, wish he had brought an umbrella!

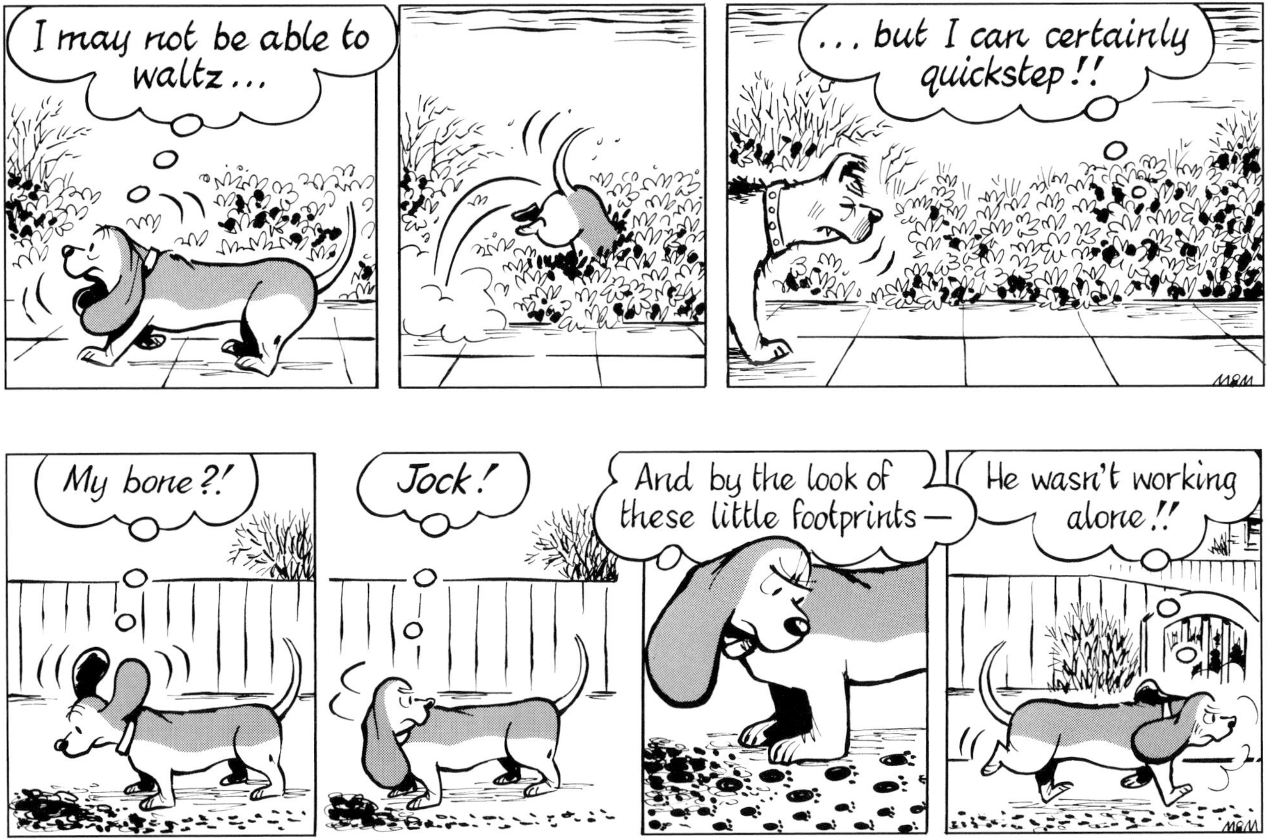
I may not be able to waltz...
... but I can certainly quickstep!!
MGM
My bone?!
Jock!
And by the look of these little footprints—
He wasn't working alone!!
MGM

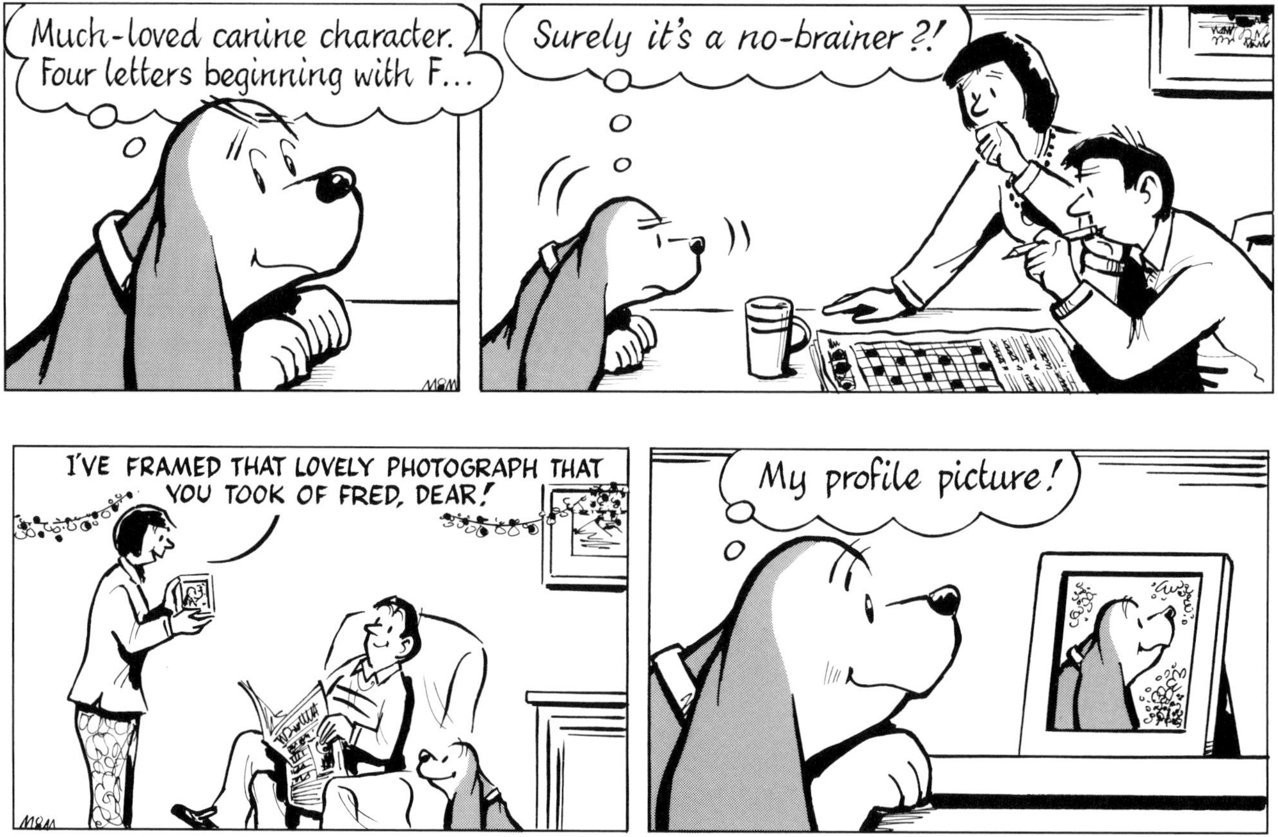

Much-loved canine character. Four letters beginning with F...
Surely it's a no-brainer ?!
I'VE FRAMED THAT LOVELY PHOTOGRAPH THAT YOU TOOK OF FRED, DEAR!
My profile picture!

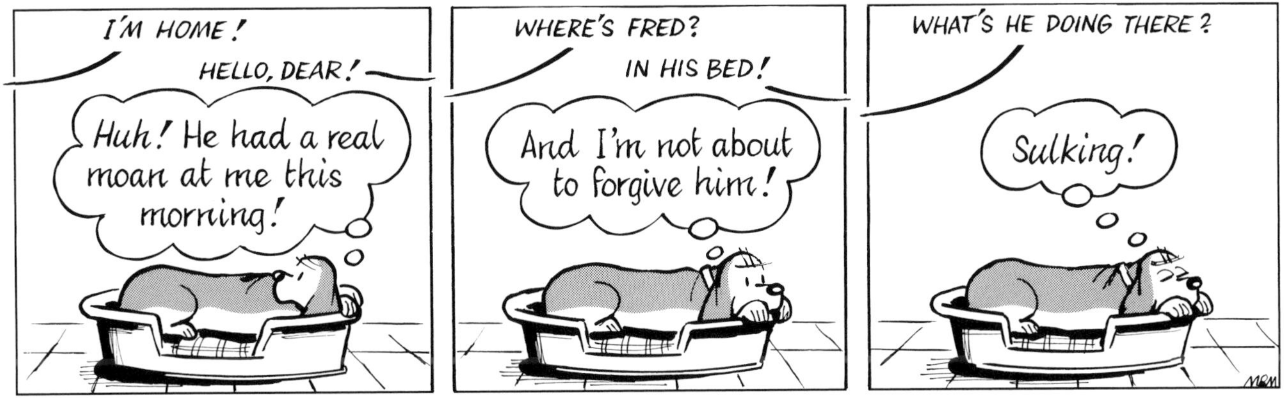
I'M HOME!
HELLO, DEAR!
Huh! He had a real moan at me this morning!
WHERE'S FRED?
IN HIS BED!
And I'm not about to forgive him!
WHAT'S HE DOING THERE?
Sulking!
M&M

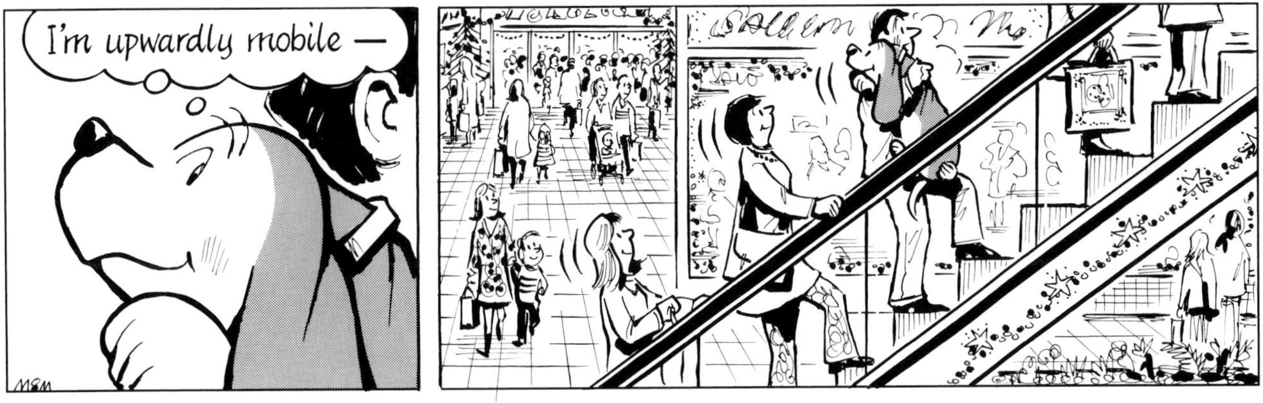
I'm upwardly mobile —
M&M

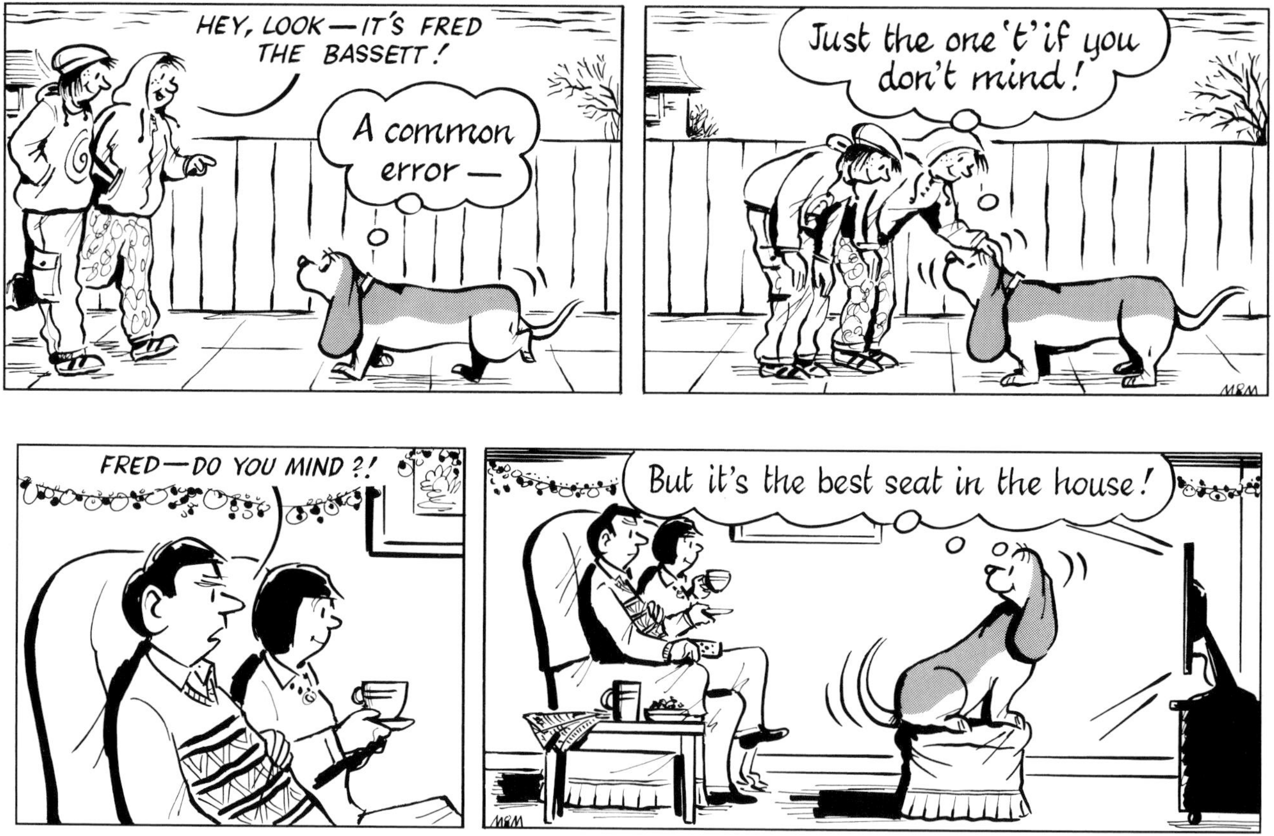
HEY, LOOK—IT'S FRED THE BASSETT!
A common error—
Just the one 't' if you don't mind!
M&M
FRED—DO YOU MIND?!
But it's the best seat in the house!
M&M

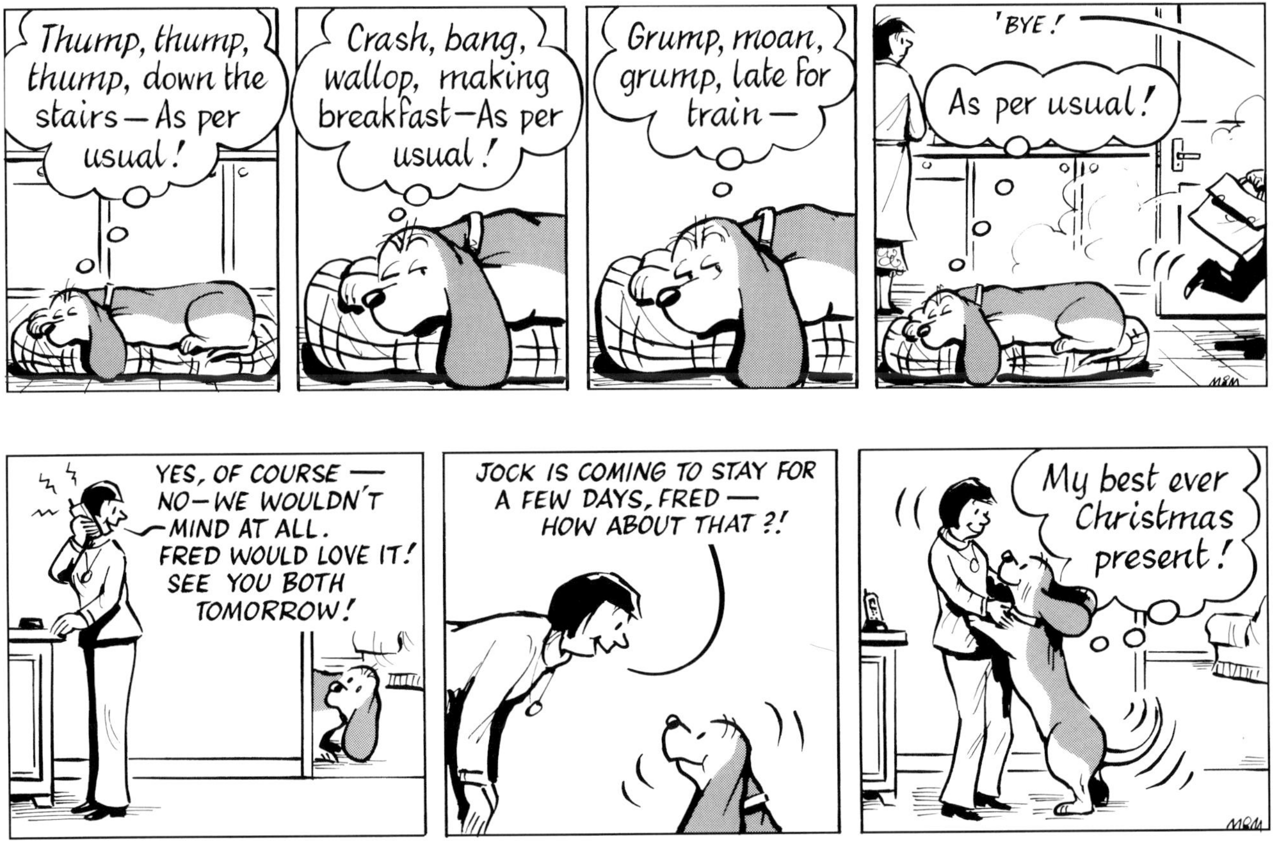
Thump, thump, thump, down the stairs—As per usual!
Crash, bang, wallop, making breakfast—As per usual!
Grump, moan, grump, late for train—
'BYE!
As per usual!
M&M
YES, OF COURSE — NO—WE WOULDN'T MIND AT ALL. FRED WOULD LOVE IT! SEE YOU BOTH TOMORROW!
JOCK IS COMING TO STAY FOR A FEW DAYS, FRED — HOW ABOUT THAT ?!
My best ever Christmas present!
M&M

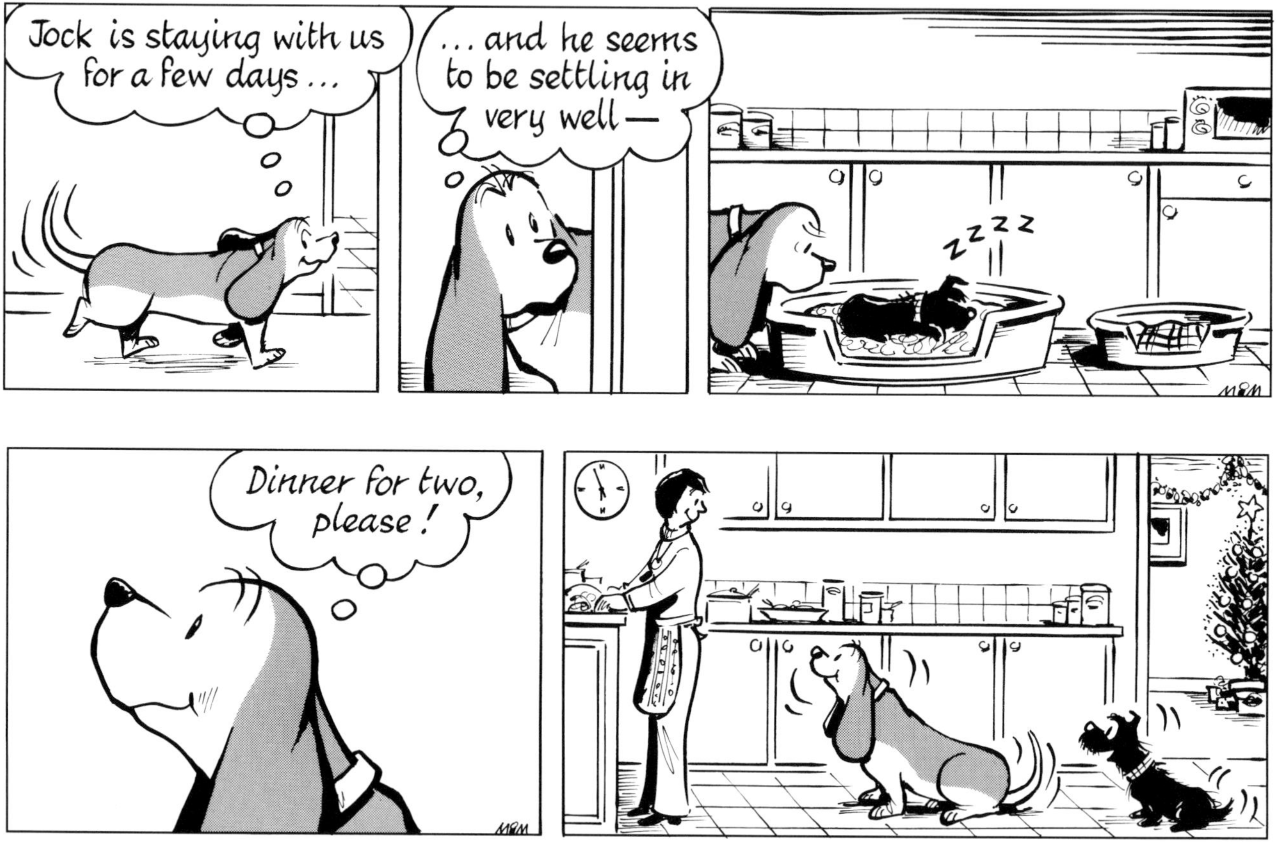
Jock is staying with us for a few days ...
... and he seems to be settling in very well —
ZZZZ
Dinner for two, please!

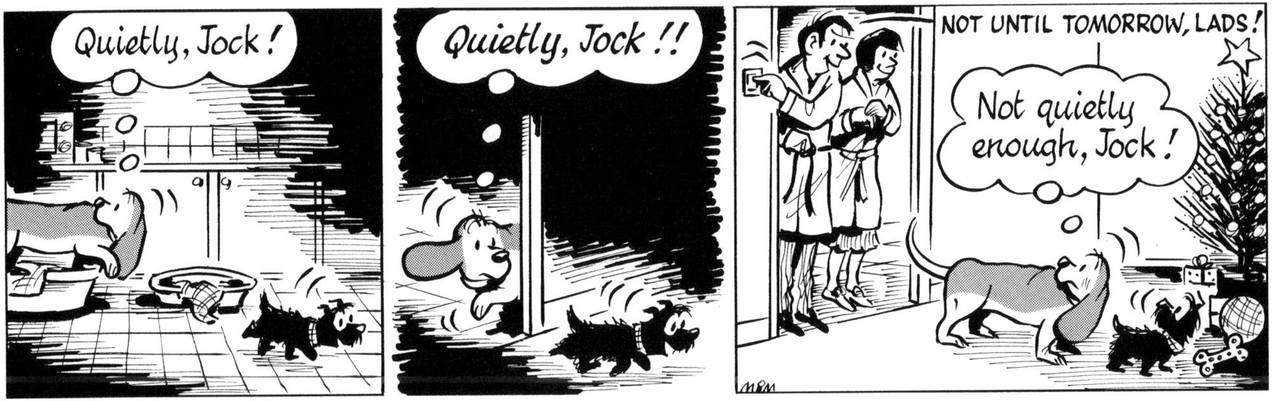
Quietly, Jock!
Quietly, Jock !!
NOT UNTIL TOMORROW, LADS!
Not quietly enough, Jock!

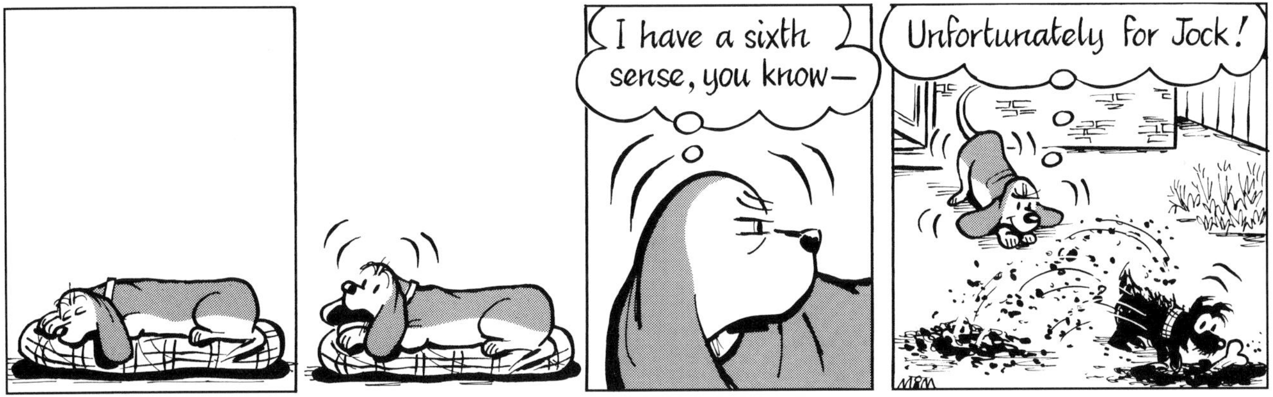
I have a sixth sense, you know—
Unfortunately for Jock!

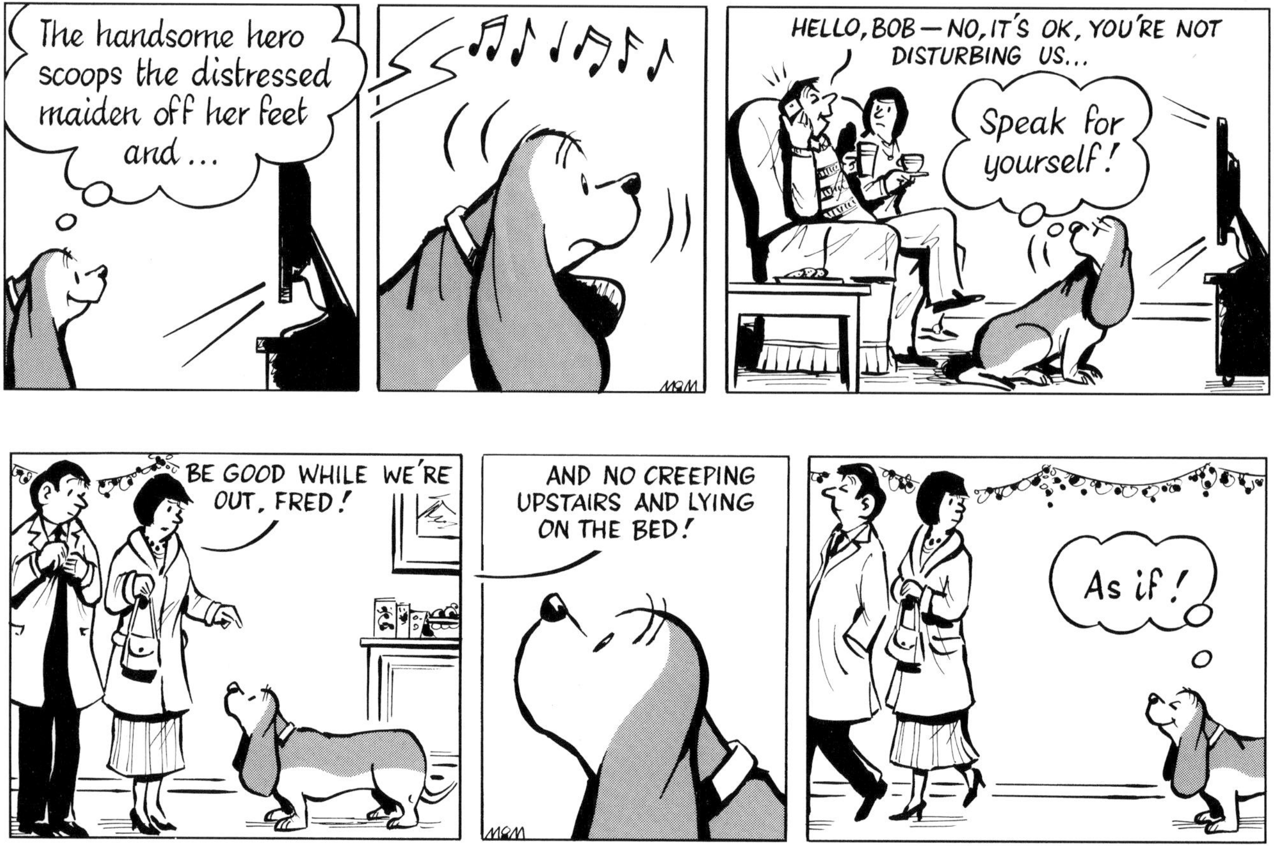
The handsome hero scoops the distressed maiden off her feet and ...
HELLO, BOB — NO, IT'S OK, YOU'RE NOT DISTURBING US...
Speak for yourself!
BE GOOD WHILE WE'RE OUT, FRED!
AND NO CREEPING UPSTAIRS AND LYING ON THE BED!
As if!